DAGGERS UNSHEATHED

DAGGERS UNSHEATHED

THE POLITICAL ASSASSINATION OF GLEN CLARK

Judi Tyabji Wilson

National Library of Canada Cataloguing in Publication Data

Wilson, Judi Tyabji, 1965-
Daggers unsheathed: the political assassination of Glen Clark/Judi Tyabji Wilson.

Includes index.
ISBN 1-894384-47-4 (bound) —ISBN 1-894384-53-9 (pbk.)

1. Clark, Glen David, 1957- 2. British Columbia—Politics and government—1991-2001. 3. Trials (Misconduct in office)—British Columbia. I. Title.
FC3829.1.C52W54 2002 971.1'04'092 C2002-911354-7
F1088.C52W54 2002

First edition 2002

Heritage House acknowledges the financial support for our publishing program from the Government of Canada through the Book Publishing Industry Development Program (BPIDP), Canada Council for the Arts, and the British Columbia Arts Council.

Cover and book design by Arifin A. Graham, Alaris Design
Edited by John Ricker

HERITAGE HOUSE PUBLISHING COMPANY LTD.
Unit #108 - 17665 66A Ave., Surrey, B.C. V3S 2A7

Printed in Canada

This book is in honour of my great-great-grandfather, Badruddin Tyabji, who dedicated his life to justice and good governance in the creation of modern India.

> *Be moderate in your demands, be just in your criticism, be accurate in your facts, be logical in your conclusions, and you may rest assured that any propositions you may make to our rulers will be received with that benign consideration which is the characteristic of a strong and enlightened government.*
>
> —Badruddin Tyabji
> Madras, 1887

Acknowledgements

My thanks to Dave Biro for his invaluable online research of articles and other tidbits, and for keeping my faith in traditional journalism and its high standards alive and well.

I would like to acknowledge the support of Rodger Touchie and Heritage House, the legislative library for assistance above and beyond, and my editor, John Ricker, for maintaining a sense of humour and perspective during the editing process.

A special thanks to Marlyn Horsdal for being a stern voice in my head during the first draft. And thanks to my husband, Gordon Wilson, for his support when I told him I had to write this book.

Contents

Foreword

The 1990s were not good for former or active premiers in British Columbia. Even Bill Bennett, who had ruled the Social Credit party for almost eleven years before resigning during the glory days of Expo '86, stayed close to his Okanagan retirement home after he and his brother were tarred with insider-trading accusations for conveniently dumping a load of stock before the bottom fell out of the market. He faced potential jail time and severe fines when his lawyers negotiated a settlement that could not hide the seediness of his actions.

When Bennett's successor, Bill Vander Zalm, glommed onto a wad of U.S. $100 bills in the early hours of August 4, 1990, while dickering over the sale of his Fantasy Gardens, he permanently soiled the image of B.C. politics and the office of premier. Neither Bennett's lawyers nor Vander Zalm's halogen smile could change the electorate's perception that both men had demeaned the office in an effort to protect personal wealth. After Vander Zalm resigned in disgrace, and transition leader Rita Johnston faced the wrath of the voters in November 1991, the NDP took power, declaring a government that would "put an end to secret deals and special favours for political friends."

New energy, idealism, and optimism were personified in Michael Harcourt, the NDP's first B.C. premier in sixteen years. But within a year of assuming office, disclosures of the "Bingogate" scandal were making waves. Eventually in 1995, after much delay, a forensic auditor, Ron Parks, painted an ugly picture of how charity funds were diverted to the NDP and of an ensuing cover-up, leading ultimately to NDP president and MLA Dave Stupich's conviction for fraud. While Harcourt was not directly tied to these misdeeds, only a month after the Parks Report was released Harcourt acceded to the wishes of powerful NDP insiders and stepped aside.

Bingogate also brought added grief to the premiership when former premier Dave Barrett and long-time political colleague Bob Williams were named in RCMP search warrants that alleged wrongdoing in a Vancouver East by-election twenty years earlier.

Amazingly, when Glen Clark was elected the new NDP leader and assumed the premier's office he was able to overcome the cynicism of the electorate and snatch a narrow victory in an election that the out-manoeuvred Liberals never should have lost.

It is fair to say that Glen Clark wore a bull's-eye on his chest from the day he declared victory in his first and only election as NDP leader. Liberal leader Gordon Campbell and the backroom Grit strategists who influenced him recoiled in shock and dismay at their pitiful election campaign performance. Their recovery was swift, however, as the substantial Liberal opposition declared open season on the NDP.

Pumped up by his new mandate and feisty by nature, Glen Clark and some of his colourful cabinet mininsters provided endless ammunition for Liberal verbal attacks. The battle that had raged between NDP and right-wing forces since the 1970s continued unabated.

Given recent history and the RCMP's apparent fascination with NDP politicians on Canada's west coast, the event that led to Clark's downfall should have come as no surprise. For many libertarians, however, their perspective of the relationship between police and politics changed on March 2, 1999, when plainclothes policemen knocked on the door of the B.C. premier's East Vancouver house while a nearby BCTV cameraman filmed their actions. As in the Shakespearean tragedy set in another millennium, with the ides of March close at hand, the strangest of bedfellows seemed to come together to assure the demise of Glen David Clark.

Ironically, while Gordon Campbell had the most to gain in the bloodletting, he had little to do but bite his lip and stay out of the way. It was a series of police, media, and NDP ministerial actions that spelled Clark's demise.

The real tragedy surrounding yet another downfall of a British Columbia premier may not, however, be obvious.

When Clark was finally charged and the lengthy process of seeking justice initiated, it was not a matter of guilt or innocence that determined his fate. It was the swaying of public opinion. With the abandonment by colleagues, the innuendo of street rumours, the aggressive actions of RCMP investigators, and the glare of media spotlights playing their parts, Clark's fate was sealed. It is unlikely that the intentions of the players or the timing of their moves will ever be fully understood, but together they add up to a single description that best describes the event—political assassination.

Judi Tyabji Wilson has gone to great lengths to explore the forces at work during Glen Clark's tenure as premier of British Columbia and the dynamics of the criminal investigation and trial that derailed his political career. Using news excerpts from local and national media to convey the impressions left on the general public, she captures the clash of political ideals and exposes the tactics that can come into play in an NDP family feud. Less clear is the role of our national police force and the relationships that have emerged with members of the press.

Judi Tyabji Wilson, seasoned by her own political and media career experiences and scarred by her own battles, has the perspective to take on a story that deserves to be told in *Daggers Unsheathed*. As one would expect, the story contains undertones of her personal passions and political idealism. At the end of her research, she has formed some strong opinions, expressed in the final chapter.

Despite their often opposing political beliefs, Judi Tyabji Wilson earned the trust of Glen and Dale Clark and people close to them and gained first-hand accounts of the impact the criminal investigation and political trial has had on their lives. In the process of gathering and presenting facts and insights she gives us a fascinating glimpse of the Clark era while seeking answers to some very important questions. And ultimately, she respects her readers as those who should decide what the future holds.

Rodger Touchie
Publisher

PART ONE

Through the Looking Glass

1

Raided

... One, two! One, two! And through and through
The vorpal blade went snicker-snack!
He left it dead, and with its head
He went galumphing back.

"And hast thou slain the Jabberwock?
Come to my arms, my beamish boy!
O frabjous day! Callooh! Callay!"
He chortled in his joy.

'Twas brillig, and the slithy toves
Did gyre and gimble in the wabe;
All mimsy were the borogoves,
And the mome raths outgrabe.

—Lewis Carroll
Through the Looking Glass

It is said that most people can remember where they were when the space shuttle blew up, or when President John F. Kennedy was assassinated, because these were events that defined an era. In British Columbia, many people can remember the day the RCMP raided the home of Premier Glen Clark. This event defined the beginning of the end of the Clark era.

It was a rainless spring night, neither cold nor warm. I remember watching the scene unfold on television like a reality show, where the cameras are assigned to the police, and crime rolls across your living room TV screen. You can watch from the comfort of your couch as the bad guys are being rounded up. It seemed completely unreal, though, because the cops were walking into the premier's home. The news reporter was saying something about a search warrant. *Did this mean the bad guys were living in the premier's house? How could that be possible?* I wondered.

I was thinking that even in the dark, the house looked comfortable; it was neat and tidy, small and cozy. *It would be awful if cameras showed up at our place*, I thought. *The yard is a mess, and under the deck there's all that wood from construction. Glen and Dale Clark are obviously much more organized.*

The police officers walked in procession single-file toward the house, up the stairs, to the front door landing, media in tow. It was such a smooth movement, perfectly executed, and their body language evoked a sombre tone, as if their feet were weighed down by the gravity of what they were doing. They were dressed in suits and ties, the lead officer in an overcoat.

This was not a casual call.

The knocks sounded on the door, and Dale Clark, the premier's wife, opened it and stood in the doorway, looking up at the tall officers. Her friendly face wore a puzzled expression, a "what's going on?" look.

The lead officer said, "There's three from the RCMP and two media, behind us. If we … could just the RCMP come in, please?"

Dale Clark didn't hesitate and moved aside to let them in. "Sure," she replied, and closed the door behind them.

The news story went on, with verbal descriptions laid over pictures taken through the windows of the Clark house. There were images of Premier Clark returning home from his office and entering through the back door. He walked in with his communications officer and someone initially referred to in the police report and the media coverage as an "unidentified female."

The footage was riveting; it was as if we were standing in the alley behind Clark's home, or on the sidewalk of his quiet street in East

Vancouver, pressing our collective noses against the window to try to see what was going on.

The cameras continued to roll; they were omnipresent, recording every visible move while commentary provided verbal speculation about what was happening. Warm lights lit the profiles of the Mounties walking through the house. The imposing images of the tall suited officers, serious expressions on their faces, were followed by the image of Clark in his kitchen, a coffee maker and wooden cupboards visible behind him. He was still in his business suit. His arms were crossed. He was shaking his head, looking puzzled, maybe frustrated, pacing the floor, unaware that we the world would be analyzing his emotions later through our television looking glass. From this vantage point, Canadians became voyeurs of Clark's moment of intense stress. We held our breath as we memorized the scenes, leaving questions about the ethics of what we were all doing for another day.

We watched intently as the drama played out. The voice-over told us the RCMP was executing a search warrant related to a criminal investigation. The entire episode was larger than life. The search went on for hours. No one was talking to the media, but the pictures kept rolling on.

What was the RCMP doing there? And how did the media come to be there with cameras rolling?

The images were fragmented and the sound out of sync. We could not make out what was happening in the house. A zoom lens only added to the confusion, as people wandered in and out of view, not providing comment. The references to casinos and criminals seemed incongruous when put together with the picture of the modest home on a quiet street on an otherwise normal evening. The premier was not being arrested, so what were they looking for in his house, and how could he have had something related to a criminal investigation into a casino?

For Glen Clark, this televised search of his home led to the final unravelling of his political career. The search would lead from a criminal investigation to criminal charges. The clock was ticking toward Clark's resignation as premier of British Columbia. It was a sound heard across Canada through our television sets, from the minute the RCMP knocked on his front door on March 2, 1999.

PART TWO

Path of a Premier: The Rise and Fall of Glen Clark

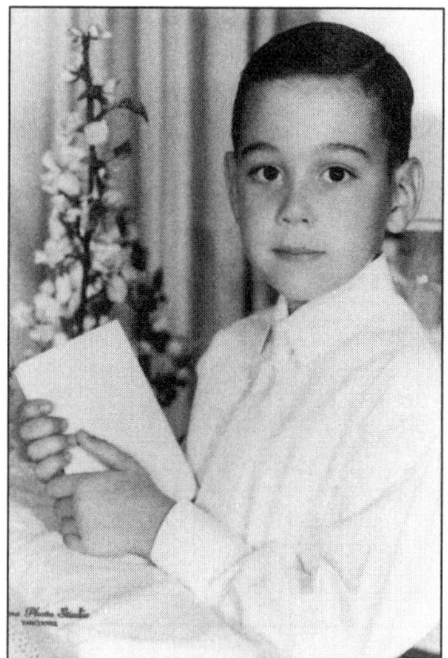

Glen Clark is seen here dressed for his first communion and as a teenager with his shaggy dog Beardsley.

Glen Clark's Grade 3 class pose at St. Jude's Catholic School. Glen (front row second from the right) spent his formative years in the same neighbourhood where he lives today.

2

A Son of Scottish Immigrants

When [Glen and Dale Clark] first met at Simon Fraser University—they took history and political science classes together—no one knew who Glen Clark was. To Dale, he was an attractive, intelligent 20-something man "with just a little bit of an edge."

"I sure didn't go out with him because of his car," she says. "He had an old beater of a Volkswagen. The windshield wipers were rigged to a string inside the car and that's how Glen had to operate them."

Their first date was an NDP dinner at the Renfrew community centre ...

"One of the things that first attracted me to Glen was the fact that he's very gentle, though I'm sure some people will have trouble believing that."

—*Vancouver Sun,* March 16, 1996

Who is Glen Clark, how did he become premier of British Columbia, and how did he end up facing criminal charges of corruption?

A son of Scottish immigrants, Glen Clark was born in Nanaimo in 1958, on the east coast of southern Vancouver Island. He was the second oldest of four children, and the only boy.

His mother, Barbara Clark (née Hamilton), came to Canada on her own when she was in her early twenties. She left the village she grew up in, Rutherglen, and took the ship from nearby Glasgow to Quebec. Then she made her way west to Vancouver. This journey was a brave move for the time, but she was determined and inspired. Her father had spent time in Canada during the Depression, travelling the country in an attempt to find work so that he could apply for landed immigrant status. He had travelled west in his search, finding the countryside and lifestyle beautiful, but was unable to find work because of the times. When he returned to Scotland, he told his children that the great beauty of Canada increased as you travelled west. As soon as she was able, Barbara traced her father's steps, eventually finding her new home on the West Coast.

James Clark, Glen Clark's father, was a large man, almost larger than life. He was six feet tall, about 200 pounds, and he travelled to Vancouver from the same village of Rutherglen, Scotland, to find work. James had known Barbara a little at home, but he was more the age of her brother, and in fact had landed in Vancouver with Barbara's brother. After James and Barbara married, Barbara filled the role of stay-at-home mom, while James worked and made time to be a passionate labour activist. Their four children arrived over a long span of years. First Leslie, a year later Glen, then four or five years later Christine, and another four years later Jeanne joined the family. Leslie now lives in Edmonton; Christine moved to Scotland; and Jeanne and Barbara live close to Glen's house in East Vancouver.

The Clarks upheld some of the Scottish traditions. The clan tartan is the Cameron tartan, and although Glen does not have a kilt, he knows the significance of it. "First footing," the traditional way to welcome the New Year, was modernized slightly by the Clarks. This Scottish tradition involves bringing a lump of coal, something to eat, and something to drink to bring in the New Year. As well, a tall, dark stranger should be the first person at your door on New Year's Day.

"We don't carry a lump of coal," Clark explained, "but we certainly follow through with something to eat and something to drink, which is usually a gift of Scotch. And it is hard to have a tall, dark stranger on your doorstep first thing in the morning," he laughed. "So every year I try to make a point of getting up early on New Year's Day, to be the first one on my mom's doorstep with some food and drink. I'm not tall, and I'm no stranger, but I'm a bit dark."

Glen Clark was smaller than many of his fellow students during his school years, but this did not keep him out of sports. He attended Notre Dame High School in East Vancouver, which he described as, at the time, a place where there were lots of small kids from poor neighbourhoods. Many were children of immigrants. "We had to work harder than anyone else," he said, "but it taught me how to be resourceful."

Clark was on the football team and took this very seriously. He claims that this experience taught him to smile in the face of adversity. "We were a small school, so everyone had to play. We fought so hard. And we won every game, even some of the games in the States, beating teams from larger, wealthier districts. I took a real beating in some of those games, being small, and that taught me one of the most valuable lessons in life. I realized that I was either going to stick it out and learn to be successful, or quit." "I don't quit anything." So Clark learned to take a beating if he wanted to win. "I like to win."[1]

How does the lesson on the football field apply to life? What would Glen Clark choose to take a real beating for in order to win? Enter Glen Clark, the political activist and advocate for labour. It was Glen's father's dedication to labour activism that taught Clark to look for the dynamics between the owners of the economy and its labourers. And it set him on an early course of ideological politics, with an ingrained commitment to the workers.

"My father believed the world of labour was black and white, and everything he saw in the conflict between owners and workers reinforced his biases," Clark said. "He insisted I go to university, and that I not end up working as a labourer for the rest of my life. He did not want me working with my hands. He believed that if I had the opportunity to rise above the role of labourer through education, then I had to take it."[2]

Clark did not believe there was any contradiction in holding an ideological commitment to the advancement of organized labour, while he dedicated his personal ambition to avoiding joining its ranks. Clark had worked briefly as a labourer and spent some time as a union

At 28 Glen Clark was a shining star as his running mate Bob Williams (middle), and federal MP for Vancouver Kingsway, Ian Waddell, endorsed the up-and-comer.

organizer. His personal ambition included studying at university. He took a bachelor of arts degree from Simon Fraser University in political science and Canadian studies. His master of arts was taken at the University of British Columbia and was in community and regional planning, which would qualify him to work as a regional planner or economic development officer. His thesis was "The History of Forest Policy in British Columbia to 1972," with an emphasis on regional planning. Clark spent a great deal of time researching the development of the forest industry in British Columbia and the inherent conflict in public versus private interests, which has been and continues to be a major issue.

Clark managed to write his thesis while working. His political interests seemed an inevitable consequence of his roots, his education, and his natural ability to speak passionately about those things that mattered to him. Clark's father, the source of so much of his political inspiration, was a heavy smoker and died of cancer at age 53, and Glen felt the loss deeply. He regretted that his father did not see him elected to pursue their common concern about fairness for workers.

When Clark joined the NDP in 1976 while studying at Langara College in Vancouver, NDP heavyweight Bob Williams was president of the local riding association. Clark joined the NDP to help in a by-election campaign, caused when Williams resigned his seat in the legislature to open the spot for NDP leader Dave Barrett. Later, when Williams returned to the legislature, he encouraged Glen Clark to run for the nomination for the other seat in East Vancouver, a two-MLA riding at the time.

Glen Clark won the nomination for East Vancouver when he was 27, and was elected to the legislature at 28 years old in 1986. He was married to Dale, and their two children, a boy, Reed, and a girl, Layne, came along a few years later after he became MLA. Dale Clark gave a peek behind the scenes in "Avoiding the glare," an article in the *Vancouver Sun,* March 16, 1996, after Clark became NDP leader.

> … She says one of the most difficult things about Glen's very public life is the constant barrage of press coverage, not all of it good …

> The Clarks try to minimize the effects of Glen's fishbowl existence on their children, seemingly with some success.
>
> With Glen delivering a rousing acceptance speech to cheering supporters at the recent leadership convention, Layne, who had just arrived with Dale's parents, climbed on to the podium and tugged excitedly on her mother's arm.
>
> "I finally bent down and asked her what was wrong," Dale says. "She looked at me and said: 'Guess what, when we were coming down on SkyTrain, I saw my swimming teacher!'"

Clark burst onto the provincial political scene with energy and an uncompromising passion for his beliefs. He was young, bright, attractive, and brash in his public comments. He soon developed a reputation for being "cocky" and was a formidable member of the New Democratic Party (NDP) opposition in the Victoria legislature.

During Clark's first five years as MLA, he quickly emerged as an outspoken critic of the Social Credit government under Bill Vander Zalm. When the NDP won the 1991 election under the leadership of former Vancouver mayor Mike Harcourt, Clark became one of the most powerful cabinet ministers in the new government. He took on portfolios that included finance, ferries, and employment and investment.

From 1991 to 1996, Premier Mike Harcourt presided over an NDP government that was rocked by one scandal after another, so that they were constantly under attack. The province's mounting debt drew criticism from the B.C. Liberals, initially under the leadership of Gordon Wilson (1991–1993), and later of Gordon Campbell. The business community was upset about financial and land-use management issues, while environmentalists were upset about the same issues for different reasons.

However, it was the nagging controversy over alleged misconduct in charitable gaming that dogged Harcourt's government. The charitable gaming controversy, known as the Nanaimo

Mixing family and politics is never easy, especially on the polarized battlegrounds of B.C. Glen, Dale, and their two children are seen posing here on budget day, 1992.

As minister of employment and investment Glen announces a road improvement project. Layne looks on.

Glen, Dale, Layne, and Reed relax on the ferry.

Relatively new to the political wars a wide-eyed Glen Clark gets an earful from the B.C. Federation of Labour's Ken Georgetti at the NDP government's 1992 budget reception.

Commonwealth Holding Society (NCHS) scandal (sometimes called Bingogate), was a complex story that evolved over time until it was hard to sort through the layers of allegations. What appeared incontrovertible was that some money that was slated for charity seemed to be missing. The public commentary was that someone in the NDP had to be held accountable for the misuse of charity money revealed by the NCHS controversy.

In a calculated political move, Harcourt resigned, citing the NCHS scandal, nicely wrapping up all the nasty elements of the story and packing them away on his back. There was public speculation that an inner circle of NDP MLAs conspired to oust Mike Harcourt, and that Glen Clark was foremost among these. Clark and the others accused have said this did not happen, and it is only relevant here to provide the context for events as they unfolded later.

At the time of Harcourt's resignation in late 1995, the NDP was all but written off as a contender for government in the coming provincial election. Its mandate was stale, since it had been four years since the previous election. The media coverage and polling had been negative for so long that few people could remember a time when the NDP was popular. Campbell's Liberals enjoyed a solid lead in the polls, and they were getting ready to take over.

Many people in the NDP were preparing for defeat, but they had a leadership race to run first. There were five contenders, including MLAs Joan Smallwood and Corky Evans. Clark said he was not sure initially that he wanted to run, but once he had decided to run, he was running to win.[3] And the race unfolded more as a coronation of Glen Clark than as a serious competition for the leadership. Clark said he could feel the momentum build throughout the campaign, beginning with an announcement from senior cabinet minister Dan Miller that he would not run, but would be backing Clark.

The audiences at the leadership debates were large and grew as the convention neared. For the first time in years, the NDP was focussed on itself, its policies, and its objectives in the coming election campaign. A new life was breathed into the party, and it emerged from its siege mentality. At the end of the leadership race, the NDP had a champion in Glen Clark and a villain in Gordon Campbell. Clark had a long list of initiatives to implement before and during the campaign, and he launched his unofficial election campaign before he was sworn in.

So did the Liberals.

On February 21, 1996, the day before Clark became premier, while the balloons were still being blown up for the celebration, the Campbell Liberals released information on a scandal concerning overseas investments by BC Hydro officials, alleging improper conduct. In short, the controversial act took place while Glen Clark was the minister responsible for BC Hydro, a powerful Crown corporation involved in a number of international deals. The allegation came from Liberal MLA Gary Farrell-Collins (later known as Gary Collins), who said that senior BC Hydro officials abused their power in a secret deal that involved NDP friends and insiders in a payoff in Pakistan. On the CTV national news on February 21. Farrell-Collins thundered: "This is about a special deal driven by Glen Clark and approved by the NDP cabinet, structured to result in significant profits for NDP friends and BC Hydro insiders. The only obvious reason for BC Hydro to form this joint venture corporation is to help its friends and find lucrative investments around the world at taxpayers' expense."

The allegation was blunt, but the details around the case were complicated. The International Power Corporation (IPC), a subsidiary of BC Hydro, was alleged to be providing a sweetheart deal to these "select few" people, who would be offered a 24 percent return on their investment, guaranteed by BC Hydro, and tax-free due to IPC's registration in the Grand Cayman Islands. The Liberals called this a "double scandal," claiming that the tax shelter status was improper. There was great moralizing, covered by every media outlet as a lead story. BC Hydro's top officials, John Laxton and John Sheehan, had their names plastered across the headlines, associated with allegations of serious wrongdoing. The newspapers, particularly the *Vancouver Sun,* took strong editorial positions condemning them for their immoral behaviour. The Liberals ran with the story at every opportunity.

The manner in which the scandal unfolded, and Clark's handling of it, set the tone of, and foreshadowed the coming election campaign. Here is an excerpt from the CTV national news of February 21.

> LLOYD ROBERTSON: A scandal at British Columbia Hydro has sent incoming Premier Glen Clark scrambling ...
>
> COLIN GRAY (reporter): This was an ambush the BC Liberals have been planning for weeks, designed to

> embarrass and disgrace incoming NDP leader and Premier Glen Clark ...
>
> Glen Clark was the Minister in charge of BC Hydro. He says he didn't know that IPC shares were going to Hydro officials and their families, and he had in fact ordered that they not. As a result he's fired BC Hydro's two top officials.
>
> GLEN CLARK (NDP premier designate): I've given specific instructions, I've been in the House, I've debated this, it's public information and my view is that the spirit of the instructions I gave were not followed and so I've no hesitation in taking the action I took today.
>
> GRAY: It's no coincidence that the Liberals released this the day before Glen Clark stepped into the premier's office. They'd like very much to see this turn into another Bingogate, the scandal that helped do in outgoing Premier Mike Harcourt ... It remains to be seen if that will be enough or if the taint of another NDP scandal will damage the premiership the man has yet to even assume.

The scandal was meant to define the new Clark regime, and to some extent it did, but not in the manner the Liberals had hoped. Clark's quick action to force the removal of Laxton and Sheehan was widely praised by the media and was seen as decisive. The Liberals were left without any further ammunition on this scandal, and they seemed almost stunned that their issue had been so quickly taken from them. If anything, the praise that Clark received detracted from the Liberals' public profile; in effect, the dropping of this scandal backfired on them. Editorials and callers to open-line radio shows commented that the Liberals appeared mean to have timed the scandal to break just before Clark's swearing-in ceremony.

Lieutenant-Governor Garde Gardom conducted Clark's swearing-in at Collingwood Neighbourhood House in Vancouver on February 22, 1996.

There is much more to this story than an explosive scandal quickly handled, however. Over the next three to four years Laxton and Sheehan would slowly repair some of the damage done to them by this incident. For three years, John Laxton was investigated by the RCMP and Special Prosecutor Paul Fraser, who was appointed by the provincial government to determine whether or not criminal charges should be laid. John Sheehan, who had served as an employee of BC Hydro for nineteen years prior to his sudden departure, was forced to sue BC Hydro for wrongful dismissal, a case he won. Both the special prosecutor and Judge Donald Brenner (later appointed Chief Justice of the Supreme Court of British Columbia) found that there was no basis for the Liberals' claims of "secrecy" or "inside dealings."

Laxton and Sheehan saw their reputations and their livelihood disappear overnight in this political scandal. Four years later, when they were exonerated, there was little publicity and almost no analysis of the incident. For the record, the deal involved the building of a power plant in Pakistan, which is operating today, to provide much-needed power to about one million people. Laxton said, "It came in on time and on budget, and is an example in Asia of an excellent power project. The great irony is that although we were accused by the Liberals of handing out bribes in Pakistan, in fact the World Bank had so thoroughly vetted our financial statements that there wasn't a penny to spare. Where would the bribes have come from? It is a tragedy that this project, which should have brought kudos to the government, was swept away in a completely false controversy."[4]

When two major investors backed out of the deal, Laxton put in his own money, about $1 million worth. This is what Farrell-Collins and the Liberals pointed to with their claims of corruption. In fact, it was a high-risk deal, and Laxton was risking his own money to save it. At the time, Laxton was taking in one dollar a year as chair of BC Hydro. He had taken on the position to serve the public. Glen Clark was blindsided by the information that Laxton and Sheehan had invested in the project, and he reacted to protect the government from what could have been a nasty scandal just before the election.

"Laxton and Sheehan were bright, and motivated by the province's best interests," said Clark. "I had not been told about their recent financing structure, and I had to act quickly." As Clark pointed out, Laxton and Sheehan's departure unfortunately appeared to support the Liberals' allegations that the men had done something wrong, an unintended consequence of their resignations.[5]

The political arena was in a state of turmoil. Clark, the dynamic new leader, was desperate to salvage his party in the waning days of its mandate. In addition to reacting to the scandal, he had many other policy-related issues in front of him and a demoralized party to rejuvenate, but in terms of the political scoreboard, he won this round.

The Liberals were having problems in marketing themselves to a cynical public. In addition to the BC Hydro bomb blowing up on them, one of their pre-election television advertisements backfired when they portrayed their leader, Gordon Campbell, in a plaid shirt.

Campbell's plaid-shirt campaign provoked mockery of the Liberal leader because few people believed that Campbell actually wore plaid shirts. Campbell, a former downtown Vancouver developer and mayor, was seldom seen in casual clothing, and he was associated with wealth, privilege, and expensive suits. The plaid shirt was an icon of the rural areas, and people reacted with laughter. This was not what the Liberals wanted and certainly not what had been foreseen. The public relations team had to move into damage control over its own advertising campaign. The issue was important enough that Gordon Campbell invited television cameras into his house to see his plaid shirts nicely hanging in his closet.

Who hangs up a plaid shirt?

In an article entitled "Campbell in the Soup," the Vancouver *Province* (March 19) provided a political opinion reflected in other major media:

> GORDON CAMPBELL got a dose of bad news last week that will require much more than plaid shirts and vague "trust me"-isms to cure.
>
> The B.C. "Liberal" leader has seen his party slip from a commanding lead in the polls to a virtual dead heat with the NDP.
>
> And it gets worse: Glen Clark has handily eclipsed Gordo as the Angus Reid poll respondents' choice for who would make the best premier.
>
> Clark is now favored by a third of those polled, Campbell by only a quarter—hardly a solid foundation for the election coronation many were predicting.
>
> What's gone wrong for Campbell?
>
> For one thing, Mike Harcourt resigned, depriving him of an easy target. Glen Clark is a much more formidable adversary who presents the opposite of Harcourt's perceived dithering. When Campbell tried a major offensive with the BC Hydro scandal, Clark wielded the axe

> quickly to stem the political fallout. It appears to have worked:
>
> The poll showing Clark on top was taken after the Hydro affair broke …
>
> If Campbell thought he could coast to victory over a self-destructing NDP, he was sadly mistaken. And if he doesn't soon pick up the pace, he could well coast to a second-place finish on election day.

And so an election that many Liberals had taken for granted became a horse race, with Glen Clark surprising the Campbell team with an energized campaign style that was a stark contrast to both Harcourt and Campbell.

Then another scandal broke against the NDP. This one had nasty overtones and hit close to Clark because of the people involved. This scandal was prominent on television and radio and in newspapers and ran as a top story for days. Television cameras showed the RCMP raiding NDP headquarters, with references to criminal activities and the need for further action. It all tied back to the controversy over the Nanaimo Commonwealth Holding Society scandal that had caused Mike Harcourt to resign, and it was like a bad penny, showing up just when the NDP was seeing some positive momentum. The TV news cameras, which happened to be on hand to catch the raid, showed boxes of documents being removed, and reporters related this back to the news stories about the NDP's alleged misuse of charitable gaming revenue.

The RCMP officer at the centre of the move against the NDP headquarters was Sergeant Peter Montague, and his comments about the raid and criminal investigations were carried across Canada. Montague was a high-profile officer who had pioneered a new form of open RCMP communication that involved a friendly accessible relationship with the media and regular communication on many police investigations. Montague first surfaced as a spokesperson in this new form of communication in a standoff with Natives in the interior over land near Gustafsen Lake. The RCMP, led by Montague, were on the airwaves for weeks commenting on what appeared to be an illegal and dangerous encampment of Natives. Montague had emerged from that with the image of a calm take-charge leader of the RCMP, prepared to face politically sensitive issues without flinching. The Vancouver media, particularly BCTV, loved him, and the public seemed to respond to his media scrums favourably. By the time of the raid on NDP headquarters, Montague was relatively famous, with an established track record with certain media.

The raid on NDP headquarters occurred two days after the NDP was shown to be neck-and-neck with the B.C. Liberals, as reported in the *Province* on March 21.

> The Nanaimo bingo scandal erupted again yesterday as police armed with search warrants swooped on NDP headquarters …
>
> Although no details were released, RCMP spokesman Sgt. Peter Montague said the warrants "allege a number of criminal offences committed by individuals and societies, including theft, fraud, misuse of charity monies, breach of trust and related corruption provisions."
>
> … Premier Glen Clark said he still plans to call a public inquiry and is not upset by the raids. If party members or others in the past did wrong and must now pay for it, "then so be it," said Clark.
>
> Liberal leader Gordon Campbell and Reform leader Jack Weisgerber called on Clark to launch the inquiry immediately.
>
> The raids, said Weisgerber, are "a timely reminder of the corruption and criminal activity associated with the NDP's Nanaimo charity ripoff scandal that will not go unpunished by voters in the upcoming election."

On March 20, CBC TV's national news also carried the RCMP comments in the context of the coming provincial election.

PETER MANSBRIDGE: Good evening. The search warrants allege fraud and corruption, and the RCMP was armed with them today, in raids on NDP Headquarters in British Columbia. It's the latest action in BC's infamous bingogate scandal. And, as Eve Savory reports, it comes just as the new NDP premier is getting set to call an election.

EVE SAVORY (CBC reporter): Smack in the middle of Glen Clark's pre-election photo ops and give-aways, the RCMP has raided seven different locations. They include provincial NDP headquarters, and the private home of a former treasurer of the Party ...

SGT. PETER MONTAGUE (RCMP): These search warrants allege theft, fraud, misuse of charity monies, and also breach of trust and related provisions in the Code for corruption ...

SAVORY: There is probably more to come. The police say there is a likelihood of more search warrants, and that means more raids ...

MANSBRIDGE: Premier Clark has also promised a public inquiry into the bingogate scandal. An announcement on that is expected soon.

In public comments reported in the *Vancouver Sun* on March 22, Gordon Campbell used Peter Montague's allegations to reinforce the perception of corruption. The raid and the allegations raised by the RCMP spokesperson and the political commentary from Campbell, all claimed possible lying, theft, and corruption by the NDP. Campbell also tried to put the blame for the scandal on the Glen Clark government by referring to actions taken in 1993, although the reference he alluded to was unclear.

... Liberal leader Gordon Campbell said in an interview that the warrants "show for the first time that the RCMP

> believe that officers of the NDP stole money from charities and lied about it."
>
> ... Campbell said the warrants contain "some very serious criminal allegations."
>
> "This happened in 1993," Campbell said. "This happened under the watch of the people who are in the NDP cabinet today. There's going to be a lot of people who have to answer for this."
>
> Premier Glen Clark told reporters before the warrants were released that he intends to call a public inquiry into the NCHS scandal soon.
>
> "I'm looking forward to a full and open investigation as soon as possible. We've nothing to hide, nothing to fear."

A few days later the RCMP dropped a political bombshell on the NDP, and more specifically on Clark. On March 29, 1996, just over one month after Clark became premier, new RCMP actions turned the focus of the media toward a criminal investigation of two of the most prominent and respected New Democrats in the province. Former premier Dave Barrett and Bob Williams were both close friends and political allies of Clark. Williams was Clark's former colleague in the dual riding of East Vancouver. The *Vancouver Sun* had detailed information on the investigations before the documents were released publicly. The Barrett–Williams investigation was, of course, a front-page story:

> Allegations of bribery, breach of trust and criminal conspiracy involving former NDP premier Dave Barrett and his long-time political colleague, Bob Williams, are contained in RCMP documents to be released today.
>
> The political bombshell prompted Premier Glen Clark to promise he will deliver early next week on his promised public inquiry into the Nanaimo Commonwealth bingo scandal.

In simultaneous press conferences in Vancouver and Victoria on Thursday, Barrett and Williams angrily rejected allegations contained in police search warrant applications that are about to be unsealed by the courts.

… In Victoria, Barrett appeared furious at being named in the RCMP search warrant, which connects him with an alleged criminal conspiracy.

He said he's trying "with some difficulty" to restrain his anger.

"What is it that I have done?" he said at a press conference in the rose garden, outside the legislature. "Nothing in the document says that stolen money was used," Barrett said. "[The warrant] says that there was a criminal act committed because he gave up his seat for me.

"The conspiracy, as I understand it, is that there was a deal struck for him to step down," he said.

Clark, who once shared the Vancouver East riding with Williams, his political mentor, tried to shrug off the latest allegations.

"It's another wild day in B.C. politics," Clark said. "This happened 20-odd years ago when I was in high school … and I'm not sure there is anything to the charges necessarily."

… Liberal leader Gordon Campbell said Clark should not delay the election call any further.

"It's like pulling teeth one at a time. How much more do we have to take before the public have their say?"

Liberal critic Mike de Jong said Barrett "offered nothing in the way of explanation for failing to take action when it was appropriate to do so."

"This is obviously a pre-emptive attempt by Mr. Barrett to dull the blow of what is about to fall tomorrow and in the weeks to come … It's very, very serious."

It is unclear how Liberal MLA De Jong could have any knowledge of "what is about to fall tomorrow and in the weeks to come," as it appears he did. Did De Jong also have information on the criminal allegations to be released later that the next day? If so, how? What was he referring to when he implied more was to fall in the weeks to come? He insinuated that Barrett was not providing a good enough defence, and hinted that the anticipated actions by the RCMP were very serious, but how would he have known this?

In fact, the RCMP documents referred to in the story were part of a search warrant application for a lawyer's office. Neither Williams nor Barrett were ever interviewed, nor were they charged in this case. After two years of investigation the special prosecutor announced that there was no foundation to the original allegations, and he deeply regretted the dark cloud the allegations had caused.

• • •

Despite the raids and criminal charges, the screaming headlines, and the maelstrom of controversy, in the political arena Clark had momentum, and Campbell was losing ground.

Clark's slogan "On Your Side," was a contrast to Campbell's appearance of cosiness with the downtown Vancouver high rollers. The Campbell slogan, "You Deserve Better," made me laugh every time I saw him on the news. Both slogans were designed for the television media campaign, and they often were on placards or attached to the podium from which the leaders would speak. Whenever Clark made a campaign announcement, under his head and shoulders it said "On Your Side." Generally speaking the announcements were about health care, education, or day care. When Campbell came on, under his head and shoulders was "You Deserve Better," which acted as a subliminal message. Campbell's announcements were often scandal-related and critical of the NDP, so there was not much relevance to people's personal day-to-day lives, and this also made him appear detached.

The theme of Clark the populist versus Campbell the elitist came up again and again, and Clark's natural affinity with workers or "ordinary British Columbians" came through in his speeches as he focussed on issues. The Campbell Liberals' strategy left them silent on many of the issues.

An important dynamic in the 1996 campaign was the competition for votes coming from the B.C. Reform party, led by Jack Weisgerber, and from the Progressive Democratic Alliance (PDA), led by Gordon Wilson, former leader of the B.C. Liberals and the man Campbell defeated for the leadership in 1993. Although the mainstream media focussed almost exclusively on the battle between the Campbell Liberals and the Clark NDP, with only occasional comments from B.C. Reform, local community media throughout the province gave more balanced treatment to the four parties with elected members. This meant that in policy debates in the ridings, the contrasts between the parties became more evident.

In many instances, the NDP, B.C. Reform, and PDA took a common position, leaving the Liberals isolated on a policy, such as the sale of BC Rail. The B.C. Liberals advocated the sale; everyone else was opposed. In addition, sometimes the B.C. Liberals sided with B.C. Reform, which made them appear to be in the extreme right-wing camp. For example, on the Nisga'a Treaty and related issues of Aboriginal affairs, Campbell and Weisgerber had opposing views to Clark and Wilson.

This dynamic also meant that in the rural areas, the B.C. Liberals were fending off the right-wing appeal of the B.C. Reform party. Campbell's statements were geared to capture as many of these voters as possible, to shore up what he perceived to be the right-wing vote. The more he spoke to their issues, the more he risked alienating the pro-environmental, pro-social justice voters in the urban areas.

Gordon Wilson had little profile in the campaign, however his focus when he was quoted was on policy issues. Wilson did not join Campbell and Weisgerber in their characterization of the NDP as corrupt and as a party of liars, and this may have helped the public temper its judgement of Clark when he talked about due process and investigations. If nothing else, it gave Clark an opposition leader he could debate on issues rather than scandal.

Regardless of why the public did not seem to jump on the scandal bandwagon, Clark weathered the controversies relatively unscathed.

Polls did show that there was one policy area where Clark had an identified weakness, while Campbell rated "strong." This was economic policy, particularly dealing with debts, deficits, and the economy. The *Province* of March 13 reported:

> B.C. is sliding deeper into debt.
>
> Provincial debt grew $1.572 billion to $28.61 billion in the first nine months of the fiscal year.
>
> … the health and social services ministries ran out of money:
>
> They overspent by nearly $180 million and are now running on special warrants.
>
> Premier Glen Clark tried to paint a rosy picture as he released the third-quarter report yesterday.
>
> "We will have a balanced budget for the 1995 fiscal year," he said. "And I am committing to a second balanced budget in 1996."
>
> But the third-quarter report showed that growth and revenues were lower than forecast.
>
> The social services ministry was $98.5 million over budget—partly because Ottawa withheld $47 million. The health ministry was $81 million over budget.
>
> The government has squirrelled away $1.2 billion that it borrowed in advance to take advantage of favorable rates, and Finance Minister Elizabeth Cull said that means it probably won't have to borrow next year.
>
> But Liberal finance critic Fred Gingell said: "They're going to call an election, and it's there to fund a few

> projects." Gingell said the third-quarter figures show that B.C. is headed for another deficit, not a balanced budget.
>
> He said it's dishonest for the New Democrats not to include more than $120 million in spending on highways and other infrastructure in the operating budget. If the accounting were done properly, he said, B.C. would be staring a $103-million deficit in the face.
>
> "The most worrisome figure is the $450-million taxpayer-supported debt," said Gingell. "That's like taking out money on your mortgage—and that's a hell of a second mortgage."
>
> B.C. Reform leader Jack Weisgerber called the increased debt "shocking." He noted that total provincial debt is $756 million higher than projected.
>
> "Glen Clark has no intention of abandoning his tax, borrow and spend approach to government," he said.
>
> Clark says he won't introduce a 1996–97 budget until the end of April and will run B.C. on special warrants when the 1995–96 budget expires on March 31.

There were many news items showcasing the NDP's controversial record in fiscal management. In each of these items, the NDP was criticized for its actions, and the B.C. Liberals were profiled in a more positive light.

On social issues, the NDP appeared to receive positive coverage; the B.C. Liberals' primary focus was not on social issues. It boiled down to a contrast in leadership and vision, and a competition for the hearts of British Columbians. Clark's father's influence on the issues Clark considered important was clearly demonstrated in the NDP's commitment to easy access to post-secondary education and jobs for youth. On March 19, the *Vancouver Sun* reported:

> ... When [Clark] took office last month, the 38-year old premier also dubbed himself minister responsible for

youth. Since then, he's surrounded himself with young faces for photo opportunity after youthful photo opportunity.

He's wobbled around on skateboards for photographers, chatted with street kids, and promised students jobs and a break on tuition.

Today, he's scheduled to show up at Simon Fraser University's Harbour Centre campus to announce operating grants for the province's post-secondary institutions. He'll also promise to keep colleges and universities accessible in a time of budget cuts.

Monday, Clark was at Langara College to announce that he'll freeze post-secondary education fees. At the same time he was making the announcement, the publicly funded Knowledge Network was running a tape of a casually dressed Clark, perched on a stool before a blackboard, delivering the same news.

Federal transfer payment cuts would have raised tuition 35 per cent if the province had not stepped in to make up the shortfall, Clark said.

... Clark seems more comfortable when he goes casual. A dressed-down Clark looks more credible than Campbell, whose appearance in a plaid shirt in recent TV ads is being mocked by New Democrats.

"I didn't know Gucci came in plaid," Clark cracked to a party gathering last weekend.

Even though Clark's personal appeal seemed to be the source of the NDP's recovery, the polls that showed the NDP and the Liberals in a neck-and-neck race also reinforced the NDP's lower credibility in managing the province's finances. The following article in the *Vancouver Sun* on March 16 is an example:

- Voters consider Campbell better able than Clark to deal with public finances and debt. His approval rating on that score is 47 per cent, compared to 40 per cent for Clark and 34 per cent for Weisgerber.

- No party has developed significant momentum. Most people say their opinion of the parties has worsened in the last three months, suggesting most are discontent with the level and nature of political debate in the province.
- NDP support is more firm than the soft support of the Liberals and Reform, leaving those parties vulnerable to more vote switching.
- Both the Liberals and NDP have done a good job of attracting back their 1991 supporters, with about 65 per cent of voters leaning toward voting again for the same party.

Clark's schedule was a whirlwind of announcements, all aimed at contrasting the NDP's social agenda with the B.C. Liberals' fiscal agenda. From Clark's swearing-in on February 22 until mid-March, his announcements (*Vancouver Sun*, March 19) included:

Feb. 23—Clark announces the appointment of Brian Smith to head B.C. Hydro.

Feb. 26—Clark announces cuts to government administration.

Feb. 29—Clark announces a new DNA lab in Vancouver.

March 4—Clark announces cuts to the highways ministry and amalgamation of the motor vehicle branch with ICBC.

March 7—Clark announces the end of B.C. Systems and the B.C. Trade Development Corp.

March 8—Clark announces steps to reduce waits for breast-cancer test results and $2.5 million in other women's health initiatives.

March 11—Clark holds a news conference on the Pacific

salmon treaty after meeting with fishing industry officials.

March 12—In Vancouver, Clark and cabinet colleagues announce the third quarterly financial report and a salmon enhancement program.

March 13—Clark speaks at a youth forum, and then later announces a program to encourage kids to get off the streets.

March 15—Clark announces youth employment and training program.

March 18—Clark announces a freeze on post-secondary tuition fees, despite reduced federal transfer payments.

The public encountered Clark either fending off scandals or making announcements geared to help youth, salmon, and social programs. Meanwhile, Gordon Campbell was frequently criticized for re-creating the Social Credit party in the B.C. Liberals and for devoting too much of his attention, and his platform, to the wealthy. The *Province,* on March 12, commented:

> The only thing new at last night's Grit gala was Nelson Skalbania's jacket.
>
> The new owner of the B.C. Lions arrived at the $250-a-plate Liberal fund-raiser sporting a fluorescent green-checked jacket, prompting some in the crowd to wonder if Skalbania is planning a uniform change for his football team ...
>
> Also spotted amid the sea of Gucci and Versacci were Phil Hochstein, president of the Independent Contractors Association, Vancouver Coun. George Puil, political fixer Patrick Kinsella, David Emerson of the Vancouver Airport Authority, former Socred organizer Brian Battison, chief Liberal strategist Greg Lyle and political schmoozer Jess Ketchum ...

> Attendance was down from last year's Grit gruel, but the price was up by $75 a plate.
>
> The price hike, according to Grit money man and master of ceremonies Marty Zlotnik, bagged the Liberal party an additional $100,000 in profit over last year's dinner.
>
> ... Campbell challenged Premier Glen Clark to call an election immediately.
>
> And he slammed the NDP government's record since coming to power in 1991, ending a 16-year hiatus in opposition.
>
> "In retrospect, the NDP told all B.C. they would be different," Campbell said. "They were different all right—they were worse."
>
> Copies of Campbell's election platform, called The Courage to Change, were on every seat in the house.

When the election was finally called in February 1996, it was almost anticlimactic, as the issues had been hotly debated since Clark's swearing-in as premier. Clark's government introduced a balanced budget, which the B.C. Liberals challenged, and they were off to the races.

The Liberal campaign had a few gaffes, such as the "Glenocchio" television advertisement with a distorted nose, in which Glen Clark was accused of lying every time he made a campaign promise. This advertisement provoked a backlash from the public, similar to the backlash against former federal Progressive Conservative leader and incumbent prime minister Kim Campbell (no relation to Gordon Campbell) when her campaign used television advertisements mocking Jean Chretien's crooked mouth.

At the end of it all, on May 28, 1996 Glen Clark astonished observers by winning a second term for the NDP. It is likely that few people were more shocked than Gordon Campbell. The Canadian national televison media (CBC TV and CTV on May 29, and CBC TV on May 31 respectively) carried stories focusing on the surprise victory:

Campaigning in Prince George in April 1996, local candidate Lois Boone and Premier Clark work at getting in step with the times.

PETER MANSBRIDGE [CBC TV]: Well, it went down to the wire in British Columbia last night …

TERRY MILEWSKI: Making government work, for Glen Clark, means a key government role in building dams and bridges and schools, using union labour. But the private sector views Clark with suspicion.

… GORDON CAMPBELL/LIBERAL LEADER: Let's just remember what happened yesterday: the largest popular vote went to the Liberal party. The only party in British Columbia that increased its share in the House was the B.C. Liberal party. We more than doubled our caucus; the NDP's was reduced.

... MILEWSKI: Indeed, with such a slim majority, it's going to be tough for Clark to get too far in front of the electorate on any issue. He does have a reputation here as a bare-knuckles union man who wants to tax the rich. But he's also known as a pragmatist who can bend when he has to. And he has to ...

LLOYD ROBERTSON [CTV]: New Democrats in British Columbia savoured their democratic but narrow election victory today and Premier Glen Clark says he'll use his renewed mandate to give B.C. a stronger voice in national politics. Voters chopped the NDP majority to 39 seats and actually gave the Liberals a greater share of the popular vote with just 33 seats in the legislature. CTV's Colin Gray reports.

COLIN GRAY: British Columbia woke up today to a second term NDP government, something nobody was predicting just a few months ago. And this is the man New Democrats in B.C. have to thank for that, having almost single handedly got the NDP back onto its feet, Glen Clark says a big priority for him will be sticking up for B.C. on the National scene ...

Liberal leader Gordon Campbell lost the election to Clark and he blew a big lead in doing so. He accepted full responsibility for the loss ...

WENDY MESLEY [CBC TV]: He's been called ambitious, feisty and flamboyant. Well, tonight we're calling him one more name: Canadian Newsmaker of the Week. He is British Columbia Premier Glen Clark, and three days ago he pulled off an election victory that many thought would have been impossible just months ago. In February, when Clark won the leadership of the provincial NDP, he inherited more than just the premier's job. He inherited a party sinking in scandal and trailing in the polls. Clark then ran an election campaign that bucked the national trend. He said it was okay to spend when other governments across the country said it was best to slash. On Tuesday night Clark proved that the NDP is still a force in Canada. The party celebrated its first back-to-back election wins ever in the province.

DAVID MITCHELL/B.C. HISTORIAN: It would not have been possible, it would not have been conceivable for the NDP to even be competitive in this election if not for the energy and the dynamism of this young leader …

My own anecdote of the 1996 general election is on a smaller scale. I had contested the election for the Progressive Democratic Alliance, having left the B.C. Liberal party when Gordon Campbell took over as leader (an episode I wrote about in my book, *Political Affairs*). I had lost my campaign, and I was very sad, since I had been defeated by my former brother-in-law, who had been a Social Credit party member and had joined the Liberals to support Gordon Campbell. During my four-and-a-half years as MLA, I had lost custody of my three children in a bitter and politicized custody dispute, and when I was defeated in the 1996 election, it seemed like everything had been a complete waste of time. I was almost inconsolable with grief; it felt like I had missed years with my children for nothing. The whole exercise seemed so pointless.

I was in our small house in Kelowna, which we had used as my campaign office. It was a cute older house with a bright kitchen and a nice yard. My sister Joy Tyabji was keeping me company, worrying over me, and trying to lift my spirits. She was also answering the phone, which was ringing quite a bit. I was not taking any calls. What was the point?

We were seated at the kitchen table, drinking tea, when the phone rang. Joy answered.

"Hello? No, this is her sister, Joy. No, it's Joy. *Really.*" She looked over and rolled her eyes. We sound exactly the same on the phone, although she is five years younger than I am. "Who's calling? *Who!* Is this a joke? No, wait, I recognize your voice. While I have you on the phone, can I just say that the tie you were wearing last night did not work. No. You need a new one."

There was a pause. She laughed. Then she said, "Anyway, hang on."

She tried to hand me the phone. "No," I said, "I'm not talking to anyone. Take a message."

"Judi, you'll want to take this call."

"No, I really don't, Joy. Please take a message."

"It's Glen Clark calling to congratulate you."

I was confused. I had lost, while he had just pulled off a stunning victory. Why would he congratulate me? Besides, we were political opponents.

"O.K." I put out my hand for the phone.

"Hang on, Mr. Clark, here she is. Oh, and by the way, *congratulations.*"

I took the phone. "Hi, Glen, congratulations to you. Good work."

He sounded pumped. "Thanks! Hey, listen, I know you didn't make it, but I called to congratulate you on your showing. I mean, that was a strong second. You must be really pleased."

"Glen, I lost."

"I know, but you were outspent and in the middle of the interior, and you still almost pulled it off. I think you surprised people. You should be proud."

"Thanks very much for the call. It means a lot." We chatted briefly, then said good bye.

"You did a great job as MLA, Judi. See you around."

This is my story of Glen Clark the morning after he won the premiership in 1996.

• • •

The British Columbia media, not known for pulling any punches, went straight to work on the newly elected Clark government. A *Vancouver Sun* editorial, May 29, commented:

> By carrying his party to a second term of government, Glen Clark has achieved what no leader of the New Democratic Party has done in B.C.'s history ... He certainly cannot boast a clear mandate—the Liberals took more of the popular vote than the NDP. Still, Mr. Clark deserves credit for taking a party that was 30 points down and mired in scandal before Premier Mike Harcourt resigned and lifting it to victory.
>
> In governing, the New Democrats will not be as weighed down by pledges as Gordon Campbell's Liberals would have been; Mr. Clark has promised to resign only if he fails to deliver on his modest income tax cut, a measure contained in the budget already introduced by the government. That budget lays out the priorities the government can be expected to follow: protecting health care and education from cuts in federal funding; investing in job creation; freezing taxes; cutting the size of government; and holding down public-sector wages.
>
> The NDP's debt management plan calls for eliminating the province's direct debt over 20 years and gradually reducing taxpayer-supported debt; we would like to see the government rein in the debt more quickly, but the issue was prominent in the campaign and many voters opted for a gradual approach ...

What is most interesting in light of the events that followed the 1996 election was the immediate publication of news stories and editorials challenging the credibility of the Clark government.

On May 29, the *Vancouver Sun* ran a column by a reporter who had covered the campaign. More interesting than the reporter's opinion and the newspaper's publication of it is the fact that the reporter clearly did not consider the expression of this opinion to be a problem for her personal integrity as a reporter. Entitled "I await the results of Clark's tendency to mislead," it reads, in part:

> With the NDP still in power, I know what to expect and I don't like it. I am profoundly disappointed that a party which once stood for ethical conduct and compassion became one of the most corrupt governments in B.C.'s history. I'm even more disappointed that it can get re-elected. I believe that some day Glen Clark's tendency to mislead will be his undoing …
>
> Like a sleeping cat, I will remain vigilant. In a democracy, it is never over.

This was not the only example. Another *Vancouver Sun* reporter was not shy in providing this editorial on May 29:

> I survived the election campaign, but I am not sure if I can survive another five years of New Democratic Party government. I think that the NDP in B.C. has proven itself to be as corrupt as a political party can get … Glen Clark will no doubt play a hands-on role in the new government. Unlike his predecessor, Mike Harcourt, Clark appears to be a strong leader with definite convictions on certain issues. He is eloquent and decisive, particularly on corrective measures …
>
> I found Clark a more effective leader than Gordon Campbell, a more charming person, more passionate on political issues but more offensive as our premier. Notwithstanding his charm and his communication skills, Clark is confrontational; you don't have to be his political opponent to be on the receiving side. During his meeting with the *Sun* editorial board, he spent an hour confronting the newspaper's coverage and its "elitist" attitude. He

Glen Clark and his cabinet (only partially shown including Moe Sihota and Corky Evans in back and Penny Priddy, Andrew Petter, and Lois Boone in front) were sworn in on June 17, 1996.

> misrepresented the *Sun*'s views as he misrepresented those of the Liberal party …
>
> I hope Campbell was wrong when he accused Clark of being unable to read a balance sheet. Already a big spender, will Clark now spend the next five years bankrupting our province? I think I have a headache.

The only other B.C. newspaper with province-wide distribution, the *Province,* ran a May 29 editorial that made it clear who was responsible for the NDP's second term:

> They ought to be hammering together the shrine to Glen Clark in NDP headquarters any time now ...
> The New Democrat victory owes more to the leader and incumbent premier than any policy or ideology the party has.
>
> Four months ago, the NDP was a shambles. Mike Harcourt was on his way out, the party mired in scandal, the Liberals looking like a shoo-in.
>
> Within weeks, Clark turned the polls on their ear. The pit bull of Canadian politics was able to focus B.C. voters on one thing: Him.

If it was conceded that Clark did not win based on ideology or policy, then these were not useful tools in targeting him. The one area that was consistently identified as Clark's weakness was fiscal policy. It was predictable that the Campbell Liberals and their supporters would launch a campaign that targeted Glen Clark based on his personal credibility, and that this would focus almost exclusively on fiscal policy. The media were primed.

You could almost hear the knives being sharpened.

3

Liar Liar

Cut deeply by repeated attacks on his credibility, Premier Glen Clark has actively considered filing a defamation suit against his tormentors ... The charge of lying surfaced in the month after the election ... Lately, Mr. Clark is discovering that, for his critics, one of the surest routes into the headlines is a frontal assault on the premier's credibility.

... But who would he go after? Liberal leader Gordon Campbell is the obvious target. He has called the premier a liar more times in more speeches than anyone else. Yet Mr. Campbell would welcome the suit, knowing that a sitting premier has far more to lose from such a messy court action than any Opposition politician.

—Vaughn Palmer,
Vancouver Sun, March 4, 1997

By the time of the RCMP raid on Clark's home in 1999, the office of premier had been under seige for years. Gordon Campbell and many others who opposed the New Democrats had trouble accepting the 1996 election result as legitimate. Campbell, his colleagues, and some of their high-profile supporters in the business community continually called for a new election, challenging Clark's mandate to govern on a number of fronts.

In official communications from the office of the B.C. Liberals, the lack of protocol was another indication that the Liberal opposition did not acknowledge Clark's mandate as premier. Parliamentary procedure guides elected members to address each other with reference to their office, for example, "the honourable member," "the MLA," "the minister," "the opposition members," "the premier," etc. However, in opposition leader Campbell's speeches and news releases, the premier was frequently referred to as "Glen," "Glen Clark," or "Clark."

In addition, references to dishonesty or wrongdoing were stated or implied almost without exception in B.C. Liberal communications. This was highly unusual, even for the volatile political environment of British Columbia. Ironically, the New Democratic Party's philosophic position on parliamentary protocol was that it was opposed to too much formality. As a result, the NDP's own lack of formality and its desire to move away from protocol may have reinforced the B.C. Liberal's undermining of the NDP's perceived authority to govern. The NDP as a government and as a party was not successful in challenging those who took the position that Glen Clark's government was illegitimate.

The popular vote, which is the percentage of vote supporting each party, was consistently quoted by Campbell as proof that the B.C. Liberals lost the election on some kind of technicality. They cited the NDP's popular support in the election, at 39.45 percent as opposed to the Liberal's 41.82 percent, as proof that the majority of British Columbians did not want the NDP to be government and did not want Glen Clark to be premier. Further, the Liberals preached a strong "unite the right" mantra, similar to that of the former Social Credit party, arguing that the 61 percent of people who did not vote NDP could unite behind Gordon Campbell and defeat the New Democrats. They courted the B.C. Reform party, the Social Credit party, and members of the Progressive Democratic Alliance. The B.C. Liberals accused all three parties of "splitting their vote" in the 1996 election.[1]

In the first years following the 1996 election, the issue constantly used to draw attention to the lack of legitimacy of the Clark government was the so-called fudge-it budget. This was a reference to the 1996 pre-election NDP budget, which was tabled in the legislature as a balanced budget by Finance Minister Elizabeth Cull just prior to the dropping of the writ. During the election campaign, Glen Clark referred to it as an example of prudent fiscal management, and it was a thorn in the side of the Liberals because they wanted to prove the NDP fiscally incompetent. Elizabeth Cull was narrowly defeated in the general election, and Clark named Andrew Petter to the finance portfolio.

Within weeks of the election, Finance Minister Petter conducted a review of the revenue to government, and he announced that the budget for 1996 would not be balanced, citing a series of reasons. He particularly focussed on the decreased revenue to government, which meant lower revenue than originally projected. This announcement set off a storm of controversy, as people claimed that Clark had misled them by fudging the budget numbers so that he could campaign on a balanced budget, and then adjusting the numbers afterward once he had a renewed mandate. The attacks against Clark were frequent, personal, and, even for British Columbia politics, quite vicious.

He was vilified in print, radio, and television stories and roundly attacked in editorials. This went on for weeks, then months, and eventually years. This story was usually given status in the media, carried at the top of the news cycle and on the front page of the "A" section of the newspapers.

Was the revised budget a result of fraud or misplaced optimism? This question was at the centre of a debate that would be taken to the courts, to the electorate, to government investigations, and to the media, over and over. It was a prolonged debate that engaged people across the province, including many people who initially claimed to be "politically neutral" in their campaign against the NDP government.

In addition to providing a public forum to discuss the financial ineptitude of the NDP government, as perceived by those attacking the pre-election budget, the fudge-it budget debate opened the door to questions about any financial decisions made by the government. Once the public debate around the NDP government's dishonesty and incompetence over the 1996 pre-election budget had been established in the public forum, all future issues were filtered through this screen, including the issue of Clark's role in the casino scandal of 1999. Perhaps the hallmark issue that emerged once the budget debate had fizzled was the catamaran ferries commissioned and constructed by the BC Ferry Corporation. The Liberal opposition and government critics dubbed the project a "fast ferry fiasco." This term was difficult to challenge in light of the years of negative publicity around fiscal management, stemming from the 1996 pre-election budget.

• • •

There was a strong overtone of morality in all the speeches and interviews of those who opposed the government, as if the unifying factor in their actions was that they were made in the best interests of the people of British Columbia. One of the earliest campaigns against the Clark government was led by Kelowna resident David Stockell, initially portrayed in the media as a non-partisan hero for the masses, taking on the NDP for lying to voters. Stockell first appeared on the public radar as a member of an audience in a CBC-TV public forum with Finance Minister Andrew Petter, a few months after the budget controversy surfaced. CBC-TV reporter Terry Milewski filed a story on October 29, 1996 about Premier Clark's slipping credibility that included this segment:

> TERRY MILEWSKI: But were they optimistic, or were they downright fraudulent? That is the question which has caused a credibility crisis for Glen Clark. Internal documents show that government officials were repeatedly warned before the election, even while Clark was campaigning on a balanced budget. And that's why the "l" word in politics right now, is "liar."
>
> UNIDENTIFIED: I've never heard of a premier in all of Canada being called a liar, as often as ours has been.

MILEWSKI: Here's how people talked back to Clark's Finance Minister Andrew Petter, in a CBC forum last night.

DAVID STOCKELL/KELOWNA BC: Isn't it time for the government to realise it lied; committed fraud, and that they should be thinking about calling another election, or at least resigning.

ANDREW PETTER/BC FINANCE MIN.: Let me say the so-called ...

MILEWSKI: Petter, like Clark, continues to say the budget forecast was a mistake—not a lie.

ANDREW PETTER: We made a mistake and we're gonna do something about it.

MILEWSKI: But that's going to be difficult, with the opposition painting Glen Clark as "Glenocchio" in its newspaper ads; what's worse, the headlines are doing the same, and the opinion polls suggest those headlines are accurate ...

By an interesting coincidence, audience member David Stockell emerged as a leading spokesperson shortly after this televised forum, claiming to represent the interests of the public at large. Stockell created the organization HELP BC, an acronym for Help Eliminate Lying Politicians, with the objective of launching a court case against the NDP to hold it accountable for projecting a balanced budget during the election campaign, and announcing a deficit afterwards. For its court case, HELP BC received funds from the right-wing National Citizens Coalition and others who opposed the NDP. Early assistance was given to HELP BC by Brian Lightburn, former parliamentary assistant to Progressive Conservative Member of Parliament Al Horning, and Gary Benson of Salloum Doak, a politically active law firm in Kelowna, associated with the Liberals and the Conservatives.

The B.C. Liberals were impatient for an election and frequently commented in support of the actions launched in the court, in the ridings, and in the media by people trying to bring the Glen Clark government down. However, there was always an effort to claim that HELP BC, David Stockell, and other government opponents were independent of party politics.

A writ was filed with the B.C. Supreme Court only months after the 1996 general election, asking that the 1996 general election results be thrown out if the courts found that certain sections of the Election Act, particularly Section 256, had been contravened. The relevance of Section 256 is its intent:

> ... to enhance the integrity of the electoral process by holding political candidates and parties to a standard of non-fraudulent dealing with the public. A vote obtained by fraudulent means is one obtained by "misrepresentations of material fact which were intended to, and did, lead voters to vote for a candidate or party for whom the voter would not otherwise have voted, and which were made by or on behalf of a candidate or political party knowing they were false, or without regard to their truth or falsity." The term "fraudulent means" as used in s. 256 would not include "statements of intention or belief, and statements which any reasonable person would attribute to mere puffery."[2]

The premise of Stockell's case was that the NDP won the election through fraud. Stockell felt that since the NDP had won by only three seats, the margin of victory was narrow enough that there should be little problem throwing Clark and his cronies out of office.

Stockell, born in Alberta as one of nine children, was a fairly recent resident of British Columbia who claimed a strong urge to fight the government for justice on behalf of the voters. According to interviews, morality was his motivation:

> Sure everybody lies, believe me I'm not perfect. I've told lies in my life but it bothers me to a point that I can't live

> with myself if they affect a person or if they hurt another person or if they do damage to another person. This characteristic that I have and most other people my age have doesn't seem to have been instilled in people like Glen Clark. That really bothers me because that's the kind of morality we're getting and this lack of morality is a serious issue with politicians these days.[3]

When asked how HELP BC would pay for a case that would cost $200,000 to 250,000, Stockell replied, "I have no doubt we'll be able to do it. We have many supporters who have said when you need help, let us know and we'll get active. These are people who have influence, connections and money."[4] In fact, the National Citizens Coalition (NCC) out of Alberta provided significant funds for the case over the years of litigation. The NCC is aligned philosophically with right-wing political parties and politicians and is active in fighting political perspectives that it opposes.

As it turned out, David Stockell *was* politically affiliated. Although he claimed that party politics was not his motivation, he was a card-carrying member of the B.C. Liberal party. He explained that he had joined the B.C. Liberals to participate in the nomination race leading up to the 1996 election, and he admitted that he had voted Liberal in previous elections. He also claimed to have voted NDP at some point in the past in Saskatchewan; however, he clearly did not support Glen Clark's government.

If HELP BC succeeded in its court application, one judge could throw out hundreds of thousands of votes. In an interesting twist, HELP BC was suing the NDP as a political party in order to toss out the government of the province. The government is a separate entity from a political party, so the intent of the case was a little confusing from the outset. The HELP BC case was not about stuffing ballots, intimidation at a polling station, or pumping people full of beer and then driving them to the polls. HELP BC's campaign was to challenge an election after the fact, on the basis of its belief that the party platform was fraudulent.

Stockell could not claim to have been defrauded by the government because he voted Liberal, so HELP BC recruited three NDP voters from three separate NDP ridings to be plaintiffs in the court case. It did this by advertising in local newspapers, asking people to come forward if they had voted NDP in the previous election because of the campaign promise of a balanced budget. Three individuals became petitioners; Leonard Friesen, Holly Kuzenko, and Mildred Umbarger were funded and supported by HELP BC. Three NDP MLAs were targeted as respondents: Sue Hammell from Surrey–Green Timbers, Graeme Bowbrick from New Westminster, and Ed Conroy from Rossland-Trail. They were sued in their capacity as NDP candidates in the 1996 election, so the New Democratic Party had to mount their defence. This was both expensive and time-consuming.

HELP BC's objective, stated publicly and repeatedly, was to have Premier Glen Clark on the stand to cross-examine him. Regardless of the success of the HELP BC court case, the constant media attention was helpful in discrediting the Clark government and drawing attention away from any of its public policy initiatives. The effect was described by reporter Julianna Hayes in her in-depth look at the HELP BC court case: "Anything positive the government has done in the months since the election has taken a back seat in the press next to the Stockell case."[5]

In January 1999, two-and-a-half years after Stockell initiated his HELP BC case, the B.C. Court of Appeal ruled that the case could go to a full trial: "In our view, holding political candidates and parties to a standard of non-fraudulent dealing with the public is in accord with maintaining the integrity of the electoral process," wrote three B.C. Court of Appeal judges.[6] From the B.C. Court of Appeal, the HELP BC case went back to the B.C. Supreme Court for full trial. The three MLAs would be called to the stand, and the plaintiffs who claimed to have been misled by them would have an opportunity to hear the MLAs' rationale for campaigning on a balanced budget when the budget was not balanced.

It was a difficult time for the NDP staff at their Burnaby headquarters. According to Brian Gardiner, provincial secretary for the NDP from 1994 until 1999, the party did not lose many members over the HELP BC case. "On the contrary, I heard many members say that their faith in the party was strong, that they believed we were right, and that we would win the day eventually. We were determined to win."[7] But HELP BC drained the party, emotionally and financially. Gardiner recollected:

> Every Monday I had to check with our legal teams to find out where we were with our case. I had good staff, which allowed me to concentrate, but this case took about one-third of my time. Some of the arguments that were made against the party were really obscure. It was like a form of torture. As you can imagine, the caucus [of elected MLAs] was very anxious to know we were going to win, especially the three MLAs who had been named.

Brian Gardiner said the Stockell story seemed to be the one that would not go away: "After a year, people were tired of the story, and the comments from the NDP and the Stockell group were getting predictable. It went on and on and never resolved. The whole case was a pain in the ass."

Gardiner explained that at any given time, six or seven out of ten British Columbians are not supportive of the NDP, as the party's core support is only around 33 percent. These people would be open to accepting the claim that the NDP was made up of liars, because they have no connection to the party.

It would be another year and a half before the case went to full trial. It was originally set for January 2000, but was adjourned in order to accommodate a related legal action. Stockell was disappointed in the adjournment, since the date of the trial was now potentially in conflict with a general election call. He was questioned about the possibility of an election interfering with the court case, and responded:

> "Trial or no trial, the issue of accountability will be part of the next election. The NDP will have to answer for their actions, if not in the court of law, then in the court of public opinion"... Stockell adds that "We have already won a major victory when both the Chief Justice of the B.C. Supreme Court and the B.C. Court of Appeal ruled that the NDP had to stand trial and we will do whatever we can to ensure that they face the music in court."[8]

It was July 2000 before the trial was held. By this time, the NDP had increased its majority by one seat, with the addition of Gordon Wilson, MLA for Powell River–Sunshine Coast and former leader of the Progressive Democratic Alliance. Wilson had joined the government in January 1999, a move that could not have been foreseen by HELP BC when it chose to target only three seats. With 40 seats, the NDP could now afford to lose three MLAs and still retain government by one vote.

In the legal process, HELP BC assisted three private persons to file a writ against three MLAs, but the case itself targeted Premier Clark and former finance minister Elizabeth Cull. In fact, the eventual ruling asserted that the three voters putting the case before the judge had no quarrel with their NDP MLAs: "Ms. Kuzenko agreed that Mr. Bowbrick was an honourable person, and Ms. Umbarger agreed that Mr. Conroy was a person of integrity. Mr. Friesen did not hear or meet Ms. Hammell during the election campaign, but did not testify to being misled in any way by Ms. Hammell herself."[9]

David Stockell was granted his wish to put Glen Clark on the stand to answer questions about the 1996 budget and election campaign. HELP BC's trial heard testimony from both Clark and Cull. Cull denied that Clark had asked her to put misleading numbers in the budget, saying that if she or the government could be faulted, it should be for selecting overly optimistic forecasts. The $355 million deficit announced after the election by Cull's successor, Finance Minister Andrew Petter, was reasonable given the circumstances. "I don't know of any business that can forecast its budget within one or two per cent, and one per cent of the B.C. budget was $400 million," Cull said.[10]

Clark's attitude before, during, and after the trial was the subject of many media stories. They consistently questioned his demeanour. Some reporters asked Clark whether he should apologize to voters for the 1996 budget.

The trial was finally concluded in July 2000, and the plaintiffs cooled their heels awaiting the judgement of Madam Justice Mary Humphries. On August 3, 2000 she ruled against HELP BC's petition. In her judgement, she made no comments with respect to the politics of the case, and it is unlikely that comments of this nature would have been well-received. The media reports did not present the public with any detailed analysis. However, Humphries' decision merits discussion because HELP BC's allegations against Clark and Cull had been instrumental in discrediting the NDP government for over four years.

> [14] Allegations of fraudulent conduct are made against the then Premier and the Minister of Finance going to the very root of their fitness to hold public office. The consequences to the Respondents are that they may lose their jobs and to the voters in the three ridings that their expressed choice at the polls may be set aside. This is not a task to be undertaken on an evaluation of probabilities. Having considered all the cases in the context of the legislation and the issues before me, I am of the view that the standard of proof must be "beyond a reasonable doubt." However, I should note that the conclusions I have reached would not have been different even if the lesser standard of proof were used.[11]

It is clear that Humphries wants to express the magnitude of the impact her decision might have on the democratic system in the event that any future court case deals with a similar issue. She lets everyone know that she is convinced about her decision regardless of the standard of proof. She states the HELP BC argument in these terms:

> [37] In respect of the revised forecast for 1995–96, the Petitioners submit that Ms. Cull and Mr. Clark, upon realizing that the surplus that had been predicted in March of 1995 was not going to materialize, picked some numbers which might have a veneer of credibility and worked the budget assumptions back to conform with them. In doing so, they ignored the professional advice of Treasury Board Staff and forced the staff to come up with unrealistic options. The Staff were so reluctant to do this, according to the Petitioners, that they insisted Ms. Cull sign off on the options statement herself, an unprecedented move. The unhappy reaction of some of Treasury Board staff to Ms. Cull's decisions was clearly evident through the testimony of Mr. Foster, chief of fiscal forecasting for the Treasury Board.

This characterization of HELP BC's case also fits the media's representation of what happened. Humphries responds to HELP BC's theory:

> [38] When all the evidence had been heard, there were some difficulties with this theory. First, the evidence demonstrated that Mr. Clark had little if any knowledge of the 1995–96 budget. Ms. Eaton, Secretary to Treasury Board, said she believed it might have been mentioned in passing at a meeting she had with him in December of 1995 when the possibility of his becoming leader of the party arose, but that the entire focus of the meeting was on Budget 96. Ms. Cull said Budget 95 was never discussed with Mr. Clark.

> [39] Mr. Clark who had assumed leadership of the NDP party in February of 1996 when Mr. Harcourt stepped down, said he knew nothing about the 1995–96 budget other than what he was told by Ms. Cull, which is that it was balanced. Aside from Ms. Eaton's belief that there was a passing reference to that budget in the December 1995 meeting, there was no evidence to the contrary.
>
> [40] The responsibility for the revised forecast for Budget 95, then, rests with Ms. Cull and it was clear from her testimony that she accepted the entire responsibility for both budgets.

Most of the media coverage during the trial focussed on whether or not Glen Clark and Elizabeth Cull contradicted each other in their testimony. This was alleged by the HELP BC lawyers, and widely reported. Humphries deals with this specifically:

> [79] Much argument was directed at whether Ms. Cull and Mr. Clark contradicted each other in such a way as to throw doubt on the credibility of each. The difference between them seems to be in the level of assurance Ms. Cull took as to the availability of the Forest Renewal funds—Ms. Cull said that, although no decision was made to use the funds, she was assured they would be available to her if the forecast and other contingency funds did not materialize, and Mr. Clark said he agreed to revisit the availability of these funds in those circumstances. Both agreed that the list of alternative sources of revenue came from Ms. Cull. Nothing Ms. Eaton said contradicted this. I can draw no conclusions adverse to the credibility of Ms. Cull or Mr. Clark from this evidence, nor can I find in the evidence any support for the proposition that Ms. Cull was forced by Mr. Clark

> to accept figures which she knew were unreasonable and unattainable.

A full reading of Humphries' Reasons for Judgement indicates that the HELP BC trial disclosed to the public the full process of government budgets and revenue forecasts. It is pretty dry reading for most people, and perhaps this is the reason why few media outlets presented this information when there were more interesting political stories to follow.

The media had speculated that Cull manipulated the numbers contrary to the information provided by staff, and Humphries dealt with this allegation:

> [57] … There is no evidence that Ms. Cull instructed anyone on her staff to manipulate or juggle figures.
>
> [58] As a result of her selections and decisions from the options briefing note, Ms. Cull added "optimism" of about $156 million to the most optimistic staff forecast, and had her staff prepare the revised forecast for 1995–96 to be included in Budget 96. The revised forecast showed a surplus of $16 million. Ms. Cull testified that she felt very comfortable in putting that figure into the budget in the full belief it would be realized as she had based it upon all the information available to her and upon reasonable assumptions. When the public accounts were published, the forecast ultimately had an error factor of 2.4%, compared to the historically acceptable rate testified to by Ms. Eaton of plus/minus 4%.

Additional revenue in the previous year had been correctly predicted by Elizabeth Cull, contrary to the forecasts of her staff. Why was Cull able to forecast more revenue and be correct in this forecast? According to the evidence presented by staff reports, the Treasury Board staff had been consistently conservative, and revenue to government had been exceeding budget predictions.

> [50] … In the previous three years, the staff January forecasts had underestimated revenues by $188.5 million, $318.8 million and $310.3 million respectively. Mr. Foster and Ms. Eaton agreed that the underestimation between the original revenue figures contained in the budgets as tabled in March of those years and the public accounts figures was even higher, reaching $800 million in 1994–95.

Humphries' decision completely vindicated Glen Clark and Elizabeth Cull. No section did this more effectively than the following (emphasis added):

> [61] … The theory of the Petitioners is, however, that a budget is a simple concept understood by everyone. Either it is balanced or it is not. Especially in an election year, the government must be scrupulously careful with any statements it makes respecting its budget. If the government is wrong in claiming a balanced or surplus budget, no matter by how little, the government has obtained votes by fraudulent means (assuming that it was this factor that caused a change in vote).
>
> [62] This simplistic approach has its appeal but it is not appropriate when the decision to be made is whether the Petitioners have proven that the Respondents or someone on their behalf acted fraudulently within the meaning of section 256 of the Act. The best that can be done, even in an election year, is that the Minister of Finance, in this case Ms. Cull, make her decisions honestly and reasonably. *I found Ms. Cull to be an honest, careful, articulate and*

well-informed witness. I accept that she believed that her assumptions were reasonable and that she was honest in her belief that the 1995–96 budget was balanced. She was ultimately wrong but she was not fraudulent.

[63] As mentioned earlier, the evidence demonstrated that *Mr. Clark played no role in setting the figures for the revised forecast.* He testified that he was busy during the early part of 1996 with the leadership campaign. He was briefed on the 1996–97 budget in February and March but had no input into and received no information about the 1995–96 revised forecast. He testified that he was told by Ms. Cull that the 1995–96 budget was balanced and agreed he wanted a balanced budget. *He said he believed the budget was balanced and he campaigned on it.*

[64] *I have found that Ms. Cull's beliefs were honest and reasonable. On the evidence before me, Mr. Clark had no other source of information available to him and accepted her statements.* He then made the public statement that the 1995–96 budget was balanced. The statement was not known to be false nor was it made without regard to its truth or falsity. In all of these circumstances I am unable to find that the representation that the budget for 1995–96 was balanced constitutes "fraudulent means" within the meaning of section 256 of the Act.

[65] If the voters in British Columbia accept the general characterization of the situation advanced by the Petitioners, that is a matter they can consider when they next come to vote, but the circumstances here do not give rise to a legal remedy.

• • •

Brian Gardiner claimed that Clark's credibility was seriously impacted by the four years of the HELP BC case claiming he was a liar. "The allegations stuck to Glen, the party, and the government, even after the judge's decision. After four years of hearing that the government had lied, opponents kept saying we lied, it became an accepted fact by the journalists that we had lied."[12]

So, why wasn't there a concerted campaign to let the members of the NDP know that a judge of the Supreme Court had vindicated Glen Clark? Why was there no attempt to put the message out to the public that Glen Clark had in fact not lied about the budget?

According to Gardiner, who had since moved on from his post at NDP headquarters, everyone wanted to put the issue behind them. "The members of the party had already accepted the NDP's comments about what had happened with the 1996 budget. If they heard what the judge had ruled, they would have felt vindicated, but they already felt they knew the truth."[13] Gardiner claimed they were tired, and their resources were depleted from fighting the case in court. There was little energy or interest to launch a public campaign.

According to the political pundits, Glen Clark had no credibility left by the time HELP BC's case went to trial in July 2000. Remember that the RCMP raided his house in March 1999, and he had resigned from office before a judge finally dismissed the evidence that supported the "liar" label.

Liberal leader Gordon Campbell and the Liberal opposition did not acknowledge Judge Humphries' ruling, and they continued to claim that the NDP had deceived people with the 1996 budget.

By the time of Humphries' ruling, Ujjal Dosanjh was premier and responded as follows:

> "What Mr. Stockell did and what his supporters did wasn't a legal case, it was a political case," Dosanjh said from Chetwynd, B.C ...
>
> The Help B.C. case damaged the credibility of the NDP, Dosanjh said.

> "Now we found out they had no legal basis to say what they've been saying."
>
> Stockell was unavailable for comment on the ruling.
>
> Dosanjh, attorney-general through much of the case before becoming premier last February, conceded the provincial auditor-general found "mistakes" in the way the government prepared its budgets.
>
> "We've dealt with issues around fiscal transparency in the last five or six months," he said. "What this decision simply reconfirms is that no legal errors had been made by the NDP at that time."
>
> The ruling came down more than four years after the NDP, led by then-premier Glen Clark, won re-election in May 1996, partly on promises to balance the budget.
>
> After their victory, Clark said the government might need some "wriggle room" on the budget, and later conceded the province's finances were significantly in the red.[14]

Dosanjh's public comments on reasons for the new budget legislation damned his own party with faint praise, since he used the word "mistake," a word not used by Justice Humphries.

In 2001, when the pre-election budget was announced by the NDP as a surplus budget, the Liberals and their allies in the business community pronounced it another fudge-it budget. They were assisted in this by the NDP leadership and Premier Dosanjh, who did not challenge this claim and who in fact campaigned by apologizing for what he chose to refer to as past "mistakes."

By the time the HELP BC ruling was made public in August 2000, Dosanjh had completed his first legislative session as premier, and he passed legislation that he claimed would address problems in the provincial budgeting process. Even though many of these problems had been identified for years and were unrelated to the HELP BC case, opponents saw the new legislation as an admission of guilt on the part of the NDP. The media referred to this legislation in the context of Humphries' ruling, and this appeared to counter some of the positive impact of the failure of the HELP BC case.

To put the entire episode in context, one only has to look at the chronology of the case. The general election was in May 1996; the exoneration of Clark and Cull in the courts was in August 2000. Clark's resignation as premier was in August 1999.

4

Under the Gun

> *... After this magazine goes to press, Auditor General George Morfitt is scheduled to release his long-awaited report into the 1996 "fudge-it budget." In addition, the technical report on whether the first fast ferry will work properly is also expected soon, probably this month. Finally, forensic accountant Ron Parks will release a draft report into allegations the NDP broke spending rules to fend off three failed recall campaigns.*
>
> *Each of these reports, especially Mr. Morfitt's, has the potential to wipe out any support Mr. Clark has built up.*
>
> —*BC Report,* March 1999

Amid the ongoing screaming headlines of B.C.'s major media, the office of the auditor-general launched an investigation into the budget issue. The auditor-general is the person responsible for overseeing the accounting of government, and Auditor-General George Morfitt took great pride in the duties of his office.

Imagine if you were the watchdog of the government's accounts, and every day the media told the public that a great fraud had taken place. The government's financial credibility was at stake, and from the perspective of an independent accounts office, there was a need to look into the allegations made against the NDP government.

Morfitt's lengthy report came out in March 1999, over a year before HELP BC was able to put the government on trial. It was an analytic report, devoid of the emotion presented in the media, and although government reports are usually "dry," this one described the context for decision-making, the boundaries of the minister's responsibility, and the political environment in which events occurred. It is worth reading in its entirety for those who have an interest.[1]

Morfitt's report challenged the constant and pervasive assertions by political opponents in the media that fraud and dishonesty were at work in the pre-election budget. His report did identify weaknesses in the budgeting process. It did *not* identify any fraud in the preparation of the 1996 budget. The report recommended legislative changes and a new process of budget accountability. In commenting on Cull's decision to table a budget with a $16 million surplus, Morfitt wrote:

> The Revised Forecast for 1995/96 reflected the Treasury Board Secretariat's "optimistic" projection of revenue, plus a further $156 million over and above the optimistic revenue forecast by the Secretariat, an inclusion that was within the Minister's prerogative. At the same time, the forecast included the Secretariat's "most likely" projection of expenditure, less anticipated savings of $41 million. Based on these amounts, the revised forecast projected a surplus for the 1995/96 fiscal year of $16 million. If either the optimistic or most-likely projections had been used for both revenue and expenditure, and if further revenue had not been included and expenditure not reduced, the result would have been a projected deficit of up to $256 million.
>
> Considering the information available to her, Minister Cull's decision to include in the revised forecast a revenue projection that was $156 million over and above the Secretariat's optimistic forecast seems inappropriate. Circumstances that may mitigate her judgement were errors in the Secretariat's reports that made the deterioration of forests revenue less noticeable to the Minister.[2]

It is interesting that although Morfitt acknowledges that the minister's forecast "seems inappropriate," he expands on this to provide the context of the decision in a thoughtful manner:

> No informed analysis of events and decisions made during any budget cycle is complete without considering the important circumstances that existed at the time and their possible influence on those events and decisions ...
>
> On October 17, 1991, British Columbians went to the polls and elected a new government for the Province—a New Democratic Party government led by the Honourable Michael Harcourt. The Social Credit Party had been in power since 1975. Over the 15 years of Social Credit administration, the Province's accumulated deficit had risen by some $1,960 million, from $140 million to $2,100 million, and the total provincial debt by $12,700 million, from $4,560 million to $17,260 million.
>
> Much of the 1991 election campaign focussed on fiscal management issues.
>
> Upon taking office, Premier Harcourt appointed the Honourable Glen Clark as Minister of Finance and Corporate Relations and Chair of Treasury Board, and Mr. Clark immediately ordered an independent review of the financial condition of the provincial government. The review was completed March 11, 1992, and reported a projected Consolidated Revenue Fund (CRF) deficit for the 1991/92 fiscal year of $2,462 million, an increase of $1,270 million from the $1,192 million originally forecasted in the 1991/92 budget by the previous administration. It also reported that much of the deficit was structural in nature, and predicted larger annual deficits in the following two years if there were no changes to policies or programs and the economy grew at a median rate. The review recommended steps to reduce the deficit

by implementing a fully integrated fiscal policy framework, reducing costs and increasing revenues.

In releasing the results of the review, Mr. Clark announced that "our first budget will begin to address the most immediate problems—controlling the deficit, cutting waste, protecting essential services like health and education, and setting spending priorities. It will be a fair budget and an honest one. And, under this government, the ongoing financial process will remain open for all to see and scrutinize." This message was echoed by the government in the March 1992 budget speech.

The audited financial statements for the 1991/92 fiscal year—the year during which administrations changed—recorded a CRF deficit of $2,355 million, an overall ("summary") provincial deficit of $2,163 million, and total provincial debt at March 31, 1992, was $20,106 million ...

On September 15, 1993, the Honourable Elizabeth Cull succeeded Mr. Clark as Minister of Finance and Corporate Relations and Chair of Treasury Board, with Mr. Clark assuming the portfolio of Minister of Employment and Investment. The Estimates tabled in the spring of 1994 by Ms. Cull reflected a budgeted 1994/95 operating deficit for the CRF of $898 million.

Every year, as required by the Financial Administration Act, the Minister of Finance and Corporate Relations must sign the audited financial statements of the Province by September 30. So, in the fall of 1994, when the government started its budgeting process for the 1995/96 fiscal year in earnest, it knew that during the 1993/94 fiscal year it had collected $528 million more, spent $92 million less, and ended up being $620 million better off in financial results than estimated in the spring of 1993. The annual growth in the provincial economy, which

> declined from 4.9% in 1991 to 3.4% in 1992, continually improved over the next two years by an average of 1.7%. The government was expecting similar or better growth in the economy and consequently better financial results for the 1995/96 fiscal year ...

In the above analysis, Morfitt points out the uncertainty of projections when it comes to budget forecasting based on the British Columbia economy. However, it is clear that in the 1993–94, 1994–95, and 1995–96 budgets the estimates were conservative, as economic projections were exceeded by actual performance. For these three years, the NDP had underestimated revenue to government. In contrast, the estimates of revenue for 1996 were overestimated. Morfitt explained the need for change in the budgeting process by outlining the events leading to the controversial budget of 1996:

> In the annual budgeting process, the period from November through February is the most crucial ... During this period in 1995/96, Ms. Cull continued in office. However, Mr. Costello and the new Secretary to Treasury Board, Brenda Eaton, often had to use their own judgement as to who, other than their minister, they should brief and who they should seek to persuade or to dissuade in regard to various operational issues. This period of uncertainty was followed by a period of hurried budget preparation activity. On February 22, 1996, the day Mr. Clark took office as the new premier, Mr. Costello—the seasoned Deputy Minister of Finance and Corporate Relations who had held that post since 1991—was appointed interim President/CEO of the British Columbia Hydro and Power Authority. And Ms. Eaton, who had been serving as Secretary to Treasury Board since July 1995, was also appointed Acting Deputy Minister of Finance and Corporate Relations. She served

> in both positions until June 1996, including the two demanding months immediately prior to Budget '96 first being tabled on April 30, 1996.

Prior to the 1996 general election, Premier Glen Clark was leading a government in the fifth year of its mandate, following years of controversy over the Nanaimo Commonwealth Holding Society scandal (and over claims of fiscal irresponsibility by the NDP). At the time the 1996 budget was tabled, there were numerous other issues confronting the government, such as the collapse of the West Coast salmon fishery and the Aboriginal treaty negotiations, including the Nisga'a agreement. As well, few forecasters could have predicted the downturn in the British Columbia economy that began in late 1995. But, after the fact, the media stories treated the allegations of a fraudulent budget as if it were the only issue facing the government when it went into the 1996 election campaign.

Morfitt describes some of the pressure on the NDP government in this manner:

> ... Our evidence indicates that Ms. Eaton and staff of the Treasury Board Secretariat were aware of the downturn in early 1996 and advised Minister Cull accordingly. However, despite their efforts to caution Ms. Cull, the Minister was not initially receptive to the news in those crucial months, as she was convinced that the Secretariat was overstating the negative impact of the economic downturn.
>
> Because its revenue forecasts in the 1993/94 and 1994/95 fiscal years were significantly below the actual revenue for those years, the Secretariat's call for a continued cautious approach to budgeting was interpreted as its insistence on being unduly pessimistic.

One final point in Morfitt's report stands out:

> ... Mr. Costello, then Deputy Minister of Finance and Corporate Relations and Secretary to Treasury Board, made a presentation to a joint meeting of Treasury Board and Planning Board ... The point, in Mr. Costello's words, was that he wanted the members of Cabinet to understand "that revenue forecasting in British Columbia is difficult, that it is a very cyclical economy with a lot of lags in the impact of the economy on revenues; it's a difficult chore but the track record was that it was getting better."[3]

All of this information was in the public arena prior to the HELP BC trial. Brian Gardiner had been following the auditor-general's investigation closely and, like everyone else concerned with the allegations against the government, was keen to know the verdict. He was delighted with the report, and he anticipated both a change in tone from the media and an impact on the HELP BC case against the NDP MLAs: "We thought the auditor-general's report was a mortal blow to the HELP BC case. It clearly demonstrated that the government had not lied. Any changes to legislation that it recommended referred to problems that had existed for decades and had not been created by the NDP."[4]

After three years of predictions that the Clark government would be held accountable for the fudge-it budget and the "lies" in the 1996 campaign, the Morfitt report actually confirmed the NDP government's assertion that it had erred in judgement and, if anything, was guilty of overly optimistic predictions. However, a new piece of information contained in Morfitt's report was that the preceding budgets had been overly pessimistic, and the NDP government felt some level of justification in over-ruling the caution of the Treasury Board staff. This action, combined with an unexpected downturn in the economy, turned out to be disastrous for the Clark government and became Clark's albatross during his next term.

Although a distant observer might expect that the Morfitt report would toss water on the fudge-it budget fire that had been burning for almost three years, it did not. Morfitt's findings were not widely publicized. The media's coverage generally consisted of low-key stories that tended to downplay the reference to the events leading up to the creation of the budget.

Stockell did not withdraw his case, and the media did not change their approach. An article from the *BC Free Press* (March 17, 1999), an online populist newspaper, sums up the response from most media outlets and NDP opponents:

> Glen, how can we help you, if you won't help yourself? Every therapist knows the first step to recovery is admitting your problem, and your problem is you're a liar.
>
> You deceived British Columbians about the budget, just as you deceived us about fast ferries …
>
> You have a problem, Glen, but you refuse to admit it.
>
> This week, Auditor-General George Morfitt's report pretty much confirmed what most British Columbians had already concluded more than two years ago—we were suckered during the last election …
>
> Clark needed a balanced budget going into the election, so that's what he gave us. A budget padded with absurdly "optimistic" revenue forecasts, that collapsed like a house of cards shortly after the election …
>
> The ugly reality is Elizabeth Cull knew exactly what she was doing. Sure, she got "cold feet" and tried to convince Clark to go with less optimistic figures. But when Clark refused, Cull tabled a bogus budget, rather than do the right thing as Finance Minister.
>
> Glen Clark may be a nasty piece of work, but Cull is no prize either. Her handling of the Parks Report and the "fudge-it" budget indicate she was as unfit for office as Glen Clark. She paid for it with her political career. She can take some comfort knowing Clark will not be far behind.

Brian Gardiner could not find anyone in the media prepared to accept the perspective that the auditor-general's report backed up Clark's position—it was optimism that led to the budget problem. Unfortunately for Glen Clark and the NDP, the release of the auditor-general's report came fifteen days after the RCMP raided Clark's home, and Morfitt's conclusions were overshadowed by the media coverage of the RCMP investigation.

The day after Morfitt released his report, an article in the *BC Free Press* (March 1999) referred to Clark as:

> ... a dictator, a slippery one at that.
>
> Which only begs the question—how did a "dictator" manage to preside over a democratic society? And how does a democratic society rid itself of such a dictator? ...
>
> The media tend to be the most effective opposition to a dictatorial government, and presently in B.C., Glen Clark is receiving the full impact of that opposition ...
>
> Clark doesn't care a whit about governance. His priority is to take care of the NDP's friends and insiders, leaving the majority of British Columbians out in the cold.
>
> Which leads us to the second question—how does BC rid itself of dictator Clark?
>
> We can't. There is simply no useful mechanism in Canada's parliamentary system to force a premier to step down, even though he's unfit to govern ...
>
> Which brings us to a third question—how do we prevent another "slippery dictator" like Clark from gaining power?
>
> The first step is to realize that one out of every five British Columbians would vote for a "slippery dictator." They don't care if Clark erodes democracy or trashes B.C.'s economy. Recent polls show Clark's NDP would get a solid 20 per cent of the vote regardless of how badly they behave ...

> These people are not living in some foreign land like Russia. They live down the street. They're your neighbours.
>
> Keep that in mind during the next election. When you cast your ballot, vote to defeat the one in five British Columbians working together to deprive you of responsible, democratic government.
>
> That's the only way a "slippery dictator" like Glen Clark can be prevented from again gaining power.

Gardiner believes that the allegations against the NDP had stood for so long that HELP BC had to continue with its court case. "They couldn't let the truth get in the way of their case."[5] The group may have believed it had a better chance in court. As well, the court case was bleeding the NDP's financial coffers, preventing the party from preparing for the general election that was at most two years away.

Since the public had not learned much about the Morfitt report, it was open to creative interpretation, and the Liberals wasted little time. They used the conclusions in the report to claim that they had been vindicated, because Morfitt had recommended changes to the budget preparation process, and he had strongly emphasized the need for more public disclosure about the assumptions made in presenting the budget. In effect, Morfitt used the opportunity of the controversy to advocate changes to the budgeting process that were long overdue.

It is interesting to note that the media reports did not claim that the Morfitt report vindicated the NDP government's position. Little of the tone of the public commentary changed. In fact, the major media jumped on the B.C. Liberals' interpretation, and the NDP MLAs appeared oddly silent on Morfitt's findings. Perhaps they were shell-shocked by the raid on Clark's home. When the report came out in March 1999, the NDP was already at record lows in the polls, and Clark had little credibility left.

The lights, cameras, and action had moved on to a new story. The only common thread was the villain—Premier Glen Clark faced a whole new round of allegations, these much more serious than those of the previous years. Whereas the accusations that had been dogging him since 1996 referred to alleged political activities used to gain votes, the accusations against him in 1999 were personal, financial, and criminal.

5

Total Recall

It [Recall] *allows well-financed, well-funded special interest groups to start to push special interest agendas ... They have enough money and influence to put into the media, on a day-to-day basis, enough misinformation, character assassination and information that is impossible to refute—because of the power and verbosity of those who put it out—to sway public opinion against that [MLA] member.*

—Gordon Wilson,
in debate on Bill 36, July 6, 1994

In the 1991 general election, the outgoing Social Credit government responded to the populist cry for political reform by placing two referendum questions on the ballot. These asked people if they wanted *initiative (referendum)* and *recall,* two political processes that would supposedly put more power in the hands of the people.

By posing these questions in the turbulent final days of Social Credit, Premier Rita Johnston could claim to be listening to the public's demand for more power, while also laying the foundation to cause considerable grief to the party forming the next government, which by all accounts would be the NDP. Critics of the Socreds speculated that recall would be an insurance policy for the Social Credit party. If the NDP won by a narrow margin, then the Socreds could target some NDP seats for recall and perhaps force another election. Few predicted that the Social Credit party would be almost wiped out in the 1991 election, or that the NDP would win 51 out of 75 seats.

Both initiative and recall passed by a comfortable margin in the 1991 election. Mike Harcourt, then NDP leader, supported them, while Gordon Wilson, then Liberal leader, opposed the questions and campaigned against them for reasons that would become obvious years later. In 1994, honouring his commitment, Harcourt's government introduced the recall and initiative legislation, which was lifting the lid on a Pandora's box that he handed to his successor, Glen Clark.

It was a ticking time bomb.

Initiative theoretically allows private citizens to advocate legislation by collecting enough public support to compel the legislature to make the private bill into law. As of 2002, no one has ever succeeded with an initiative, because the threshold for numbers of signatures per riding has been too high.[1]

Recall legislation allows an individual or group of individuals to allege wrongdoing by an MLA and then collect enough signatures of residents in that member's riding to force the MLA out of office. A by-election would then be held, and the person who was turfed out of office would be eligible to run. Keep in mind that the legislation does not require any independent hearings for the person charged with wrongdoing. He or she would not have a day in court, nor access to any non-political process for a fair hearing.

At the time that the recall and initiative legislation was passed in 1994, Gordon Wilson was an opposition MLA representing Powell River–Sunshine Coast. He voted against the bill, and the debate that occurred foreshadowed a great irony in British Columbia's political history. Wilson began:

> I remember history classes that talked about when people—mostly women—were charged with being witches. The masses would rise up, rush out and say: "That person is a witch." They would be asked, "How do you know?" and answer: "Because they look like one." That may be enough to bring up a stake, put them there and burn them …

> That's what recall is. It's a travesty. This is not democracy; it's counterproductive to democracy. It allows well-financed, well-funded special interest groups to start to push special interest agendas ... They have enough money and influence to put into the media, on a day-to-day basis, enough misinformation, character assassination and information that is impossible to refute—because of the power and verbosity of those who put it out—to sway public opinion against that member. That's what this bill is all about. It's wrong. It's a fundamentally anti-democratic process.[2]

In response to these comments, Glen Clark, then a senior cabinet minister in the Harcourt government, entered debate:

> I think there's a certain demagoguery as well in [Wilson's] remarks—and maybe, when you listen to his comments, even a bit of a martyr complex. He clearly has said that he's a victim of public anger, a victim of the establishment; he's taken a principled position on issues, and look where it's got him ...
>
> Where I share his view is the danger of initiative and recall being used by powerful special interests, by the media or by organized interest groups, those who can raise funds, etc. ...
>
> With this bill the government is saying that the wisdom of the average British Columbian is important, and that we are not afraid when government makes tough decisions. ... they [the public] will have the wisdom to make those choices. They may choose to try to organize recall and initiative, but at the end of the day, that's a battle in which governments have to be prepared to engage in the 1990s.[3]

Ironically, a few short years later, Premier Clark would lead a government forced to engage in this battle. In another irony of B.C.

politics, the only "successful" recall attempt was not against an NDP government member, but against Liberal opposition MLA Paul Reitsma, who was accused of inappropriate conduct. Enough signatures were collected on a petition within the given time frame to force him to step down, however Reitsma resigned before the signatures were counted, so technically the recall process has yet to oust an elected member.

Recall was not pursued prior to the 1996 general election.[4] Almost immediately after the election, two recall campaigns were launched against NDP MLAs: Paul Ramsey in Prince George North and Helmut Giesbrecht in the riding of Skeena. Both of these campaigns received province-wide media attention, and their proponents were given considerable news coverage. Both campaigns failed. After the failed recall campaigns, anti-NDP rallies began to occur in various places in the province. These were followed by two more attempts to recall NDP MLAs: another challenge against Paul Ramsey, and a new one against Evelyn Gillespie, MLA for Comox Valley.

This ongoing publicity provided a platform from which to criticize the government. The theme of "lying" and "corruption" was almost identical to that of the HELP BC campaign.

• • •

While the HELP BC lawsuit was slogging through the maze of the court system, a new challenger to the NDP government came forward. In November 1998, a champion of the masses emerged in Kevin Falcon, a young man who claimed to be independent of the B.C. Liberals and who stated he wanted truth and justice to win out in our democratic system. Falcon captured the imagination of the media with the name of his campaign (taken from an Arnold Schwarzenegger movie, *Total Recall*) and its goal. With the help of unnamed financiers, he was going to head up a public-relations campaign named Total Recall, which would take aim at every sitting NDP MLA. The people of B.C. would have a chance to force all 39

MLAs out of office, thus negating the results of the 1996 general election. The Total Recall campaign began with a rally at Cloverdale in November 1998, put together by a new organization, the Concerned Citizens of B.C. The group appeared closely connected with the Surrey Electors Association. In an interesting footnote, a young woman named Rachel Barkey, associated with the Surrey Electors Association, became Gordon Campbell's constituency assistant. She resurfaces later in this story in connection with the casino scandal.

And so Total Recall was another campaign attempting to invalidate the results of the 1996 provincial election. Again the media carried stories about a person taking on the government. Falcon claimed to have few political ties, but he gained support from high-profile members of the public. He launched Total Recall with a rally against the NDP. On the evening of November 26, 1998 thousands of people showed up at the Cloverdale fairgrounds. This rally launched the Total Recall campaign with fanfare, and Total Recall would be in the news frequently. On November 27, in an article entitled "Rally could prompt recalls: Turnout surprises organizers hoping to oust NDP gov't," the *Province* newspaper provided prominent coverage of Falcon's rally at Cloverdale:

> Organizers of an anti-NDP crusade hope to convert the zeal of public discontent into a recall campaign to bring down the Glen Clark government.
>
> About 5,000 people who jammed into the Cloverdale Fairgrounds last night whooped and hollered their support for knocking Clark out of office.
>
> They flooded the Agriplex for a rally organized by the Concerned Citizens of B.C. … "We started to realize from the phone calls and faxes we were getting that something bigger was happening than we expected," said Falcon, co-chairman of the event, who worked for the Liberals in a recent byelection …

> "It takes [the defeat of] four NDP MLAs to bring about the collapse of the government.
>
> "If there is strong support for [recall], then we will begin a campaign to target the four MLAs where we have the best chance to make that happen."
>
> He did not identify any New Democrat MLA who he thought might be vulnerable.
>
> Falcon estimated the cost of last night's rally at $50,000, about $15,000 of which was reportedly raised through donations at the Agriplex.
>
> He said he will disclose the full amount of contributions but will not divulge the names of individual donors.
>
> Other speakers last night were David Stockell, the Kelowna lawyer suing the NDP for its campaign budget promises, economist Dr. David Bond and Troy Lanigan, executive director of the Canadian Taxpayers Federation.

Although the article mentioned that Falcon worked for the B.C. Liberals in a recent by-election campaign, there was no analysis of his political affiliations, nor was there third-party commentary about Mr. Falcon's actions and comments. The other speakers at the rally were known opponents of the NDP. Further, the media did not appear to pursue the matter of who provided the $35,000 for the rally. Who was the piper calling the tune? The *Province* profiled members of the public attending the rally who expressed varying degrees of anger or disgust with the NDP. But the article did not say if attendees had voted NDP in the 1996 general election

• • •

At the time of the Total Recall campaign, former NDP Member of Parliament for Prince George–Bulkley Valley, Brian Gardiner, was the provincial secretary of the NDP, the senior staff person. He claims that in both the HELP BC case and the Total Recall case, the party was placed in a difficult position. The party was under attack over issues that were 100 percent the responsibility of government. For example, the NDP as a political party is responsible for setting general policy on issues including the environment, day care, fiscal responsibility, and many other matters. The party raises funds, recruits candidates, sets up political advertisements, organizes conventions, and generally provides the backdrop for the MLAs and the candidates in their ridings. The bone of contention in the Total Recall rallies and the HELP BC court case was the deficit budget, which was in the government's domain.

The party has nothing to do with the day-to-day operation of government, the implementation of government programs, or the provincial budget. Government MLAs work with teams of bureaucrats and civil servants to establish the budget. Party staff learn about the contents of the budget and the legislative agenda at the same time that the public learns about them.

However, in both the HELP BC and the Total Recall campaigns, the party found itself having to respond to detailed allegations made against the NDP as a political party, even though the attacks were against the "NDP government" and its budget. This meant that resources used to counter the actions and comments of Falcon and Stockell had to come from party headquarters and from individual members of the New Democratic Party. Gardiner elaborated: "Why the party was being held responsible for the government was a mystery to us, but the court case led to an increasing financial burden that was in the hundreds of thousands of dollars. We had no choice but to incur the costs. We were the defendants."[5] Ironically, staff from headquarters had to be briefed on the actions of the government before they were qualified to answer questions, even if they felt it appropriate to respond. This made a counter-campaign very difficult. As well, the focus of the Total Recall campaign—the 1996 election budget—was in front of the courts. Most lawyers advise their clients not to comment publicly on anything before the courts, and this muzzled the party officers. Discretion may work well from a legal perspective, but can be deadly in the political arena, which moves at a much more fluid pace than the justice system. NDP headquarters was overwhelmed by the constant attacks and the need to muster an ongoing defence.

• • •

The *Province* and the *Vancouver Sun* were the only two province-wide newspapers at the time of the Total Recall campaign, both owned by Pacific Press. *Vancouver Sun* articles on the rallies and recall efforts were similar to those in the *Province.* In addition to the print media covering the anti-NDP efforts, there was television and radio coverage by: BCTV, CHEK TV (Victoria) and CKNW radio all owned by WIC, the public broadcasts of CBC TV and CBC Radio, and others.

In the debate that preceded Harcourt's recall legislation, recall was not considered a tool to re-fight a general election campaign by targeting enough MLAs to eliminate the government's majority. It was intended to provide protection against individual MLAs, based on allegations of specific indiscretions. But in the commercial and public media there was no public debate about the appropriateness of Total Recall. The tone of the broadcast media was consistent with that of the *Sun* and *Province* and tended to cover the anti-NDP forces with little commentary from the NDP.

Brian Gardiner noted: "Few media outlets were interested in hearing from us. It was difficult to be heard amongst the deluge of negativity. It was as though even the reporters had made up their minds. They were tired of the 'spin' from the NDP."[6]

Gardiner was enormously frustrated by CBC Radio as an outlet that ran stories without the perspective of the NDP: "So many of our members and supporters listened to CBC Radio, and I would turn it on and only hear these really negative stories with absolutely no input from the NDP. I had to make it a habit to phone CBC Radio to try to get them to cover us. I didn't have a lot of success."

• • •

After two high-profile regional recall attempts failed in Prince George and Skeena, and before the Total Recall rally at Cloverdale, the *Sun* ran a front-page story about a rally in Prince George. The article referred to Alberta as an economic model for B.C. to emulate, without mentioning Alberta's thriving oil and gas industry of the time, and it included comments from those attending the rally. The reporter was a member of the press gallery in the B.C. legislature, one of a select few who could have provided an independent analysis of the government. Excerpts from his *Vancouver Sun* article on November 9, "Anti NDP sentiment finds rallying cry," gave insight into his perspective:

> Their goal is to tear down the government with a wrecking ball of public disgust.
>
> Their tool is a slogan: "Have you had enough yet?"
>
> The expected answer is a resounding, "Yes, I've had enough," according to Bill Lynch, the 52-year-old Prince George real-estate agent who helped organize a rally in September that got that response from between 2,500 and 3,000 northerners.
>
> Their anger is aimed at Premier Glen Clark and the governing New Democrats, but the message is for the parties in opposition: Forget your differences and figure out a way to work together to get rid of the NDP …
>
> "We simply want to take back our province for British Columbians," said Steve Cook, who is helping organize the next rally, set for Nov. 19 in Terrace …
>
> "We've just had enough, it's as simple as that," he said.
>
> Cook said he's had enough of unkept promises and of jobs heading east to Alberta, where mills are working "24 hours a day, seven days a week and we can't seem to work a month or six weeks at a time here without a shutdown."
>
> He added: "We've got the resources, we've got the technology. Something just is not right."

The Prince George rally, like the others it has spawned, was organized as a non-partisan event. Lynch admits he once was a member of Social Credit, and last summer he joined the B.C. Liberals. But he says the rally was for people who might never have put a label on themselves, who shared a common sense of disgust with Clark and the government in far-off Victoria.

Cook's citizens group is like others that have been forming around the province in a loose underground network of people who are no longer content to wait for the anti-NDP political parties to tackle a government they are disliking more and more.

"I'm just somebody who absolutely hates this government and I'm going to do whatever I can to get rid of it," said Kevin Falcon, a developer whose newly formed Concerned Citizens of British Columbia is planning a rally at the Cloverdale Fairgrounds Agriplex Nov. 26.

Falcon, who has been converting apartment buildings into condominiums in Alberta but does no work in B.C., said he has supported the Reform Party federally and worked to elect Liberal Gordon Hogg provincially in the Surrey-White Rock byelection last year.

His organizing team includes Liberals, Reformers and people with no affiliation, but the rule is, "If anyone wants to push any kind of political agenda, they can get the hell out."

This is an anybody-but-the-NDP campaign, offering no solutions beyond the demand that the so-called free-enterprise vote be brought together.

"My view is that the voters are going to take care of that for us," said Falcon. "Ultimately, the voters are going to go up to the ballot box and say, 'Okay, who has the best chance of knocking off the NDP candidate in my riding?'"

Lynch said if an election were called tomorrow, he would support Campbell ...

> In Comox on Vancouver Island, a local citizens' group called People B.C. is hoping to stage a rally this spring.
>
> Margaret Grant, a retired harbourmaster who now lives in nearby Fanny Bay, said the message from Prince George resonated with her as soon as she heard it.
>
> "I've had enough," said Grant, who has worked for Liberal candidates in past campaigns …
>
> [The article quoted Liberal leader Gordon Campbell:] "I see this as a way of focusing the public's attention on how disastrous the NDP's economic policy is and they automatically take the next step and say, 'How do we make sure that we defeat this government?' Individuals will make their own choices, but I'm very pleased with the ones who have come to us."

How can you be non-partisan when you openly oppose a political party? Organizers talked about non-partisan efforts in one breath, while professing a "common sense" hatred for the NDP in the next. For example, Kevin Falcon emerged from the series of rallies as the champion of the cause. He claimed to be non-partisan, but in the next sentence pointed to the purpose of the rallies, which was to defeat the NDP. He also acknowledged partisan political ties by saying he worked to help B.C. Liberal Hogg win his seat.

Falcon and his cohorts Lynch, Grant, and Cook all said their efforts were not openly tied to one particular political party, however when pressed, they were all either directly affiliated with or supporting the Campbell Liberals.

• • •

The stories from the provincial media eventually had an impact in small communities in remote parts of the province. Erda Walsh, Kootenay MLA from 1996 to 2001 commented that at first the Falcon stories were removed from the day-to-day comments in the

East Kootenay region that she represented. Walsh said that people tended to acknowledge that the actions were politically motivated, and they disregarded them at first.

> However, the "fudge-it budget" phrase was constantly in the media, and eventually it was picked up by locals in letters to the editor and critical public comments. People would say to me, "You guys lied about the budget and revenues." It became constant, and seemed to be part of every criticism of what we were trying to do. References to the fudge-it budget were always linked to comments that it was time to dump the government, that people wanted the government dumped.[7]

Walsh said that as the government's critics picked up momentum, the same comments would start to come up in their letters and statements on the radio. "They began to say that they used to support me, that they had voted for me, things like that. I knew some of them had never ever supported me or the NDP. I would have had 100 percent support if all of their votes had been counted for me." NDP members were confused by the media coverage. Walsh added: "They thought it was pretty clear that the recall campaigns were politically driven and could not understand why the media didn't mention this. The people I spoke with didn't think the recall would ever work anyway, and they figured that since the election was over, the critics should just wait until next time."

In the Prince George area, anyone who spoke out about the inappropriateness of the recall campaign as a political tool was attacked in public. This happened to former mayor of Prince George John Backhouse and to former Social Credit MLA Len Fox, who commented against the abuse of the recall process.

According to Lois Boone, the NDP MLA for Prince George–Mount Robson at the time, attempts to focus the anti-NDP forces on public debate were a waste of time. Boone, an experienced MLA, witnessed the recall attempts against her colleague Paul Ramsey in Prince George North from close quarters. Boone claimed that the recall attempts against Ramsey were intensely negative, and they focussed exclusively on personal attacks on his character and competence. "It was one of the nastiest campaigns I've ever seen; it upset me considerably," Boone said. "And it was incredibly hard on his family."[8] Boone said that Ramsey was labelled a liar by his opponents and was constantly targeted.

"He was creamed by the media," said Boone. "It was an all-out attack. It became so that no one was prepared to say anything; they were too afraid they would become the next target. Paul [Ramsey] finally had to sue Ben Meisner for slander. He won the case in the end, but at what cost to his family?" (Meisner was a prominent Prince George radio talkshow host who covered current events, who was found by the courts to have slandered Paul Ramsey.) Boone added:

> The media was constantly running stories saying the government had lied about the 1996 budget, and then it reached a point where the label "liar" was just accepted. The same thing happened to Helmut [Giesbrecht] in Terrace [Skeena riding]. No one wanted to debate anything real, they just stood up over and over saying "liar." How can you have an intelligent discussion about education or health care when every time you open your mouth you are called a liar? It was awful.

Boone contended that the media stories were so focussed on the attacks against the government that not only was it the main story, it was the only story. She claimed it was tough on morale to see some of her colleagues targeted and watch the party's credibility erode more with each attack.

• • •

Few media articles seemed critical of the Total Recall campaign, nor did any of them question the wisdom of restarting recall campaigns in Prince George North and Skeena, when one recall campaign had already failed.

In happier times Glen Clark serves coffee to Lois Boone on the campaign trail at Prince George in 1996.

Besides the characterization of the NDP government as a group of liars and cheats, there was a second common theme emerging in Falcon, Campbell, and Stockell's comments This was a belief that if they could get rid of the NDP government, either through the courts, the recall campaigns, or the court of public opinion, we in British Columbia could enjoy Alberta-style prosperity. According to them Alberta had a thriving economy, better health care, balanced budgets, and tax cuts.

It was like Disneyland.

But no one asked Falcon and the Concerned Citizens of B.C. the obvious questions. If the anti-NDP forces were successful in ousting the government how were they planning to achieve Alberta-style prosperity? Was it a non-partisan goal? Given that Alberta and its prosperity was a common theme, it was reasonable to anticipate a forum to debate the assumption on many fronts, including:

- How did British Columbia's economic indicators compare to Alberta's?
- How did British Columbia's tax regime compare to Alberta's?

- Was the NDP government to blame for the economic circumstances of British Columbia, particularly in the rural regions?
- If the NDP was responsible for the problems, what were the specific solutions, and who was planning to implement them?
- Could British Columbia cut taxes to match Alberta's without the oil and gas revenues that went to the Alberta government?

This public debate did not take place. Was it the media's fault? Members of the media would argue that they showed up for large rallies and covered what was presented to them. They would have covered any pro-government rallies, too.

When Falcon's Total Recall campaign finally died, Falcon received a soft landing from the media, and stories citing fund-raising problems and the proximity of the next election circulated in the news. Although Falcon acknowledged that he had failed to raise the $250,000 needed for such an ambitious undertaking, he blamed the NDP for the failure of Total Recall. According to wire service stories, Falcon said the lesson he learned was that "the government is a bully that intimidates its opponents."[9]

Public Service Minister Moe Sihota disagreed with Falcon, saying, "I think Mr. Falcon got the signal from the public," says Sihota. "They don't think it's appropriate to use recall legislation to try to bring down a government when it was intended to bring down an MLA that was guilty of wrongdoing."[10]

Regardless of the eventual failure of the recall campaigns to force NDP MLAs out of office, they were successful in discrediting the Clark government to the extent that few people doubted that Clark had lied about the budget in the 1996 election campaign. The HELP BC court case, the auditor-general's investigation, and Total Recall all fuelled the media fire critical of the Clark government. The media focussed on these controversies for the first three years after the 1996 election, and these controversies provided background for numerous editorials.

The controversies had a profound effect on the Clark government's ability to receive credit for public policy initiatives. They also opened the door to a widespread feeling of contempt for the Clark government and to a general culture of disrespect. Lois Boone observed: "Guys like Falcon and Stockell did a good job of influencing people and killing off Glen. Their constant comments went unchallenged, and by the time the decisions came out, it was way too late. People's minds were already made up."

In the 2001 general election, Kevin Falcon ran for Gordon Campbell's Liberal party and was elected to office. Despite Falcon's high profile as the supposedly independent, non-partisan organizer of Total Recall, the matter of Falcon's credibility was not an issue in the general election campaign. After the election, Campbell appointed Kevin Falcon the minister responsible for government deregulation.

The Total Recall cloud finally lifted from the Clark government in May 1999, but few people noticed because this was two months after the RCMP raided Glen Clark's house. Now the discussion had turned to speculation about when Clark would resign over the casino-licensing scandal.

6

The Undercurrents

British Columbians are sick and tired of NDP lies and excuses and abuses.

Drop the writ, Glen.

They're tired of an NDP government that doesn't know right from wrong.

Drop the writ, Glen.

They've had it with a government that willfully breaks the law.

Drop the writ, Glen.

—Gordon Campbell, leader of the opposition,
Langley Civic Centre, May 2, 1998

In late 1998, the Clark government's fortunes were stabilizing. The public had heard of the budget scandal for so long that it was stale, and the media had begun to focus on public policy statements on health care, Aboriginal treaties, and post-secondary education. Total Recall and HELP BC were losing steam. Even if they were of occasional interest to the media, the initiatives did not seem likely to succeed. Turfing an NDP government almost three years into its mandate was not as provocative as trying to derail it at the beginning.

Glen Clark was not one to sit idle, and he had already begun to ramp up policy work on some of his favourite subjects. Ironically, the one issue that had run as an undercurrent throughout Clark's term was Aboriginal rights. One of the most controversial events of the NDP's first term occurred shortly before Harcourt's resignation in

In one of their more civil moments Glen Clark and Gordon Campbell and a host of visiting students celebrate the hundredth anniversary of B.C.'s parliament buildings.

1995, and one of the century's greatest breakthroughs occurred in the last year of Clark's term in 1999. Both involved Aboriginal rights.

How one determined what was "policy" and what was "politics" in British Columbia tended to be based on how much attention a government decision received from interest groups. Aboriginal rights were a hot political issue because there was very little middle ground when it came to treaties with Natives. Either you supported the concept of treaties, or you didn't. Sometimes support was simply a function of whether one lived in an urban or rural area. Generally speaking, it was believed to be good politics to be against treaties in the rural areas, where a treaty would have an impact on land-use jobs like forestry and mining. In voter-rich urban centres, public support tended toward resolving the treaty issues.

The Aboriginal treaty issue was a complex problem. Moderate Native leaders involved in treaty negotiations had to show their community members that they were delivering a "win." At the same time, militant leaders were saying that nothing short of indigenous sovereignty would be acceptable. In 1992, the Charlottetown Accord was the much-hailed constitutional agreement advanced by the federal and provincial governments, and it had a provision for a "third order of government" for Natives. This concept was undefined and created considerable controversy in British Columbia, the most heavily affected province. Most of the land in B.C. was under Aboriginal claim. The Charlottetown Accord was defeated in British Columbia, to some extent because of the undefined Aboriginal provisions. Even many B.C. Aboriginal leaders were opposed to it.

• • •

When British Columbia joined the Canadian confederation, it did so with the commitment to negotiate unresolved treaties with the indigenous peoples. This commitment related to B.C.'s fiduciary obligations and the responsibilities of the Crown or state. Originally Vancouver Island and the Mainland were separate Crown colonies. After the Cariboo gold rush in 1858, the two colonies merged into the single colony of British Columbia under Governor James Douglas. This colony joined Canada in 1871. The matter of resolving Aboriginal land-title issues, which originally was the responsibility of the British Empire, passed to Canada with very few treaties signed. Notable exceptions were the treaties on Vancouver Island negotiated by Governor James Douglas and the Treaty 8 agreements in the Peace River region. Otherwise, the land issue was unresolved. In the late twentieth century, this meant that the Governor General, represented by the federal government, had a legal obligation to settle the land-claim issue. Some Natives assert that it is Queen Elizabeth, as Queen of Canada, who has sole legitimate authority to negotiate treaties with them.

University of Lethbridge professor Anthony Hall provided a relatively simple analysis of the legal situation when he gave evidence to an American court in an extradition case:

These [treaty] negotiations are very political exercises, whose very existence serves to illustrate that the Aboriginal land title in British Columbia is an extremely charged subject of political controversy, where the future disposition and rights to almost unimaginable natural-resource wealth hangs in the balance.

While these treaty negotiations are political exercises, they proceed in an environment where the domestic courts of Canada have created some of the parameters within which the bargaining is taking place. In 1973 in the Calder ruling, and in 1997 in the Delgamuukw ruling, the Supreme Court of Canada addressed the question of whether or not the Indigenous peoples of the province hold an existing Aboriginal title to most of British Columbia. While there is much ambivalence and paradox in both rulings, basically the courts have gradually vindicated the positions of generations of Indian activists, who have consistently argued that British Columbia since its inception has not developed according to the rule of law of British North America. Following a flood of Californian gold miners into the Hudson's Bay fur trade preserve west of the Rockies formally known as New Caledonia, British Columbia was made a Crown colony in 1858. The southern boundary of Crown territory and the northern boundary of US jurisdiction were negotiated in the Oregon Treaty settlement of 1846.

The headway made by Indian people in the courts has been extremely hard won. Many delegations of British Columbia Indian leaders have over the last 125 years made representations to the Dominion government in Ottawa and to the monarchy as well as to the House of Lords and the House of Commons in London, seeking to call attention to the failure of Crown authorities in BC

> to address the Indian title of the First Nations through the negotiation of treaties. That recognition of Aboriginal title was codified and entrenched in the founding document of British imperial Canada, namely the Royal Proclamation of 1763. The response of the Canadian government to this mobilized Indian lobby was in 1927 to amend the Indian Act to make it illegal for registered Indians to raise money for their own political organization or to hire a lawyer to pursue an Indian claim. That draconian law stayed on the books until 1951.[1]

In the waning years of the Social Credit government, Indian Affairs Minister Jack Weisgerber (later to lead the B.C. Reform party and oppose treaties), along with Prime Minister Brian Mulroney, and the First Nations Summit signed on to the B.C. Treaty Commission—a body formed to facilitate treaty negotiations. Very little occurred immediately after the signing ceremony since both the provincial and federal governments changed soon afterwards. The new governments, the Harcourt NDP and the Chretien federal Liberals, were more committed to the treaty process than their predecessors and work on the treaty negotiations went into high gear.

The Aboriginal community was deeply divided on the treaty issue. Some groups maintained that the province had no legal right to be involved in negotiations. Other groups declared that they would retain sovereignty, and most of the leadership tried to advance the interests of their communities, while facing criticism from all sides.

• • •

Native unrest came to the fore in the summer of 1995, during the Gustafsen Lake standoff between a small number of Secwepemc, or Shuswap, people and the RCMP, backed up by the Canadian military. The conflict took place in a remote part of the interior, on a ranch, and began with a Native sun dance. The provincial players in this 1995

Aboriginal-rights drama were reunited in the drama that unfolded in the premier's office almost four years later. The tactics employed at Gustafsen Lake foreshadowed some of the political events to come.

In a 1995 cabinet shuffle, Mike Harcourt moved a relatively unknown MLA from his short stint in the portfolio of minister of government services into the office of attorney-general. Ujjal Dosanjh, the MLA for Vancouver–Kensington, was elected to the legislature for the first time in 1991 when Harcourt took the NDP to government.

Dosanjh impressed many people with his understated style in the debates. He was fresh, articulate, attractive, and professional in his presentation. Born in the Punjab, India, his past history included working in a lumber mill, which led to a workplace injury to his back. Unable to continue as a labourer, Dosanjh became a lawyer. In his new profession he took on social justice issues on behalf of farm workers. In the first three years of the Harcourt mandate, Dosanjh demonstrated consistency and intelligence without flash, which earned him an entry-level position as minister of government services. He was low-key and remained non-partisan in the legislature, cautious in all his comments.

I was MLA for Okanagan East, sitting in the opposition for the Progressive Democratic Alliance, when Harcourt put Ujjal Dosanjh into cabinet. I was very happy for him and sent a note across the floor of the house that said, "It's about time!" He acknowledged the note with a smile and a wave. He and I had jousted in debates over the years, and I had enjoyed matching wits with him. He seemed to be a good choice for attorney-general.

Dosanjh would soon be tested in a conflict over land and Aboriginal rights in the Cariboo region on a ranch owned by Lyle James. The Gustafsen Lake confrontation escalated quickly into a military operation and a media feeding frenzy. The Gustafsen Lake standoff was one of the most disputed, controversial, and nasty battles over Aboriginal rights and territory to occur in British Columbia. Managed by the RCMP, it saw the largest deployment of military might on domestic soil in contemporary Canadian history.

The standoff was followed by a series of court battles, with many details sealed to this day by the presiding judge. The CBC ombudsman, in a lengthy review, determined that much of the information fed to the media by the RCMP was false.

It was in July 1995 that Natives sought title to a portion of ranchland in the Cariboo owned by Lyle James. They occupied the land for their sun dance and did not want, or plan, to leave. A team of RCMP officers, including some Aboriginal officers, moved in to try to resolve the conflict. On August 18, someone fired a shot at an RCMP officer, and three Native RCMP officers were immediately removed from the case.

The Gustafsen Lake standoff landed on Ujjal Dosanjh's desk while the Harcourt government was in summer recess, and the relatively new attorney-general soon had a major crisis on his hands. Along with RCMP Sergeant Peter Montague, Dosanjh appeared on the CBC and CTV newscasts regularly. Both men projected well on camera, and their public profiles grew. Montague, as the public spokesperson for the RCMP, controlled all public communication and worked directly with the media. It is reasonable to believe that he was also the contact or a source for the attorney-general's office, based on the public statements made by both Montague and Dosanjh. It is difficult to know the extent of the working relationship, since the judge in the resulting court case did not allow this line of questioning.

On August 19, the day after a shot was fired at an RCMP officer, the RCMP flew Lower Mainland media into the Gustafsen Lake area to cover the story. BCTV reporter John Daly somehow managed to bypass the RCMP roadblock and travel into the camp to interview Native protesters directly. At the same time, police reports said the Natives were armed and very dangerous.

The political climate of the time was precarious. The B.C. Reform party, not a supporter of Native rights, was outspoken. It called for a strong response to put down Native protesters. People who lived in the interior tended to be strong supporters of a "law and order" response to the Native protesters. As an interior MLA,

I heard from many people who felt the RCMP should remove the Natives from James' land.

It was a major test for Dosanjh, the new attorney-general, and from the public's reaction to his actions he won it hands down. He acted quickly, provided resources to the police, contacted Ottawa for back-up, and spoke in unequivocally negative terms about the Natives involved in the standoff. He stayed in close contact with the RCMP and provided briefings to cabinet that were supportive of the RCMP actions. The media covering the story awarded Dosanjh kudos for his tough response, and political observers tended to see this as a positive move from a government that was, in other matters, foundering. For Mike Harcourt's NDP government this was the first positive news coverage they had received for some time.

This high-stress situation brought together a number of players for several weeks, including Peter Montague of the RCMP, John Daly of BCTV, and Attorney-General Ujjal Dosanjh. But what really happened at Gustafsen Lake? Many facts have come to light in the years since to raise questions about the sequence of events and who was making the decisions. In retrospect, it appears that much of the information passed on to the media, and through the media to policy makers, was part of a deliberate campaign of "disinformation."

The *Province* of May 17, 1997 summarized the findings in the trial:

> It could have been a bloodbath—or at least another Oka. But the final tally in the 30-day Gustafsen Lake armed standoff was: one dead dog, one bullet in the arm of defendant Suniva Bronson, and one hot slug allegedly lodged—and subsequently thrown away—in the pants of an RCMP officer.
>
> "It was a miracle no one was killed," says Kamloops lawyer Don Campbell, who represented five of the accused. "From some perspectives the RCMP operation was comical—but only because no one was killed."

Unlike the 1990 Native standoff in Oka, Que., which left one police officer dead, Gustafsen ended quietly on Sept. 17, 1995.

But the ensuing 10-month trial pulled an official veil from the RCMP operation headed by Kamloops Supt. Len Olfert. It raised eyebrows, prompted demands for a public inquiry and blackened the image of Canada's national police force.

Yesterday, RCMP Sgt. Peter Montague said police "would do substantially the same thing" given another standoff. "In the face of violence you try to contain the situation and deal with it," said Montague, who was the Mounties' media officer during the standoff.

During testimony, jurors heard of the RCMP plan to drop oats laced with poison from aircraft to kill the Natives' horses—a never-used scheme intended to stop the animals from alerting the camp by neighing.

Court also heard that the RCMP released criminal records of shadowy camp figure "Johnny Guitar" at a press conference—while the man listened from the back of the room.

Then there was the RCMP reference to the camp's "early-warning canine detection"—noisy dogs to the rest of us.

More unsettling was evidence of information manipulation, a buildup of military-style assault weapons and descriptions of assault plans on the camp.

"The RCMP were on a war footing" with Natives, defence lawyer Sheldon Tate alleged.

The court heard that RCMP:

- Released juvenile criminal records of some of those believed in the camp—normally done only for sexual predators or fugitives. RCMP denied this was part of their "misinformation" and "smear" strategy jokingly referred to in meetings. Montague admitted he lied when he told a reporter most of those in the camp were murderers. Media were urged not to talk to other RCMP, to maintain the "official messaging," as Montague described it.

- Used military lingo and tactics, including describing sites as "Zulu" and "Hanging Tree." There were plans to use up to 4,000 officers to "neutralize" the Native camp, which held about 40 people.
- Secretly brought in Bison armored personnel carriers borrowed from the Canadian Forces to be used to "assault" the camp, a plan later cancelled. Search warrants usually required were never obtained. The RCMP had submachine-guns, night-vision goggles, "sniper" rifles, trace flares and stun grenades.
- Fired from an aircraft at a Native in an agreed-upon "safe zone." The bullet narrowly missed the man. An internal investigation was promised.
- Ordered five more APCs and an additional 20,000 rounds of .222 ammunition after Sept. 12 as people started to leave the camp. A request for .50-calibre sniper rifles was turned down, but guns were later obtained from an RCMP museum in Vancouver and a gun dealer in Phoenix.

The most notorious line out of Gustafsen Lake was a statement made by media contact Sergeant Montague and taken from an internal police video, that "smear campaigns are our specialty." He stated at the trial that his comment was taken out of context. Nevertheless, the statement was controversial, one of the few verbal faux pas by the RCMP's first national media star.

By 1997, the general election had passed, with the NDP winning a second term, and the headline political news was fudge-it budgets, total recall, and financial mismanagement. Gordon Wilson, as leader of the Progressive Democratic Alliance (PDA), called for an inquiry into the Gustafsen Lake controversy, but this did not receive much attention. The political fallout from Gustafsen Lake was quietly buried.

Prior to Glen Clark's resignation, and certainly during the subsequent leadership race, there were more calls for an inquiry into Gustafsen Lake. With no personal up side to further conjecture about the event, Dosanjh did not want to talk about it, and he certainly was not prepared to consider an inquiry. In the end, the controversy disappeared into the internet and academic papers.

The great irony in the handling of Gustafsen Lake is the fact that the NDP put considerable resources and energy into trying to make the B.C. Treaty Commission work, dealing with the federal government and the 50-plus Aboriginal bands who had signed on to the treaty process. In order to do this, the provincial government faced constant criticism from the B.C. Liberal and the B.C. Reform parties. The heavy-handed approach to the Natives at Gustafsen Lake, managed by the RCMP and candidly endorsed by Dosanjh, created friction. It was the opposite response to the NDP's approach through negotiations.

Gustafsen Lake was a challenging story for the media to cover and a difficult issue for politicians and decision makers to address. There have been many calls for an inquiry into the Gustafsen Lake standoff to clear the air of many disturbing questions. Some elements of the Gustafsen Lake standoff are relevant to set the stage for events that would appear later during the Clark NDP government.

• • •

The need for success in treaty negotiations was increasing with each Supreme Court decision. The Delgamuukw ruling, referred to earlier, made it clear that some legal precedent existed for Aboriginal claim to the land, and if the governments did not succeed in negotiation, then the courts would impose solutions. A court-imposed solution would not only be expensive, divisive, and controversial, but it was also seen by many in the political arena as flying in the face of democracy.

The public controversy around treaties was having an impact and was beginning to draw attention from the international community. British Columbia's economy was dependent on natural resources and "secure tenure" to the land. Before investing, forest, mining, and other natural resource companies wanted to know that they would not be bumped by a land claim from an unresolved legal obligation. The matter was referred to as "certainty." One objective of the treaty process was to bring certainty to the land base.

The B.C. Treaty Commission negotiations were still in their infancy when the Gustafsen Lake standoff occurred in 1995. However, in a separate negotiating process the Nisga'a Treaty had reached approval-in-principle stage. It was a political hot potato supported by the NDP and PDA, but opposed by the B.C. Reform and B.C. Liberal parties. The NDP, with Clark's fancy footwork, won its second term in 1996, and the Nisga'a Treaty negotiations continued.

By 1998, the B.C. Treaty Commission had made slow progress, only tangible to those directly involved. The Nisga'a Treaty, on the other hand, was complete. It was identified as a "wedge issue." In politics, especially in a two-party political system like B.C.'s, wedge issues are manna from heaven. A wedge places the two parties on opposite sides of an issue, with little or no middle ground. It is generally bad for one party, to the direct benefit of the other. Properly timed, a wedge issue can deliver critical momentum in the months leading up to an election, or in the short four weeks of a B.C. election campaign.

For a beaten and battered political party with a feisty leader looking for an urban wedge issue, Nisga'a was perfect. It might become a plank on which to rebuild some of Clark's credibility. It was generally conceded that Clark had evolved into a passionate advocate for Native rights and for a progressive approach to treaties. This was an appealing part of his persona. But it was an even better wedge issue than that. The Nisga'a Treaty had the support of the federal Liberal government, and the NDP knew that many federal Liberal supporters were likely to be upset with the B.C. Liberals if they opposed the treaty. B.C.'s party politics is complicated, but it is widely known that many federal Liberals wait to see which provincial party is closest to their own beliefs before casting a provincial vote. NDP strategists knew that they could create internal division within the B.C. Liberal party if they forced Gordon Campbell to take a strong negative position on Nisga'a. The NDP was looking forward to it.

Michael Izen came out of the Nisga'a Treaty implementation office, and as a partisan supporter he felt that the Nisga'a Treaty and post-secondary education were both good "wedge" issues between the NDP and the Liberals. According to Izen, the Nisga'a Treaty would benefit the NDP in the urban ridings around Vancouver, where they desperately needed to regain or retain support. Izen said:

> The Liberals had launched a court challenge to the Nisga'a agreement, which was not sitting well with some of their members, and which was not likely to succeed, while the NDP took the high road. Even though the public did not seem to be aware of the details of the Nisga'a Treaty, we felt that an information campaign would see the public onside.[2]

Glen Clark's pro-Nisga'a stance, lining up on the same side as the federal Liberals, appears to have won the next generation.

Clark as premier during the good times at the Western premier's conference in May 1997: Western premier's photo op, fishing with son Reed, and Clark with salmon—winner of the competition among premiers.

The NDP's only chance of recovering popularity in the polls was to force Campbell to debate Clark on issues. When Clark began as premier, he had identified youth issues as important, and his early commitment to post-secondary education had not waned. In late 1998, he moved some new workers into the premier's youth office and gave them an ambitious mandate. He dared them to dream and to develop policy for students. Michael Izen worked in the premier's youth office from November of 1998, joining just as the mood of the government was turning upbeat. He remarked:

> The premier had programs for youth—and although it's true that the youth did not know or care who was putting the programs in place, these were good public policy initiatives to take to the voters. Plus, we were looking at the elimination of tuition—not just freezing it. Premier Clark was the driving force behind the tuition policy—he had the support of caucus, the support of cabinet.
>
> He was battered but it was mid-term; it's to be expected that a government is at its least popular at mid-term. We believed he would have the support of the public as soon as he was back on his issues.

Even if this might have seemed optimistic to outside observers, it is important to note that there were many motivated party workers who believed they could improve the poor standing in the polls with Clark as leader. In light of the surprise 1996 election victory, it may not have been an unrealistic belief.

Education, post-secondary education in particular, was another wedge issue that the NDP felt they could use because the B.C. Liberals had a policy to cut several popular government programs. The NDP, in a controversial deal overseen by Clark, had also imposed a teacher's contract earlier that resulted in smaller class sizes.

• • •

In January 1999, when the NDP was at a historic low in the polls, the volatile world of British Columbia politics underwent another dramatic change that took observers by surprise. Gordon Wilson, former leader of the B.C. Liberal party and the only elected member of the PDA, crossed the floor of the legislature to join the New Democratic Party as a cabinet minister. He walked directly into cabinet, a move almost unprecedented in the NDP, a party known to focus on seniority as a key consideration for party positions. As well, Wilson was rated the most popular leader in British Columbia. Izen commented:

> Wilson crossing the floor was a show of strength—a show of potential public support. The mood of the staffers was positive about this, even though many staffers saw Wilson as an outsider, or even as someone who had been a political adversary for a number of years. You had to like the move to join us. We had momentum.

The deal to wrangle Wilson into the NDP government unfolded in complete secrecy, with only a handful of people involved. It followed a by-election in Parksville–Qualicum, where Paul Reitsma had resigned with a recall initiative hanging over his head. The PDA ran an aggressive and well-financed campaign to see what the party could achieve with an effort focussed exclusively on one riding. Although the PDA gained momentum and polls indicated popular support, the final tally of less than 15 percent of the vote was a severe disappointment to Wilson and his closest supporters.

Former premier Dave Barrett had preliminary meetings with Wilson's senior aide, Tony Cox, to discuss a possible deal. After a few meetings, NDP heavyweight Moe Sihota entered the discussions and began meeting with Wilson and Cox. For the final agreement, Premier Glen Clark joined the group to confirm the arrangements that would bring Wilson into the NDP cabinet and oversee the dissolution of the Progressive Democratic Alliance.

Wilson moved from the political frying pan into the fire and took on two of the most controversial portfolios: Aboriginal affairs and the BC Ferry Corporation. The Nisga'a Treaty was coming up for debate in the legislature, and the Campbell Liberals had launched a strong opposition in the political arena and in the courts. The B.C. Liberals had filed a writ in seeking to have the Nisga'a Treaty derailed. In addition, the BC Ferry Corporation was facing strong public opposition around the issue of the new fast ferries. As well, the ferry corporation was in rough shape financially.

Prior to the 1996 election, the NDP had embarked on a program to design and construct high-speed catamaran ferries, known as fast ferries or "fast cats." This decision was somewhat controversial at the time, however the NDP proceeded with the program. By 1999, the first of the ferries had been built, but the cost was significantly over budget, and there were problems with the design. When information came out in 1998 that there were substantial cost overruns, the fast ferry controversy escalated dramatically. The B.C. Liberals referred to this as the "fast ferry fiasco." When added to the fudge-it budget discussions, the decision to build three high-speed high-cost catamarans reinforced the public image of the NDP as a fiscally irresponsible government.

Ironically, Wilson had been the strongest opponent of the program from its inception, and he was now the minister responsible for launching the new ferries and trying to convince the public that they were a viable option for the coast. Wilson represented Powell River–Sunshine Coast, a ferry-dependent riding, and he had been vocal about repositioning the BC Ferry Corporation as an extension of the highways. With his appointment as minister, the government was giving him a hot potato. There was little left to lose if he dropped it.

• • •

At the same time that public attention turned away from the fudge-it budget and toward more policy-oriented discussion, it was rumoured that the imminent auditor-general's report would deal with legislative

With the Nisga'a people, Clark makes an historic Nisga'a Treaty announcement in August 1998.

changes and would not assist the government's opponents in advancing their campaign about the 1996 budget. For the first time since the 1996 election, it appeared that the budget cloud might finally lift enough to change the political dynamic in Victoria.

News coverage had become critical on policy issues rather than political ones, moving from a debate on the premier as a liar to a debate over the future of the BC Ferry Corporation. This was an improvement from Clark's perspective. Policy was an area that many felt was a weakness for the Campbell Liberals, and a policy debate could provide the chance the NDP had been waiting for to recapture the public's attention and rebuild some of the government's shattered credibility.

Erda Walsh was on the inside, and she remembered the change in dynamics that occurred in early 1999. The NDP recalled the provincial legislature to pass the Nisga'a Treaty, and the Liberals faced off with the NDP in question period and debates. Walsh recollected: "The year looked great. One B.C. Liberal MLA, who would not want

Gordon Wilson's move to the NDP came as a surprise to many, and he quickly became a senior minister that Clark relied heavily upon. Still many in the party painted him as an intruder.

to be named, said to me 'if Glen is around in the next election, he will wipe the floor with Campbell.' We had such a strong showing in question period, Clark was slamming Campbell on his policies."[3]

Walsh believed that here could be a repeat of the 1996 election when Clark came from behind to defeat Campbell. She also thought Clark had a trump card in his hand:

> When Wilson joined, there was increased fear in the opposition Liberals because now they faced two pit bulls. Both Glen and Gordon were good on their feet and could hold their own in debate or with the media. You could see it on their faces when one of them was responding in question period. Here was one of their former leaders, a Liberal, supporting Clark after all the controversies had died down.

The stage was set for the coming election, later that spring.

7

The Albatross

And I had done an hellish thing,
And it would work 'em woe:
For all averred, I had killed the bird
That made the breeze to blow.
Ah wretch! said they, the bird to slay,
That made the breeze to blow!

... Ah! well a-day! what evil looks
Had I from old and young!
Instead of the cross, the Albatross
About my neck was hung.

—Samuel Taylor Coleridge,
"The Rime of the Ancient Mariner"

It was March 2, 1999, and the RCMP, led by Officer Bud Bishop, arrived on the premier's doorstep in Vancouver and began a search of his house. This search was authorized by a warrant issued from the B.C. Supreme Court. The Associate Chief Justice of the Supreme Court, Patrick Dohm, the second most senior judge in British Columbia, issued the warrant. The warrant and its contents were sealed to the public until much later.

The raid was captured on television by BCTV. What was unique in Canadian political history was that repeatedly during the next week, the people of Canada watched the same surreal images of RCMP officers showing up at Glen Clark's home, a modest house in East Vancouver. There was no security to prevent access, nor was there any physical barrier to prevent the cameras from catching each moment—from the time the door opened until the moment the police left the house. It was high drama—and no doubt had high ratings.

Dale Clark, the premier's wife, greeted the RCMP at the door, and we could read the expression on her face. She later acknowledged that she was terrified at the sight of the officers, assuming that her husband had been hurt. She soon learned that the officers were there to search the house and question the premier.

Premier Clark was not yet home. The television audience was able to watch the premier arrive home with his communications officer, Geoff Meggs, and his lawyer, Richard Fowler. And once he was inside, we were able to witness the premier's surprise, the concerned body language, the pacing to and fro, and the movements of the officers. The Clark house was easy to watch as the television cameras peered through windows.

The public was told that the search warrant had been issued for the premier. We were also told by BCTV that in a "parallel" criminal investigation, Dimitrios Pilarinos, a neighbour of Clark, had been charged with operating an illegal gaming house.[1] The BCTV news story included pictures of the gaming tables being confiscated from the illegal gambling house.

It all seemed exceedingly seedy.

Two evenings after the raid, the seediness was compounded when BCTV's Tony Parsons introduced the two top stories, on his 6 p.m. newscast on March 4, both related to RCMP investigations. The first continued the story on the premier and was reported by Keith Baldrey. It featured Clark's new lawyer, David Gibbons, who was vigorous in his defence of the premier and in his condemnation of the media. His candour gained few friends in the media, but may have convinced them to be more cautious in their coverage of his client. Next came a story filed by John Daly, the reporter who had been present at the premier's house when the RCMP appeared on his doorstep. Tony Parsons introduced John Daly's March 4 story in this way:

> The raid on the premier's house is the link between two separate but parallel police investigations ... Tonight, in our continuing investigation, reporter John Daly uncovers the connections between the two police probes and some strip clubs on the lower mainland.[2]

The connection was Pilarinos. The RCMP charged him with various criminal activities. It would be some time before all the criminal charges against Pilarinos related to illegal gambling and strip clubs were dropped.

At the time of the raid on Clark's house, no information was made public about what had prompted the investigation. We were not told the contents of the search warrant because this information was considered to be too sensitive for publication. The RCMP told us that the premier himself was not under investigation.

• • •

Following the raid on Clark's house, Conflict of Interest Commissioner H.A.D. "Had" Oliver was called on to investigate the allegation that the premier had breached the Conflict of Interest Act. The first part of the complaint centred around the question of whether or not the premier had received a free and direct pecuniary benefit. An example of this kind of conflict of interest was demonstrated by Liberal MLA John Weisbeck when he received a free ski pass at Big White, because he was the MLA for the region. It is notable that in this instance of a clear receipt of benefits, there was little pressure from the media for Weisbeck's resignation. Instead, the MLA was compelled to return the pass, but without penalty. In Clark's case, the question revolved around whether or not he had been "gifted" work on his sundecks at less than market value. The investigation centred on the assessed value of the work versus the amount paid; the implication was that Clark received a significant benefit.

The second part of the complaint concerned whether or not the premier exerted the influence of his office, in cabinet meetings or other venues, to ensure the casino licence connected to Dimitrios Pilarinos gained approval in principle. If it was proved that Premier Clark had received a gift, and in exchange he had influenced the consideration of the casino licence application, then a conflict of interest had occurred.

Commissioner H.A.D. Oliver's investigation would go on for several months, and his final report was sealed.

• • •

The trail of breadcrumbs to trace the casino scandal against former premier Glen Clark is complicated, perhaps because some of the breadcrumbs were eaten by those not keen in having the path lead to their door. The story begins in August 1998, with an anonymous allegation that Premier Clark was being offered bribes in exchange for a casino licence for the North Burnaby Inn. This was an explosive allegation, with enormous ramifications, both criminal and political. The information provided to the RCMP indicated that Glen Clark had been approached by a neighbourhood friend, Dimitrios Pilarinos, who was one of the applicants in the casino licence application for the North Burnaby Inn.

Further, the information about the bribes seemed to have a foundation. Pilarinos was a contractor. Clark had just renovated his house and his Penticton holiday cabin, adding sundecks. Pilarinos had apparently constucted both of them. The allegation was that Clark had not paid for them, but had instead applied political pressure to advance Pilarinos' casino application. This was a payoff, said the informant.

The investigating team was joined by a special prosecutor, someone appointed to insulate the attorney-general from judicial proceedings that have a political aspect. The special prosecutor worked with the deputy minister to the attorney-general, Ernie

Quantz, in order to ensure that objective treatment was given to the file, even though it was the premier himself under investigation.

On December 18, 1998 the government of British Columbia awarded approval in principle to a number of casino licence applicants. The North Burnaby Inn, which was under criminal investigation for illegal gambling, received approval in principle for a casino licence. However, the B.C. government's guidelines for reviewing casino licence applications were specific—no applicants under investigation were eligible for a casino licence.

In the review process, the North Burnaby Inn should have been disqualified immediately. But it was not. Something questionable was certainly going on. How could the rules be ignored in this one instance? The approval in principle granted to the North Burnaby Inn was a fact. It was all the evidence that the RCMP needed for further investigation of the allegation against Premier Clark—that he might be engaged in a breach of trust in helping a friend obtain a licence under special circumstances.

The team of RCMP officers and the special prosecutor continued the investigation by applying to the courts for a search warrant of the premier's house. Given the sensitivity, the case was "seized" by Associate Chief Justice Patrick Dohm, meaning no other judge could hear matters related to the search warrants. Dohm granted two warrants and sealed their contents. All of this took place behind the scenes until the night of the raid. Then it burst into the public arena like a festering sore, exposed to the world in all of its ugliness.

Geoff Meggs was the director of communications for the premier's office in 1999. He had worked for Glen Clark since shortly after the 1996 election, taking the place of Bill Tieleman. Meggs' past experience was in the fishermen's union and the Hospital Employees' Union, and he explained that he had a steep learning curve from the time he joined Clark's team, just as the fudge-it budget campaign began in 1996. He worked closely with Adrian Dix, Clark's chief of staff and friend.

Meggs was with Clark the night of the raid on the premier's house. An interview with him a year and a half later revealed that a residue of frustration existed over missed opportunities to manage the political communications crisis that unfolded after the raid. The RCMP and media blindsided the premier's office so completely that the only option left was to react to an investigation that was clouded in secrecy. Although it was Meggs' job to handle the communications, so many emotionally charged external factors were at work that it was like trying to manage an avalanche. Meggs said:

> The first indication we had that something was wrong was the information that a warrant had been served on the Ministry of Employment and Investment. Also, when we watched BCTV news at five o'clock, we saw the raid on the North Burnaby Inn, and we noted a really high degree of media attention on this one story, which was strange.[3]

At that point no one knew about any connection between the two events. The information that a search warrant had been served on the Ministry of Employment and Investment was bothersome, and it was some time after the news item about the raid on the North Burnaby Inn that the RCMP showed up at the Vancouver provincial cabinet offices in the Vancouver Trade and Convention Centre on the waterfront. Premier Clark, Meggs, and Dix were preparing the spring legislative agenda when Inspector Bill Ard showed up to speak with the premier. Ard briefed Clark on some of the details of the criminal investigation into the casino licence application, and he stressed that the premier himself was not under investigation. Clark does not remember Ard notifying him about the search warrant issued on his home, and Clark said Ard did not mention that the RCMP were at that very moment acting on this warrant.

Following this brief meeting, Meggs, Clark, and Dix discussed what they should do in the wake of the information that an RCMP investigation affected the premier's office and a ministry of government. They decided to retain the firm of Gibbons Fowler, a well-known and respected legal firm. Richard Fowler joined Meggs and Clark at the cabinet offices before they returned to Clark's house. While Glen Clark was in discussion with Inspector Ard, Dale Clark had called to tell Glen that the RCMP were at their house. Clark was concerned for his family and extremely upset about this unexpected and shocking information that a criminal investigation was so close to home that it was in his home. His one comfort was that he had been told by the RCMP that he was not under investigation. Still, it was extremely upsetting.

Clark gave as much direction as he could to his staff about the legal and internal political responses needed. He was eager to return home to find out what was happening. When Clark, Meggs, and Fowler arrived at Clark's house, they noted an unmarked van parked nearby and assumed it was part of the RCMP investigation. They had no idea that they were being filmed by BCTV for the evening news. Dale Clark told them that the camera crew was there and had been trying to gain an interview, and she was extremely concerned that they would catch their son Reed returning home. He was too young to be caught up in this mess, and she did not want the media intercepting him outside, catching him on camera, or interviewing him.

According to Meggs, BCTV reporter John Daly was banging on the door of Clark's house loudly, demanding an interview. Meggs was able to negotiate with Daly to ensure that Reed was not captured on camera. It was the only concession that Daly made to the Clark family.

According to John Daly, he was adamant that Clark should provide his perspective of events as they were unfolding in order to counter the media story about the raid on the North Burnaby Inn and Clark's house.[4] Daly felt that without Clark's input, the public would fill in the blanks of the criminal investigation using their imagination. Daly admitted to an aggressive pursuit of an interview, saying that he leaned on Meggs to convince Clark that he should talk to BCTV on camera. Daly said:

> We were told we would have a chance to speak with the premier as soon as he was finished with the RCMP. Then later we were told that wasn't going to happen. Personally, I think that was the biggest mistake they could have made. They let the story escalate until it was out of control. A simple comment would probably have put a different spin on things.[5]

• • •

There has been much speculation about how a major television news crew could have been parked outside the premier's house when the RCMP walked up to the front door to act on their search warrant. It was after normal business hours when most newsrooms are running on few cameras. Usually at that time they are reserved for emergencies such as fires, large accidents, or shootings. BCTV had not one, but two cameras camped outside Clark's house—almost unprecedented for an unplanned event.

Is it credible to believe that BCTV just happened to be ready with two cameras on the night of March 2, 1999, waiting outside the premier's house hoping for a story? Is it possible to believe that BCTV could have operated independently, without a tip from the investigating officers?

John Daly insisted that there was no direct tip-off from the RCMP, although he admitted that the knowledge of the allegation that the premier was caught up in a casino licence application involving the North Burnaby Inn was widespread. The same anonymous fax that initiated the RCMP's investigation had been circulated to some of the media outlets. Some reporters had discussed the information in the fax with some members of the RCMP.

Daly acknowledged that he knew that if the North Burnaby Inn had been raided, he should keep an eye on two other locations nearby: the premier's house and the home of Dimitrios Pilarinos, one of the men involved with the suspect casino licence application.

Daly's story of what happened on March 2 begins with the context of the news day. It was the day after Jack Webster's death. Jack Webster, a giant in the British Columbia media, the man who gave British Columbia the Webster awards for excellence in journalism, was a much-loved curmudgeon who was both a tiger and a pussycat. He was an icon of good reporting, and the day after his death the newsrooms across British Columbia were taken up with stories about his life and times, and reminiscences of his best performances on radio and television during his long-running talk shows.

It was an awkward day, cold, and raining, and Daly had been told to work at home, since nothing much would be going on in the newsroom the day after Webster's death. The retrospectives had already been prepared, as Webster's death was a sad but not unanticipated event. Daly was working in his basement office, feeling blue and low-energy, when he received the call that the North Burnaby Inn had been raided.

This was something Daly had been waiting for, and he immediately left his home to join BCTV cameraman Gary Hanney, who was filming the removal of tables and other items from the North Burnaby Inn. Daly claimed that the story was over when he arrived, and there was little left that he could do. He knew that the two other locations to watch were Clark's and Pilarinos' house, and he felt it was much more likely that the RCMP would be making a move on Pilarinos. Daly tried to convince Hanney to leave with him to check out the other locations, but Hanney was keen on catching some more images at the North Burnaby Inn.

Daly was sure that the RCMP would make another move right away. How was he so sure? Daly claimed he knew the contents of the original allegations in detail, and in his discussions with the RCMP they indicated the connection was likely to play out in their search warrant activity. Since Pilarinos' and Clark's houses were on his way home, he decided to stop at each location to see what, if anything, was happening.

Daly left the North Burnaby Inn and called his desk from his car. He spoke with Dale Hicks in the BCTV newsroom and told him he wanted a camera assigned to him to scope out Pilarinos' house. Hicks told him he would try, but by this time the cameras were almost all booked out for the day. As it turned out, Karl Casselman was heading home and was asked to join Daly at Pilarinos' house en route.

Daly checked out Pilarinos' house and saw that nothing was happening. He called Casselman to let him know that he was moving from Pilarinos' house, and that there may not be anything to film. But now Casselman was interested in the story, and he decided to meet Daly at the premier's house. Daly claimed that Clark's house was hard to find because the streets were confusing, and he had to stop and ask directions.

Glen and Dale Clark's house sits on an unexceptional street in East Vancouver. When Daly located the premier's residence, all was quiet, so he parked in front of the house. Casselman arrived shortly after Daly, and although Daly was ready to leave because he did not see any evidence of activity, Casselman informed him that an unmarked police van was parked at the corner of the street with two police officers in it. Casselman parked where there was good visibility, and Daly joined him in the media van that was also unmarked. They waited to see what the police would do.

According to Daly, the police made their move, and BCTV rolled the cameras. The rest of the drama played out on the evening news later that night.

• • •

Clark's lawyer, Richard Fowler, first met Clark the night of March 2, 1999, when he accompanied Clark to his home to protect his client. He remembers that there were journalists banging on the door of Clark's house. It was Fowler, with his loose shoulder-length hair, who was mistaken by the police for an "unidentified female" accompanying Clark. Coincidentally, Daly initially reported that Clark entered the house with his communications person and an "unidentified female."

Defense lawyer Richard Fowler had an understated courtroom style.

Fowler explained that, as Clark's lawyer, he was less concerned about journalists chasing a story and more concerned about how they happened to be there when the police were raiding the house.

> Given the nature of the story, Daly's enthusiasm was understandable—it was a huge story—but my concern was, how did Daly happen to be there? ... The police have an obligation to investigate allegations thoroughly, fairly, and impartially, but in this case, when the background of the person under investigation was in politics, acting carelessly could indicate a serious bias. The police had to know there would be an impact on the premier if they raided his house, especially if the media were present. The only reason to tip media is to ensure that there is maximum exposure and damage to the person being searched.
>
> I don't think our system of justice is based on the end justifies the means.[6]

Although Fowler stated that photographing the inside of Clark's home was reprehensible, and the images should not have been broadcast, he said that it did not change the dynamic of later events. Two issues stood out for him on that fateful night of March 2.

> First, the time and date of any police search is highly confidential. This is only a matter of common sense. If police did not keep the details of a search confidential, the suspect could easily be tipped off, which has a serious negative impact on the investigation. Second, the conduct of the police in tipping off the media has to be questioned for motive, because if it cannot further the investigation, the question has to be asked, "Was this done to smear the reputation of the person under investigation?"[7]

On March 22, 1999, *Time Magazine* commented:

> In truth, there seemed something very questionable about the high-profile Mountie raid on the home of the provincial premier. The R.C.M.P. had stated after the search that Clark was never the object of a criminal investigation, and that there was no question of his culpability in anything ...
>
> But if that was so, why did the Mounties make the evening visit without affording Clark the chance to hand over the documents they were looking for ... Who masterminded the raid, and who approved it?
>
> ... R.C.M.P. spokesman Frank Henley justified the search, even with the media presence. "Just because it's the premier, we're not going to leave. As soon as we do that, the perception is out there that we're playing favorites."
>
> ... Last week, journalists learned that Peter Montague, the head of the crime unit that conducted the search on Clark's house, was invited by Liberal leader Gordon Campbell back in 1997 to run in the riding of Surrey–

> White Rock in an upcoming provincial by-election … Clark's supporters were quick to underscore the incident. "That is where my concern about the politicization of the RCMP comes in," says B.C. aboriginal affairs minister Gordon Wilson.

After the cameras had left, and a shocked British Columbia public had been treated to yet another traumatic political scandal, a quiet incident occurred late in the night of the raid that was not reported, but may have foreshadowed coming events. According to a number of accounts, the RCMP officers went through Clark's home looking for evidence related to home renovations undertaken by the Clarks on their house and Penticton cabin. They searched in the desk, kitchen drawers, and other places for records such as cancelled cheques. Although they found some records, they left with little evidence that bills for renovations had been paid. After the RCMP left, Clark and his lawyers continued to work their way through the debris left from the police search.

On the floor under the desk they found a stack of papers related to the renovation that appeared to have been overlooked. Among them were the cancelled cheques paying Dimitrios Pilarinos thousands of dollars for renovations. This felt like a breakthrough, and Clark's senior lawyer, David Gibbons, thought this would clear up any misunderstanding and demonstrate that there was no basis to the allegations that the work had been "gifted." Gibbons called one of the RCMP officers, Inspector Ard, to tell him he had important evidence that had been overlooked. Then Gibbons delivered a package to the investigating officers sometime after midnight that evening. When he handed it over, the receiving officer looked thunderstruck as he saw what the package contained.

Gibbons departed with the impression that the RCMP had not expected to see any cancelled cheques.[8]

• • •

In the days and weeks following the raid, a debate took place over the ethics of the police and the role of BCTV in broadcasting the raid.

It was clearly a difficult period for Clark, who for the first time showed public signs of sadness and fatigue. He made it known that it was a hard time for his family. Public sympathy appeared to be with Clark, and even his detractors commented about the unfortunate circumstances at his home. Clark also received supportive comments from some members of caucus, and the party rallied behind him as the 1999 legislative session continued. Once Clark was able to state that the RCMP were following a process, and he was co-operating, the issue died down and took a back seat to pressing public policy issues like ferry cost overruns, the health care system, balanced budgets, and a myriad of other issues.

After awhile, Clark seemed to regain his composure and his unswerving optimism, which appeared to have the effect of reducing public sympathy. There were calls for Clark's resignation in the wake of the raid, and calls from opposition leader Campbell for an election.

8

Rats from the Sinking Ship

Clark weathered the scandal, and began to rebuff renewed calls to step down. In fact, since a caucus retreat in early July where several cabinet ministers asked him to leave office, he has been working hard to shore up support and shut down critics. He even recruited NDP heavyweights such as former B.C. premier Dave Barrett and Burnaby/Douglas MP Svend Robinson to lobby on his behalf. On July 8, Barrett was seen leaving the office of Attorney-General Ujjal Dosanjh—regarded as a credible successor to Clark—after questioning Dosanjh about his leadership ambitions. "It was a very short meeting," Dosanjh snapped later. "I heard him and I'm absolutely certain he heard me. It was a very frank exchange of views."

—*Maclean's*, August 2, 1999

When did Attorney-General Ujjal Dosanjh know that Premier Glen Clark was under criminal investigation? Only Dosanjh can answer that question, a question that he has never been asked under oath. He did not respond to a request for an interview for this book. Dosanjh may have known about the investigation in January 1999 when the special prosecutor was appointed to oversee it, since this appointment came from the attorney-general's ministry. He would almost certainly have known the terms of the criminal investigation by March 2 when the premier's house was raided.

The special prosecutor was appointed as a result of the large-scale RCMP investigation into a casino application that involved the premier. The RCMP called this "Project Ezra." It required additional resources from the attorney-general because of the size of the investigation and its special costs. When the RCMP were seeking a search warrant for Clark's house, they chartered jets to Palm Springs, California on two separate occasions. They wanted to be heard in front of Associate Chief Justice Patrick Dohm, who was on holiday there at the time. Later this move became controversial, but was justified by the RCMP, apparently due to the sensitivity of the investigation and the fact that Dohm had seized the case.

The appointment of a special prosecutor was prompted by the award of approval in principle to a casino licence to the North Burnaby Inn through Employment and Investment Minister Mike Farnworth's office. The North Burnaby Inn was still under investigation by the Gaming and Audit Investigation Office, a branch of Attorney-General Ujjal Dosanjh's office, and the approval in principle drew the attention of the RCMP.

Later information suggested that Dosanjh's office had, at best, failed to inform Farnworth's office of the investigation into criminal activities. At worst, news of this investigation was deliberately withheld from Farnworth in order to trigger the approval in principle and create the perception that something crooked was underway.

• • •

Within the NDP there were many stories that Dosanjh had started his party leadership campaign at the beginning of 1999, talking to MLAs about the need for a new leader and testing the waters to see if they would support his bid. Gordon Wilson had this story of his experience with Dosanjh and his supporters:

> Within a matter of weeks of my crossing to the NDP I was approached by several MLAs, most notable among them Sue Hammell, feeling me out on the question of Glen's leadership, and my ambition. By late February [1999] it was clear that there were a number of MLAs

who had been working on an alternate leadership plan to that of Glen Clark. I became aware that there was "something big" about to fall on Glen by mid-February of the same year.

I was active in moving Nisga'a through the House [1999], along with Dosanjh, who was clearly upset at my joining the party, and he tried to take the lead in the debate. I had seen the signs before in 1992–93 as leader of the Liberal party, and my suspicions were confirmed when I was invited into Dosanjh's office one evening to partake in a single malt scotch.

His plan to oust Glen had been brewing for some time. Ujjal had suggested at the conclusion of our regular caucus meeting that I should take a moment and join him in his office later that evening. I had been around the circuit enough times to know that he was not offering me a "welcome aboard" drink. When we met, he poured me a healthy scotch and raised the matter of Glen's leadership and the plight of the party. He was keen to know if I planned to contest the next election, and hearing that I had made that commitment prior to crossing the floor, he then suggested that I should go to Glen and convince him that for the good of the party he should step down.

When I refused to do so, he suggested that perhaps I should be one of three or four to approach Glen. I suggested to Ujjal that the problem with the party and government was that there was no fight within them to counter the barrage of negative press that was coming at us daily. He then told me that something may be afoot that would force the premier to resign, and that it would be better for Glen to have already resigned for "the good of the party, province, etc." Dosanjh was never specific as to what it was, except that Glen was involved with unsavoury elements.[1]

Speculation about Dosanjh's ambitions and strategy had not been charitable. Fred Steele and Ken Charlish were long-time members of the NDP who became embroiled in legal battles with NDP headquarters during the leadership campaign in 2000. Steele recalled:

> Dosanjh and his supporters were running bulk memberships into the party before Clark resigned. He let them [his supporters] continue with the bulk memberships while seeking advantage for himself, knowing that he could come out anytime and make the statement that Glen was under investigation, and this would force him to resign.[2]

Politics in British Columbia is a medium of strange and unpredictable alliances, and they were beginning to form in the NDP by the summer of 1999. Attorney-General Ujjal Dosanjh was seen to be advancing his leadership ambitions, because the Sikh temples in the lower mainland were rife with stories of Dosanjh's speeches, public appearances, and membership drives. From the time of the raid on Clark's house, Dosanjh's political supporters were not hiding the fact that Dosanjh had leadership aspirations. His leadership team was made up of many Harcourt-era NDP members. Former finance minister Joy MacPhail, a probable contender, was also making many appearances and rekindling contacts in the labour sector.

• • •

My observations of the tension between the leading players in the party revolved around a fundraising dinner at the Pan Pacific Hotel in May 1999. The Progressive Democratic Alliance (PDA) had some debt outstanding, and one of the conditions of Wilson crossing the floor was that there would be a committee put together

Premier Clark, Attorney-General Dosanjh, and prominent British Columbian Rick Hansen announce the B.C. Neurotrauma Fund in 1997.

to raise this money as soon as possible. As Gordon Wilson's wife and one of the founders of the PDA, I had my own interest in seeing the debt retired. By February 1999, nothing substantial had happened, despite repeated enquiries to the leading players. It was obvious that there were several very different political agendas at play. The NDP as a party wanted nothing to do with the dinner and would not participate. John Pollard, Sue Hammell's husband, worked with the government and was supposed to head up the dinner committee, but there was no activity. I was as keen as Gordon was to see the PDA debt put to rest, so I decided to become more involved and put a committee together to set up the venue and sell tickets.

At that point, Pollard and the people working with him became almost a parallel committee, and some of them were very helpful. However, they also took exception to the location we chose, the Pan Pacific Hotel, the ticket price of $150, and the tickets that we had printed. They insisted that all print materials carry a union label, even though the event was clearly not officially supported by any union, or by the NDP. Pollard leaned on us to move the event to a hall in Surrey where we could hold a buffet and sell $30 tickets. Eventually there were a number of tickets sold by Pollard's committee members, most of them at the last minute, and it was hard for us to track the process.

It was frustrating. Sometimes we were sandbagged by people who were working on the dinner, and it was impossible to know who was doing it. A notable example was the sale of a table to a large cigarette company. I remember this clearly, because the table was sold by a prominent NDP lobbyist, against my wishes. When I told him that I thought we might be criticized, I was almost patted on the head with a "There, there, this is how you do *real* politics. You'll learn."

When the media found out that a cigarette company had bought a table, they were all over the story. I had received a warning call from Par Sihota, ministerial assistant to Gordon Wilson and long-time New Democrat. He was helping with the dinner and was also working hard behind the scenes. He wanted to make sure I was ready for a media call. The controversy erupted on a day when the legislature was sitting, and I was going to the buildings to meet Gordon for lunch. Gordon knew almost nothing about the dinner, but since it was in his honour and to pay off his former party's debts, the media were swarming him. They were asking him, quite legitimately, about the hypocrisy of taking money from tobacco companies when the government was taking them to task for selling cigarettes. As a former MLA, I had access to the legislative corridors, so I took a deep breath and inserted myself into the media scrum to answer questions. I took full responsibility for the mistake, since I was overseeing ticket sales. I apologized and at the prompting of a reporter, committed this $1500 to the B.C. Cancer Agency. My cousin Mark Devereux had been president of the Kelowna chapter, making this extremely ironic for me.

Although major ontroversy was averted, the incident reinforced my feeling that it might be dangerous to trust some of our committee members. How had the media found out about the table sale so quickly? Was the whole thing a set-up? I also had to keep my mouth shut (often a challenge for me) about the internal problems with organization and communication, which were many.

Thanks to the hard work of everyone involved, the dinner began to come together. It was billed as "An Evening with Gordon Wilson." And due to the strict regulations of Elections BC, it was held under the umbrella of "The Friends of Gordon Wilson." We had sold over 500 tickets in advance. I could feel the momentum building in the days before the event. There was an excellent cross-section of people present, from Aboriginal leaders to small business owners to union executive members, all supportive of Gordon Wilson as a politician.

The issue of protocol came up. Since the seating was set in advance, I had been hounding the government representatives on the committee to find out which cabinet ministers would be present. I did not want any of them seated in the "cheap seats." This was a gala event and had the potential to generate some good publicity at a time when we all needed it. I had heard that Attorney-General Ujjal Dosanjh was coming and asked many times for confirmation. I was finally told that he was not available.

The evening unfolded beautifully, with one exception. The attorney-general did show up, at the last minute, with some guests in tow. There were no seats left for Dosanjh. As soon as I saw him I pulled Angie March aside, who was overseeing all our dinner evening details, and I asked her to arrange for a table and full place settings to be set up at the front of the room, near the head table. Angie, always unflappable and organized enough to put Martha Stewart to shame, had this taken care of immediately, and Dosanjh was able to take a seat. Dosanjh worked the room quite a bit that night, and he had his picture taken with many guests.

We had reserved a seat at the head table for the premier, and the dinner organizers had purchased boutonnieres for the head table guests. Clark showed up on his own, a little rushed, and he seemed to be quite nervous. He had not picked up his boutonniere, so I fetched it from the front and pinned it on him while we were seated at the head table. I tried to relax him by talking to him, but this only seemed to make things worse. Eventually he seemed to enjoy the evening, and he made a few jokes.

It was a good dinner, but an odd hybrid of an event, with a keynote speech from Gordon Wilson that dealt with "coming together to advance progressive ideas."

There were many people who assumed that Gordon Wilson was organizing a leadership bid of his own from the time he joined the party in January 1999, and we did nothing to dissuade people from this opinion. As long as everyone could see Wilson's loyalty to the current leader, future ambitions seemed less relevant. And there were many outside the party who were happier to accept Wilson's crossover to the NDP if there were future leadership prospects. In addition, Wilson and Clark worked well together, with Wilson serving as his backup whenever necessary. Wilson was still seen as an outsider and somewhat non-partisan, yet he provided enough support to Clark on certain policy issues, such as the ferries, Nisga'a, and the budget, to help stabilize Clark's fortunes. As long as Wilson had leadership ambitions and remained loyal to Clark, he helped keep the wolves away from the door.

The evening reminded me of a story of great palace intrigue, where no one knows who still supports the king and who conceals a dagger under a cloak, where every move is watched and analyzed by every faction. And the king does not know whom to trust.

• • •

Many people had speculated that the RCMP raid on Glen Clark's house and the subsequent investigation might prompt his resignation. But the RCMP were quick to point out that the premier himself was not the subject of the investigation, and although the RCMP investigation was a serious political concern, it was generally considered a non-political issue. For a few months the NDP was enjoying the first reprieve from political controversies and scandals since the 1996 election. By the summer of 1999 Clark appeared to be emerging in a position of some authority. As well, summer was playtime in B.C., and people were forgetting about the scandals of the previous spring. The S.S. *NDP* was still tossing about on rough water, but observers were musing that perhaps the ship was sound enough to keep going forward. Internally, questions were circulating about the captain, and that was when serious unrest began. As so many politicians have done, some of Premier Clark's colleagues began to sharpen their knives and prepare for mutiny. Exactly when preparations started is the source of considerable debate.

While Dosanjh nurtured a public image of competence and sound reasoning, his leadership aspirations would reveal that he also knew something about political warfare.

During the spring legislative session, it was no secret that meetings had taken place in Victoria between Joy MacPhail and Ujjal Dosanjh, with Sue Hammell prominent in organizing an anti-Clark faction for Dosanjh.

In July, Finance Minister Joy MacPhail resigned from her cabinet post, citing "personal reasons," as well as stating that she had no interest in the leadership of the party. This resignation dealt a hard blow to Clark, and it brought NDP scandals and controversy back to the front page of the newspapers. Clark shut this controversy down relatively quickly. In a surprise move, he appointed Gordon Wilson minister of finance, temporarily making him the minister responsible for Aboriginal affairs, BC Ferries, and finance. This was unexpected enough that it was a distraction from MacPhail's resignation.

Unfortunately, MacPhail's departure was shortly followed by the resignation of Parliamentary Secretary Graeme Bowbrick, MLA for New Westminster. Bowbrick was a low-profile MLA best known for being one of the respondents in the HELP BC case.

The second cabinet minister to resign was Sue Hammell, women's equality minister and MLA for Surrey–Green Timbers, and, coincidentally, one of the other two respondents in the HELP BC case. Hammell, never a strong performer in the public arena, issued a three-line statement to announce her resignation from cabinet.

These resignations put Clark's leadership back on the front burner as an issue for the party. But Clark still did not resign; his will to move forward appeared to baffle many people. His opponents within the party now seemed more determined to receive his resignation than the opposition Liberals, who were notably, and uncharacteristically, quiet about the NDP in-fighting.

The next move by Clark's opponents within the NDP was to apply pressure by sending a letter to Clark from outside the caucus, signed by former MLAs and other party heavyweights. Copies of this document were then leaked to the media, and anonymous party sources were quoted on the internal dynamics of the party. The media loved the story—full of intrigue, betrayal, and power plays. Reports began to appear that presented speculation as fact. Media outlets engaged in it, competing to have stories first. On July 19, 1999 the Canadian Press wrote:

> On Monday, a senior New Democrat in former premier Mike Harcourt's government confirmed some party members plan to put their concerns about Clark in writing in letters to party officials.
>
> "There are a lot of us intensely concerned about what is happening to the party," said the source to the Canadian Press.
>
> "It would be unlike us to sit and do nothing."

One Vancouver TV station reported Monday that as many as 20 New Democrats have signed a letter to NDP president Bruce Ralston calling on Clark to quit.

Ralston said he had not received any such letter though he conceded it might not yet have reached his office.

"It may be in existence," he said. "It may not. I don't know."

BCTV also reported Monday that a second similar letter was sent to Clark signed by 11 of his own caucus members.

Teresa Wat, a spokeswoman for the premier, said Monday she could not find any relevant letters in the files at Clark's office in Victoria …

"It's a team effort that gets you into a mess and it's a team effort that gets you out," said Public Services Minister Moe Sihota.

"People are worried about the state of the party and what they should be doing is pulling up their socks—me included …"

The NDP has been battered by trouble in various files. The economy is slumping badly. An NDP-pushed project to build three fast ferries has run about $235 million over budget. Plans to build a badly needed convention centre in Vancouver have collapsed.

"There are obvious concerns about the continued leadership of Glen Clark," said Leonard Krog, a former NDP MLA who is reported to have signed one of the concerned letters to Clark.

Deputy premier Dan Miller criticized New Democrats who are questioning Clark's leadership, saying the critics are only hindering the government's ability to be re-elected …

"My advice to these dissenters is that they should really stop doing what they're doing because they're really just making it worse for all of their colleagues," he said.

However, behind the scenes the unofficial leadership race was already on. Not everyone had their ambitions on hold, and those who supported Dosanjh were trying to set a course toward the next election. The biggest obstacle they had to putting in place a general election strategy under Dosanjh's leadership was Clark's refusal to resign. They may have felt Clark owed it to the party to resign, in the same way that Harcourt had resigned and taken the Nanaimo Commonwealth Holding Society scandal with him. Many media articles made comments, such as these in the *BC Free Press* of July 1999:

> An apparent alliance between two of the NDP's main leadership hopefuls is putting pressure on Premier Glen Clark to make a decision about his future.
>
> Two of the NDP's three serious leadership hopefuls—Attorney-General Ujjal Dosanjh and former Finance Minister Joy MacPhail—appear to be working together to bring down Clark ...
>
> The only new wrinkle is that the NDP's "significant other" leadership aspirant, Ujjal Dosanjh, appears to be working with the feminists to up the ante. MacPhail seems to have convinced Dosanjh that neither of them has a snowball's chance in hell unless they can force a reasonably early leadership convention. Only Clark and Wilson have the provincial profile and name recognition to lead the party into an election at this time ...
>
> Dosanjh is a bit of a ditherer in the Mike Harcourt tradition, and Clark's been successful browbeating the meek and mild ... in all likelihood, Dosanjh had already cut a deal with MacPhail and could see no benefit, either personally or to the party, in helping Clark hang on to power ...
>
> The next day in caucus meeting, John Cashore demands Clark step aside, supported by Dosanjh and

> several other MLA's. It's a similar tactic used by MacPhail a few months ago ... Leadership hopefuls MacPhail and Dosanjh prefer to employ others to confront the premier, lest they alienate members of caucus from whom they will need support in a future leadership race.
>
> Then suddenly, the Monday after the caucus meeting, MacPhail tells Clark she's resigning from the Finance Ministry portfolio ...
>
> MacPhail's feigned lack of interest in the NDP leadership is nonsense. She wants a leadership convention so bad, she can taste it. She also knows there is nothing to be gained by remaining in cabinet. Now, she can muster support among NDP MLA's without being perceived as a disloyal cabinet colleague.
>
> It's too early to tell how far Dosanjh and MacPhail are prepared to go to support each other, but it doesn't matter much at this stage ...
>
> And what of Dosanjh? Like Mike Harcourt, he's a likeable loser, nothing more ...
>
> ... Glen Clark probably believes he can pull off another win over the Liberals' Gordon Campbell.

Speculation about what would happen next ran rampant. The July 1999 issue of *BC Report* ran a damning article comparing Clark to former premier Bill Vander Zalm, who some argued was the leader who presided over the destruction of the Social Credit party, at one time the most powerful political party in B.C.

> The 1990s are ending the way they began: a premier labouring under the weight of innumerable scandals, accusations of criminal behaviour, collapsing caucus support and historically low poll numbers. In 1995 Premier Mike Harcourt faced a remarkably similar set of circumstances and chose to "take a bullet for the party."

… B.C. Supreme Court Associate Chief Justice Patrick Dohm is expected to release the search warrants he authorized the RCMP to use in March to search the homes of Mr. Clark and the other principals in the Pilarinos affair. The raid followed the issuing of a temporary charity-casino licence to Dimitrios Pilarinos, Mr. Clark's neighbour and friend, and strip-club owner Stephen Ng …

… At a July 20 press conference, [Clark] dashed many NDP hopes when he announced he would soldier on. "I'm not here for a good time, as you obviously can tell," he admitted. "I'm here because I care deeply about what I campaigned on and the people I represent, and I want to continue doing that, as long as I have the support in caucus and the party."

That support is marginal at best. The press conference came at the end of a tumultuous week that saw the resignations of finance minister Joy MacPhail, women's equality minister Sue Hammell, NDP provincial secretary Brian Gardiner and Mr. Clark's parliamentary secretary, Graeme Bowbrick. It was then revealed that Mr. Clark had earlier received a letter from former MLA Leonard Krog and Bernie Simpson, the latter a party fundraiser nicknamed "The Bagman." The letter-writers urged the premier to step down for the good of the party; they claimed support from at least 20 NDPers, including such heavyweights as former cabinet ministers Alex Macdonald, Bill Barlee and Darlene Marzari. Mr. Macdonald said publicly, "Glen should take the lead and have a leadership convention. This present attitude of 'come and get me' is bad for everyone."

… Now that Brutus has become Caesar, Mr. Clark knows just how Mr. Harcourt felt. Electioneering by Mr. Clark's would-be successors has already begun …

> The first-ever NDP premier, Dave Barrett, now acting as a party fixer, has reportedly warned Mr. Dosanjh that his apparent campaigning for his boss' job is unseemly. Mr. Dosanjh and Ms. MacPhail are among the dozen or so MLAs that have called on Mr. Clark in caucus to resign ...
>
> But Mr. Clark's problems are more serious than mere policy. A great many British Columbians consider him dishonest—a fatal perception that dispatched Mr. Vander Zalm, just as it did Brian Mulroney. To put it bluntly, they think he is a liar ...
>
> Backbencher Rick Kasper, considered by some a maverick, dismisses the calls for a leadership change ... [he] remains angry that NDP plotters are taking "a family fight into the streets of the neighbourhood." "It's bad form," he says. "These people saying these things—I didn't see them at the convention. Glen Clark was not supposed to win the 1996 election. He did. Now there are people out there gunning for him to be gone; they know he could win the next one."
>
> University of Victoria political science professor Norman Ruff thinks that extremely unlikely. He argues Mr. Clark is designing his own timetable, buying time ... Until then, Prof. Ruff contends, "He is basically saying, 'If you want me, you'll have to get me in March.'"

In B.C.'s turbulent political environment, with its two prominent parties, the governing party was now in a state of turmoil, with its leader holding onto the leadership while fighting off dissidents in his own party.

There was nothing to compel him to resign. Yet.

9

The Resignation

... But now old friends are acting strange
They shake their heads, they say I've changed
Well something's lost, but something's gained
In living every day

I've looked at life from both sides now
From win and lose and still somehow
It's life's illusions I recall
I really don't know life at all ...
—Joni Mitchell, "Clouds," 1969

"The premier is under criminal investigation in the context of the information released by the court today."[1] Glen Clark's life as premier ended on Friday afternoon, August 20, 1999, with this statement from his attorney-general, Ujjal Dosanjh. At the time of the raid on Clark's house five months earlier, the RCMP had announced that the premier was not under investigation. The same strategy of disinformation that had been used to "manage" the media during the Gustafsen Lake standoff was in play again.

The morning of Dosanjh's announcement, there had been a conference call with the majority of NDP MLAs in order to tell them that the premier was under criminal investigation, and that Dosanjh felt he had no choice but to inform the public immediately. A heated debate took place, as a number of MLAs asked Dosanjh why he felt compelled to tell the public. Dosanjh maintained that once he had informed the caucus, he felt the public had a right to know, and if he did not tell them, people would think there had been a cover-up.

Dosanjh told his caucus colleagues that he wanted to set up a press conference to announce the criminal investigation of the premier. In fact, this press conference had already been called for the same afternoon. The attorney-general understood the implications of his announcement.

The deputy minister to the attorney-general, Ernie Quantz, was informed of the investigation on January 14, 1999, about six weeks before the raid on Clark's house and about seven months before Dosanjh made this information public. Quantz, as Dosanjh's first lieutenant, was responsible for the decision about how much to tell the attorney-general and when to tell him.

The special prosecutor, appointed to safeguard the attorney-general from any real or perceived political interference, had not yet reported back on the Clark case when Dosanjh made his public announcement. This raised questions. Why did the attorney-general feel compelled to make any kind of public comment about an investigation being handled by a special prosecutor? Why did he not let the special prosecutor proceed with his investigation and report when he was finished? Or, alternatively, if Dosanjh felt compelled to make a statement, why not do this in March, right after the raid?

Former NDP cabinet minister Moe Sihota, a powerful ally of Clark in the inner circle of government, was with Clark the night of the announcement. Sihota said:

> The night before his resignation, Glen stayed overnight at my place. We knew the media would be looking for him ... so I suggested he stay with me, because this was a safe spot for him. Prior to Ujjal's announcement, I had been urging Glen to hang on, but once it was public that he was under criminal investigation, there was no choice, he had to resign ... I felt an eerie sense that the party was

> dead. Glen was the glue that kept it together ... At the time that Glen was forced to resign, there were serious divisions in the caucus. For example, at the end of the conference call with Ujjal (when Dosanjh told us that Glen was under criminal investigation, and he was going to hold a news conference to announce it), some members of caucus were spitting mad at Ujjal; others thought he had taken the high road. We were already split down the middle. To some people, Ujjal was a saint.[2]

Sihota said that the statements of the RCMP and the attorney-general that Clark himself was not under investigation were key points in the NDP's political strategy discussions during the summer.

> Prior to Ujjal's announcement [inAugust], we were all working from the presumption that Glen was not under criminal investigation. In fact, we had held a caucus retreat at Dunsmuir Lodge in July that was pretty intense, and we felt that we had set out our agenda for the next year.
>
> At the retreat, all caucus members had a chance to speak their minds; everyone took turns. And even though Ujjal, Joy, and Corky all wanted Glen to go, once everyone had spoken out, the caucus took a decision that Glen would stay until December. And if the polls didn't turn around, he would resign and make way for a leadership convention the following spring. That would give the new leader about a year to take a run at turning things around.
>
> I remember that after we took the decision, some of us were out on the terrace; it was a nice sunny day, and I was talking to Ujjal, and he accepted the decision. If Ujjal knew that Glen was actually under investigation, it was unconscionable that he could have participated in the discussions and not told anyone. If Ujjal knew in

> March that Glen was under criminal investigation and started organizing then, and there's some evidence of this in terms of the courting of other MLAs to his campaign, it puts a new light on what was happening in caucus.
>
> I heard at the time, and I have heard over and over in the months since, that the Dosanjh supporters were in full panic when Wilson was appointed minister of finance. They were worried that if Wilson had any time in that portfolio, then he would build a head of steam and be unstoppable because he would attract public and party support. If Glen remained until December, and Wilson had from July until December to do this job, he would have showcased his skills sufficiently to take over the party. And he would have overcome his biggest internal problem of being too new to the party to lead it.
>
> It was in the Dosanjh team's interests to have their convention in the fall of 1999, giving Wilson the least amount of time. If Dosanjh knew that Glen was under investigation, then he pulled the plug in August to prevent Wilson from organizing a credible leadership bid.

The manner of the announcement suggested_that the attorney-general was not insulated from the politics of the investigation. Certainly, Dosanjh took charge of the policy direction of this investigation from the time of his news conference until he no longer held the position of attorney-general, some months later.

One well-known political commentator who took exception to the attorney-general's actions at the time was CKNW radio talkshow host Rafe Mair, a former Social Credit cabinet minister. Mair, who maintained that he thought that Dosanjh was "a decent guy" who was simply "badly advised on this matter," was very upset at Dosanjh's handling of the investigation and the announcement. "Dosanjh knew all along that there was a criminal investigation and that the premier was the subject." Mair said that Dosanjh was overtaken by loyalty to his party in waiting to make the announcement about the investigation. Mair declared:

> If the premier was under investigation, it was the obligation of the attorney-general to call for his resignation—if the premier had refused to resign, it was incumbent on the attorney-general to resign himself. This is the tradition of British parliament, and it is not negotiable. This was a clear-cut case of abrogation of ministerial responsibility.[3]

At the time, Dosanjh maintained in interviews and on Mair's open-line program that he was constrained from making a public comment by the Crown Counsel Act. According to Mair, Dosanjh said this act restrained him from interfering with the investigation. Mair didn't accept that reasoning.

> This was a red herring because the act says nothing about the attorney-general's very different responsibility to advise the head of government of criminal investigations concerning members of cabinet, including the premier. I never said Dosanjh should make an announcement publicly; he should have met with Clark in private to advise the premier of the investigation and demand his resignation.

As Mair pointed out, when Dosanjh made his announcement on August 20th, he knew no more than he knew on March 2nd. The only difference was that Dohm was going to release the contents of the search warrant that led to the March 2nd raid. The search warrant would reveal that the premier was actually under investigation, and that knowledge prompted Dosanjh to do what he should have done five months earlier:

> It's no different for a minister than for the premier. Let's say Dosanjh had been told by his staff that a minister was facing criminal investigation for child molestation—clearly he would be obliged to provide legal advice to that minister that he should resign. If the minister did not resign, the attorney-general would be forced to call a news conference to state that he was resigning because his legal advice to his cabinet colleague had been ignored. In the case with Clark, maybe there wasn't such a big outcry because it was more of a "white collar" allegation, but it's the same principle.

Mair cited a precedent during the years of the Social Credit government. At that time cabinet minister Jack Davis was under investigation, and Attorney-General Garde Gardom had advised Davis that he should resign pending the outcome of the investigation. Davis refused. Gardom then had to go to Premier Bill Bennett and tell him that one of his ministers was under a cloud.

> My understanding is that Gardom told the premier. The premier went to Davis, who refused to resign, so Bennett walked straight into the floor of the house and announced that Davis was no longer a minister in his cabinet. This was in 1976. Bennett did this to protect Gardom's integrity, because otherwise Gardom would have been forced to resign.

Mair said that bypassing parliamentary procedure did not have the impact it should have. He believed Dosanjh should have resigned as attorney-general for his failure to deal with the matter in March 1999.

> This should have been on the record when he ran for leader.

> But clearly the long-term implications of sitting on the information were not big for Dosanjh, because he became premier of the province a few months later.

According to former MLA Erda Walsh, it is unusual for an attorney-general to report publicly on information related to the premier's office. She claimed that her research into the practices of attorneys-general in other provinces indicated that normally an attorney-general will take information directly to the premier, and either receive the premier's resignation or tender his or her own. When the decision has been made regarding resignation, the reasons are made public.

> If the premier is seen to be doing something questionable, the attorney-general should tell the premier to step down pending an investigation, or the attorney-general will resign. To hold a news conference to announce that the premier is under investigation is inconceivable.[4]

Former provincial ombudsman Stephen Owen was quoted in the newspaper as supporting Dosanjh's actions in informing the premier of the criminal investigation. From a *Vancouver Sun* article on August 23, 1999, it is unclear whether Owen agreed that a news conference was the appropriate venue to make this declaration.

> While Dosanjh has known since March about the investigation into the casino affair, he was prevented from speaking to anyone about the case for fear of prejudicing the criminal justice process.
>
> Legal expert Stephen Owen, the former head of B.C.'s justice branch, said it appears Dosanjh conducted himself properly and well within the role of the attorney-general by first telling Clark, then NDP caucus and then the public about the criminal investigation.

> "Someone has to stand up and put the public at ease that the justice system is working properly and that person is the attorney-general. If he takes political heat for that, well, that's just one of the knocks of the role," Owen said Sunday while on a business trip in Brazil.
>
> He said if Clark hadn't quit, Dosanjh might have been forced to resign himself.
>
> "When he tells a premier he is under criminal investigation, he's in effect telling him he can't remain. If the premier doesn't take his advice on that and resign, the attorney-general has to resign. He finds himself in a constitutional crisis where his legal advice to the premier isn't being accepted."

This information matches the events that took place during the Social Credit administration. Attorney-General Brian Smith took his concerns to Premier Vander Zalm and requested that the premier tender his resignation based on these concerns. When the premier declined, the attorney-general resigned.

Why did Dosanjh wait to make his move? Dosanjh claimed that he timed his announcement to coincide with the release of information on the search warrant used to search Clark's home. The search warrant was the one issued the previous spring by Associate Chief Justice Patrick Dohm, and it had been sealed. In August 1999, few people knew why the warrant was issued that allowed fourteen locations to be searched, including the premier's home in East Vancouver. Premier Clark's legal team, headed by David Gibbons, had applied to Dohm to open the warrant, and on the morning of August 20, Dohm agreed to allow some of the information out. The rest of the warrant remained sealed. For the first time since the March 2 raid, some of the search warrant's contents were available to the public. The man who was the RCMP's source of information in obtaining the search warrant remained unnamed, but his allegations became public. The media ran stories on this public part of the warrant, including CBC TV's national news program, August 21, 1999:

> The warrant was issued as part of a police investigation into the way a casino licence was awarded to Dimitrios Pilarinos, one of the premier's friends. The unnamed source alleges Clark received renovations to his home in exchange for political influence.
>
> According to the warrant, a police informant said Clark turned down a bribe to approve a casino licence. Clark was allegedly offered a 15 per cent take of the profits from a casino in exchange for helping get the gambling licence approved.
>
> But Clark declined the offer, the informant said.[5]

Most observers overlooked the anonymity of the source, because the person's credibility was clearly satisfactory to RCMP case officer Peter Montague, Associate Chief Justice Patrick Dohm, and the staff from the attorney-general's office.

On Saturday, August 21, 1999, Glen Clark resigned. The press release issued was uncharacteristically short:

> Premier Glen Clark advised Lt.-Gov. Garde Gardom today that he is tendering his resignation as government leader effective as soon as caucus confirms the selection of a new leader. Clark met briefly with reporters, then delivered his resignation to the government caucus meeting in Victoria.

Clark's statement to the media was more detailed.

> First of all, I just talked to the Lieutenant-Governor and tendered my resignation effective when the caucus chooses a new leader. It's been nearly six months since the search

of my house on the evening of March 2, 1999, and of course I have known right from that date that it was likely I would be having to do this today or at some point. In the intervening months, British Columbians have wondered what information or allegations lay behind the events of that evening. They had wished, as I had, that the entire affair would be completely laid bare, every question answered and every judgment assessed in a report by an independent special prosecutor. In short, they want to know what is going on. How can the premier of the province's house be raided by the police?

Only 10 days ago, I was permitted to read the allegations against me and the wiretap evidence accumulated by the police in the course of the investigation. They contain scurrilous and unfounded allegations, many of which have already been disproved and others of which, of course, I categorically deny. I want to repeat some of what I told them that day.

First of all, I was completely insulated from the decision-making process regarding the North Burnaby Inn casino proposal. I had no interest in the application of any sort. I paid in full and, I believe, full value for the renovations at my home and at my cottage. I did not direct the applicants in any way, shape or form. I did nothing to intervene in any way, shape or form in the process with which the application went through, some of which has already been proven. But I wanted to speak clearly about that for you. The decision to provide the conditional approval was made by Mike Farnworth alone and he alone, and of course, he has acknowledged that.

While I'm certain I've done nothing wrong, the information to obtain makes it clear that a friendship has been portrayed in a despicable manner. When I read the information to obtain, it clearly looks terrible. I had taken

> steps to ensure my actions were not misinterpreted and the mistake is my responsibility and I accept that responsibility.
>
> ... I'm completely confident that I'll be exonerated and cleared. And I must say there has been lots of support in caucus for that. But even though I'm convinced I will be completely exonerated and cleared and that no premier should be driven from office by the existence of an investigation that remains incomplete and much of which has already been disproven, I've concluded it would be wrong for me to continue and that's why I, of course, took the action I took today. So. I like being the underdog, but this is getting ridiculous.[6]

This was the premier's first opportunity to respond to the allegations made against him that led to the police raid on his house five months earlier. Because a portion of the contents of the search warrant had been sealed, he could not specifically respond to some of the allegations, because he did not know what they were. The premier's response was overshadowed by the news of his resignation.

Regardless of Glen Clark's comments on whether or not he committed a criminal act, most commentary in the British Columbia media, both in news articles and editorials, appeared uniform in its condemnation of his actions to date. Two notable exceptions, the Victoria *Times Colonist* and the *BC Free Press,* explained that the resignation was the result of an investigation, and Clark was innocent until proven guilty.

Glen Clark was the third British Columbia premier out of the previous four to resign amidst a cloud of controversy.

• • •

Remarks by NDP MLA Moe Sihota, a high-profile and controversial minister, inflamed the media commentary around the resignation. A *Province* editorial on August 25, 1999 stated:

So now, as Premier Glen Clark steps down from office amidst investigations into criminal misconduct, it is richly ironic that Sihota should be the one to point the finger of blame at us. The idea behind his words—that our expectations are too high—is wrong.

But, there is some truth that must be acknowledged as Sihota points the finger of blame to British Columbians.

At first thought, it is hard to imagine that we could be at fault. All one has to do is take a sweeping glance at the political scandals and corruption that have pervaded the governing processes across our country during the past decade or so.

In Saskatchewan, 21 members of Grant Devine's Progressive Conservative government from the 1980s have been charged with defrauding that province's taxpayers of $1 million.

So far, 15 have been convicted.

In Manitoba, Premier Gary Filmon's staff tried to influence the outcome of the 1995 provincial election by financing the campaigns of independent Aboriginal candidates in an attempt to draw votes away from NDP incumbents in key ridings. Clever ... but stupid.

In B.C., 1986 was the last time that an elected premier actually finished a term without having to resign in disgrace. First Bill Vander Zalm, then Mike Harcourt and now Glen Clark. During Clark's brief reign, there have been deliberate and misleading lies about budgets and other projects, and the NDP is now being taken to court by its citizens.

What a rich legacy we have in the political scandal business.

We used to arrogantly assign such political scandals and corruption to Latin America and other developing countries. But here is ample evidence that Canadian

> political leaders have stolen from their people, and that, like the foreign dictators that they publicly oppose, they are willing to utilize whatever tactics are necessary to ensure that they retain power.
>
> Last year, a study on politicians and ethics showed that Canadians have little tolerance for lies and hypocrisy in the public lives of our politicians, but are willing to overlook such behaviour in their private lives.
>
> This acceptance of a separation of ethics in the public and private lives of politicians could be attributed to our willingness to protect the private lives of our politicians. But, it is also foolish, naive and, as we have seen, ultimately destructive.
>
> How can we expect our leaders to govern with honesty and integrity, when we so willingly accept a lack of those qualities in their private lives?
>
> Our apathy over personal integrity in the private lives of our leaders has become an open invitation for them to cast aside honesty and morality in their public lives. Private and public morality cannot be separated and, as long as it is, we will be victims of political corruption and scandals.
>
> Ultimately, each politician is responsible for ensuring that his own conduct does not violate the public trust. Glen Clark has no one to blame but himself.

But if politics is the art of manipulating perception to influence public opinion in the pursuit of power, perhaps the politician facing condemnation is simply, in the given instance, the poorer artist.

10

The Dosanjh Factor

Thousands of new British Columbia NDP members still have a chance to play a role in the selection of their new leader.

The party's provincial council chose to include members who sign up as late as Dec. 22 as possible delegates at next year's leadership convention.

A resolution proposed at the council meeting would have barred members who joined after Sept. 22 from becoming delegates ...

That front runner is Ujjal Dosanjh, B.C.'s attorney-general. His campaign signed up thousands of new members, many from the province's South Asian community ...

The resolution to change the cut-off came after a week of allegations that overzealous Dosanjh supporters had signed up the new members—without their permission or knowledge ...

"I said before that it's up to the provincial council to make a decision and I accept that decision," said Dosanjh.

—*Vancouver Sun*,
December 12, 1999

The official leadership race to replace Glen Clark was immediately underway. Three candidates declared in the fall of 1999: Joy MacPhail, Attorney-General Ujjal Dosanjh, and Agriculture Minister Corky Evans. Finance Minister Gordon Wilson did not announce that he was running until January 2000. Len Werden, a labour activist, also joined the race, but was not a significant factor.

MacPhail had resigned from cabinet in July, and Dosanjh and Evans retained their portfolios.

Dan Miller, who had become interim leader of the NDP and premier on August 25th, moved Wilson from the finance portfolio to education, saying this would allow him a chance to focus on his campaign. At this time, Wilson had not declared or decided to run.

It was a nasty leadership race.

Dan Miller, seen here with his wife Gail at a political reception, acted as caretaker premier until Ujjal Dosanjh was chosen NDP

Shortly into the leadership race MacPhail abandoned her campaign and joined the Dosanjh team adding her voice to those critical of Wilson as a candidate. Even before Gordon Wilson declared he found himself facing repeated and varied personal attacks in prominent newspaper, radio, and television stories. One involved an allegation of debt owed to a woman described consistently in the media as "the widow." During this controversy the *Vancouver Sun* ran Wilson's personal financial statements from a court case several years earlier in its newspaper. The woman in question, the famous widow, was businesswoman Sajida Shah. However, the story did not originate from her, and she was not promoting it; the story had originated in the office of a Liberal MLA.

Sajida Shah was an intelligent, attractive woman of strong character and sound business sense, probably in her late 40s at the time the story ran. She was a powerful person, not the helpless woman conjured up repeatedly in the publicity around the controversy. Since she was not advancing the story, no one ever saw or heard from her. Meanwhile, the Liberals played the story up so that it appeared Wilson was the world's biggest cad, running off with money owed to poor, quiet, decrepit widows.

In addition, the Liberals filed an official complaint with the conflict-of-interest commissioner, who was obliged to investigate. Now Wilson was under investigation for the allegation that he had not disclosed the original debt properly, and it was alleged that he was in serious legal trouble.

Eventually this story died out when it was obvious that Mrs. Shah was not behind it, and when the conflict of interest commissioner cleared Wilson and found that he had followed the rules. By then, enough had been said that there was considerable damage to Wilson's campaign.

Another attack hit very close to home, and this one was much worse than the first. This second attack against Wilson was levelled at him through his son, also a formidable political organizer in the leadership race. Mathew Wilson was an intelligent, hard-working young man with a keen sense of humour and a manner that attracted the respect of anyone who knew him. His even-tempered nature in the face of adversity was to his credit, and people frequently commented on how much he was like his dad. Mathew was in his final year of his university degree when an allegation was brought against him that led to the attorney-general's office.

A special prosecutor was appointed by the attorney-general's office just prior to the NDP leadership convention to proceed with a criminal investigation of Mathew Wilson, and the RCMP interviewed members of his family. This incident dragged on for months. Shortly after the leadership race, all allegations were dropped due to no evidence. It was a devastating episode for the Tyabji and Wilson family, especially for the children, and it resonated for some time.

A third attack against Wilson was an allegation, later traced to one of the NDP MLAs in caucus, that he had fabricated his biography in his book, *A Civilized Revolution*.[1] This generated considerable controversy, regardless of the facts. Wilson found himself stuck on the flypaper of anonymous allegations. There was little scrutiny of the source of allegations or the motives behind them. It was a horribly difficult time for him and his family, and he remained in the race, perhaps out of sheer stubbornness, perhaps to see it through and to put a lie to the allegations.

Shortly after these scandals died down, prominent NDP supporters of the Dosanjh campaign—including former premier Mike Harcourt and former attorney-general Colin Gabelmann, publicly questioned Wilson's integrity. CBC TV reported on January 13, 1999:

> Former Premier Mike Harcourt says Ujjal Dosanjh has what it takes to be NDP leader—and premier.
>
> "I'm here today to endorse a very good friend of mine ... a man I respect ... Ujjal Dosanjh."
>
> Mike Harcourt says Ujjal Dosanjh has the character, the commitment and the leadership skills to be premier.
>
> Harcourt says he'd planned to stay out of the NDP leadership campaign—but all that changed when two other former NDP premiers got involved.
>
> Dave Barrett and Glen Clark have been working on Gordon Wilson's campaign.
>
> Harcourt says he still has questions about Wilson's character and integrity—and questions the commitment of a man who's been a New Democrat for only a year.

Gordon Wilson's mantra at the time was that only through a coalition of centrist forces with the traditional left could Campbell and his supporters be defeated. He stayed in the race.

• • •

In order to become the next party leader, a candidate had to receive the majority of votes at a leadership convention. Voters at the convention were delegates selected by members who attended their local meetings. For example, a Victoria resident who was a member of the NDP would attend the "delegate selection" meeting in his or her riding, either to vote for a delegate or to try to become a delegate for the convention. The number of delegates that any given riding could send to the convention was determined by the number of paid-up members in that riding. What became clear, even before Glen Clark resigned, was that the candidate who signed up the most new members in key ridings could win based on "increased delegates." In short, whoever signed up the most new members would win. The weekend that Glen Clark resigned, the race to sign up new members was officially on.

There are two potential problems with the mass sign-up of new members: first, they are not proven, loyal party supporters; second, they could be from the political opposition. In order to understand the internal dynamic of the NDP leading up to the leadership convention of February 2000, both potential problems bear examination.

The problem with the new, unproven party members begins with their motivation. If the motivation is to elevate a member of their community for community pride, this in itself is not a problem. For example, if people from the Sikh community sign up because they would like to have an Indo-Canadian premier, this may not be a problem. However, once that person becomes leader of the NDP, if the new members bail out, then there is a problem. The new leader may be abandoned by the new sign-ups and left with embittered long-time members who will not work for the new leader in an election campaign.

The membership drive and delegate selection processes for the NDP leadership race unfolded in 75 ridings. The number of delegates that a riding was entitled to send was based on the number of members signed up in that riding by a certain date. Some ridings had hundreds of new members by the deadline, entitling them to select many more delegates than they would have had otherwise.

This method of signing up new members was highly controversial, and later ineffectively challenged.

Choosing delegates in a riding was relatively complicated because there was ongoing negotiation between organizers in certain ridings, and "slates" (lists of potential delegates) were assembled. Although in theory a delegate would be neutral, during the delegate selection process organizers for each candidate handed out slates naming their potential delegates, and those potential delegates would be wearing buttons, touting their chosen leadership candidate, and sometimes they would speak in favour of one candidate or another.

It was a winner-take-all process. For example, if only 50 members showed up to vote for 40 delegates, and one leadership candidate received 26 votes, he or she would receive all 40 delegates.

Confusing the issue were the lifetime members of the NDP, who may have been unaffiliated but wanted to attend the convention. If they were not on a slate, they would not be given a delegate spot. This meant that in many ridings, people who had put their hearts into the party for decades watched as newcomers were voted into delegate spots. This caused hard feelings in many cases, and many longtime members tore up their cards or launched complaints to party headquarters over alleged irregularities.

Yet another controversy was the allegation that in addition to the mass sign-up of unproven newcomers, there were significant numbers of Liberal supporters signing up to vote for the Dosanjh slates. Liberal membership lists were cross-referenced with NDP membership lists because, according to the NDP constitution, a person could not be a member of both parties.

Since the days of the Trojan Horse, plots have been cobbled together to fool people into positions of vulnerability. The Dosanjh campaign argued that allegations of Liberal sign-ups were a red herring. On January 24, 2000, CBC TV reported:

> David Schreck speaks for Ujjal Dosanjh's leadership campaign, and he said information about dual

> memberships was leaked to the media in order to discredit Dosanjh:
>
> "There is a very suspicious side to the fact the story was spun in such as way as to try to harm Mr. Dosanjh ... it's timed with the first big weekend for delegate selection."
>
> And Schreck says if it's true Liberals or former Liberals are signing up with the NDP, it could be an indication of Dosanjh's success in winning converts.

However, the controversy over B.C. Liberals joining the NDP became significant enough that former NDP candidate Ken Charlish and longtime NDP member Fred Steele threatened an injunction that would prevent the NDP leadership convention from going ahead. In response, the party appointed former B.C. Federation of Labour president Ken Georgetti to investigate. He reported the night before the vote, but it was not a substantial report and did not alter any of the dynamics of the convention. Some members of the NDP continued to want this matter investigated further, even after the general election.

• • •

Controversy over mass sign-ups and dual memberships began bubbling over in the Indo-Canadian community, which is more politically active than the public at large. It is a point of pride for Sikhs that they have strong connections to members of the federal and provincial governments.

The Sikhs represent the largest proportion of British Columbia's Indo-Canadian community, unlike in India, where the largest religious population is Hindu, followed by the Muslims. The Sikhs are a significant but minority population based mainly in the Punjab state in the north. For decades there has been political tension between some members of the Sikh community and the Indian government. One of the most well-known events was the raid on the Golden Temple in Amritsar, when former Prime Minister Indira Gandhi ordered troops in.

Sikhs have been a force in British Columbia since the early pioneer days, when many of them arrived to open up agricultural areas and work in the forest industry. Many Sikhs in British Columbia are third- or even fourth-generation Canadians, and although they may continue to have family ties in India, many are active and productive members of the political and business elites in B.C.

In recent decades Sikh temples have often been used as recruiting grounds for aspiring political leaders. Prime Minister Jean Chretien was one of the earliest recipients of large-scale Sikh sign-ups and delegates when he became federal Liberal leader at a convention in Alberta in 1990. In this case, there were no proxy votes or electronic ballots, so individuals attended and cast their votes in person. This was not a particularly controversial process, although some members commented on the large number of recent members from one community.

In 1993, Gordon Campbell was criticized for obtaining high-profile support from the Indo-Canadian community in his leadership bid, as I detailed in *Political Affairs*.[2] In Campbell's case there was a televote to determine the leadership, and any member, old or new, could vote by paying $25 to receive a PIN number. Hundreds of Sikh names were signed up as new members, many using post-office-box addresses. These mass sign-ups were connected to mass phone-ins using PIN numbers to vote for the leadership of the party, so many of the new members did not have to show up at a meeting, and there was little accountability.

In the case of the 1999 NDP leadership race, the Sikh element was significant, controversial, and divisive. There was no televote, so new members had to show up at meetings to vote. However, the central issue became one of "delegate entitlement." The signifance of having so many new members was that some ridings were entitled to many more delegates then they would have been a few months earlier. Three prominent members of the NDP caucus were from the Sikh community. Ujjal Dosanjh, Moe Sihota, and Harry Lali were cabinet ministers and well-connected to the Sikh organizers. Sihota and Lali were supporting Gordon Wilson, and some of the controversy over mass sign-ups of Sikhs splashed onto the Wilson campaign. Most of it, though, was directed at the Dosanjh campaign, particularly regarding new members who were also allegedly active members of the B.C. Liberal party. Enter the Sikh temple membership lists, and the cohesive and politically charged Sikh community. Add to this scenario an experienced political organizer named Raminder Dosanjh, Ujjal's wife and fellow activist, and there was a potent mix.

Sihota was close to some of the key organizers in the Sikh community at the time of the mass sign-ups. He said he found the mass sign-ups from the Indo-Canadian community to be shocking:

> At the end of August my wife and I went to Shuswap Lake for a holiday with the family, and at that time the phones were ringing and everyone was talking leadership—about who should run. Svend Robinson [NDP MP] wanted to run, and he called me. I talked to him at some length, and during the discussion the concern was raised that Ujjal would sign up vast numbers of Indo-Canadians and take the convention that way. People said if I ran I could do the same ...[3]

Sihota decided to follow up on these conversations as soon as summer ended, and he went to the Sikh temple in Surrey to meet with Balwant Gill, who was the president. Gill was late for the meeting.

> I looked down on his desk, and there were stacks and stacks of hundreds of NDP membership forms, all filled in, and all with transfer forms stapled to them. The ones I read all transferred the memberships from all over the province into Sue Hammell's riding [Surrey–Green

> Timbers]. And that's when I realized the extent to which Ujjal had been organizing, because it was less than two weeks since Glen had resigned, and there's no way you could have signed up that many people that quickly. Obviously they wanted to transfer the memberships into one riding to make it really easy to organize the delegates. At that time, the convention was slated for November, so this would have made it impossible for anyone to match the Dosanjh camp for memberships or delegates.

What Sihota saw appeared to be evidence of a mass sign-up in the temple, taking names from the temple membership lists and adding them to the membership lists of the New Democratic Party. In many instances people were signed up without their knowledge and consent. This would boost the delegate entitlement dramatically. Sihota went on to describe his meeting with Gill and other community leaders.

> So Balwant Gill arrived, and I had the meeting with the moderates. I told them I was thinking of running, to see what reaction I would get. They were literally shell-shocked, and finally what I got from them was, they said, "we heard that you and Harry [Lali] and Ujjal had a meeting, and had decided only one of you would run, and this would be Ujjal, and the other two would support him." I asked them where they had heard this, and they told me it was when Ujjal's family representatives had come to see them in July.

It was after Sihota's meeting with the moderates that a group of senior New Democrats began organizing to have the fall convention put off until the spring, to try to create a less volatile situation within the party. The decision was made at the provincial council meeting in Prince George, and it was at this meeting that the debate over the structure and timing of the leadership campaign became heated. Sihota said:

> While I was in Prince George for the provincial council meeting, the Indo-Canadian fellows there told me that Ujjal's campaign had signed them up as NDP members over the summer, and they had filled out transfer forms for Surrey. So that showed that there were organizers travelling all over the province before Glen even resigned. If you add to that the idea that Ujjal was the only member of caucus who may have known that Glen was under criminal investigation, the whole thing is unconscionable.
>
> Anyway, the motion to delay the convention until the spring passed after quite a bit of debate. Ujjal was furious. He used some pretty colourful language with people there. You see, with the sign-ups from the community, he had a lock on the leadership. Once the convention was delayed, the Dosanjh camp took the transfer forms off most of the new membership applications, and the organizers worked on a number of key ridings.

• • •

In the 1999 NDP leadership contest, there were several public forums for the candidates in different parts of the province. Glen Clark may have taken a back seat to the leadership process, but he was kept alive through commentary in the public forums. Attacks on his record became a dynamic in the race.

Dosanjh stood out as the candidate with support from many former MLAs and some members of caucus. He was the sole candidate to take on Clark directly. In the NDP, it was unusual for a former leader to be singled out for personal attacks. Previously

Corky Evans was the last roadblock on the Dosanjh drive to the premiers chair. His challenge and the "stop Ujjal" movement fell short.

The NDP leadership race featured an aggressive campaign by Ujjal Dosanjh and some unfortunate memories for Gordon Wilson, the target of assorted mudslinging.

differences were kept in-house. However, Dosanjh and his supporters must have thought that an anti-Clark strategy would gain them a political win in the short term. On January 24, 2000, CBC TV commented:

> Many pundits predict Dosanjh will win the party's leadership, partly because he has spent a lot of time bashing his old boss. Glen Clark resigned last year when his name surfaced in a police investigation into how a casino licence was granted.

At the leadership convention, only two candidates were left when it came time to vote. Len Werden and Gordon Wilson had dropped off the ballot to join Corky Evans, but this was not enough to put Evans over the top. Ujjal Dosanjh won the leadership of the NDP on February 20, 2000, becoming the first Indo-Canadian premier in Canada. He was quick to distance himself from the politics and policies of Glen Clark. CBC TV carried the story on February 21, 2000.

> But [Dosanjh] said he's in no hurry to call a vote, preferring to focus on other issues. "I want to make sure that once I'm sworn in and we have a cabinet, we work hard on a budget and a throne speech and we have both of those ready by the end of March," said Dosanjh.
>
> The new leader also said he would be preoccupied with "cooling down the hot politics in British Columbia."
>
> He promised a change in style from former premier Glen Clark. He blamed Clark for being too combative and accused him of centralizing power in the premier's office.

Former premier Glen Clark did not attend the convention. He was under criminal investigation.

11

Death by a Thousand Cuts

In the latest chapter of an ordeal he has described as "torture," former B.C. premier Glen Clark was charged Friday in a casino licensing scandal that forced him to resign from office a year ago ...

"I've got a lot of emotions," he added. "I'm angry, I'm shocked, I'm disappointed. But in some ways I'm also relieved because it's just been torture to have this dragging on and on and on without being able to deal with it."

... The case centres on allegations that the former premier used his influence to help Pilarinos get the gambling licence. After the accusations surfaced, the licence was revoked.

... Clark, who still has a seat as a member of the British Columbia legislature, also said he is prevented from discussing the case in detail while it's before the courts.

"I had nothing to do with that casino licence application," the former premier repeated Friday. When asked if he thought the charges were "politically motivated," Clark told reporters he "would love" to respond to the question but couldn't.

—CBC TV, October 21, 2000

On October 20, 2000, former premier Glen Clark was charged with criminal breach of trust and accepting a benefit in the form of discounted renovations to his home and cottage. This occurred while the Dosanjh government was continuing its work in the months leading up to the anticipated general election. The charges generated little publicity, since the Clark trial was not expected until fall 2001, some time after the election.

The year 2000 had already been a challenging one for the New Democrats, who continued to slump at historic lows in the polls, despite a new leader, a new team of people running government, and a new policy direction for the province. But how much was new?

Dosanjh's advisors were largely recycled from the Mike Harcourt government, restating policy directions that Harcourt had espoused. They were overwhelmingly from the Lower Mainland, which was reflected in the decisions that increasingly alienated rural communities.

The new deputy premier was Joy MacPhail. This post may well have been negotiated before she collapsed her leadership campaign to support Dosanjh. MacPhail had been a prominent member of the NDP government's inner circle throughout both the Harcourt and the Clark governments. She was well-known to the people of B.C. as a feisty, clever politician and a good debater. MacPhail represented a low-income riding in East Vancouver and was an outspoken advocate of urban and feminist issues. MacPhail always left an impression—good or bad, most had an opinion of her.

When she ran for leader of the NDP, she had the backing of only one member of caucus, Graeme Bowbrick. Further, even though MacPhail came out of the union movement, she did not draw significant support from the unions. The Canadian Union of Public Employees (CUPE) were still upset with MacPhail for what they considered her betrayal when she legislated them back to work. In making MacPhail his deputy premier, Dosanjh increased friction within caucus, even though it rarely bubbled over publicly.

The Dosanjh government returned to the Harcourt-era "consensus" decision-making. Consensus decision-making meant major decisions would often be referred to committees of stakeholders for review, which was not only time-consuming, but a political nightmare. The term "stakeholders" referred to unions, environmentalists, business owners, and others who felt they had a stake in the decision. By this time, cynicism with government was rampant, and few were willing to spend time at the meetings needed to achieve consensus. In addition, most business owners thought that the Dosanjh government was on its way out, so they were not interested in working with it. This left the environmentalists and the unions—mainly private sector unions like the IWA. Both groups traditionally supported the NDP, but they did not have a lot in common. Fights broke out that pitted loggers against environmentalists at land-use hot spots, such as Mount Elphinstone on the Sunshine Coast and Hasty Creek near Silverton in the B.C. interior. They inevitably led to government intervention, with little possibility of a political "win."

The NDP received negative public commentary from the environmentalists and the unions and had difficulty finding anyone to say positive things about the government and its decisions. As well, the Green party was gaining strength from both defecting members of the NDP and also new, significant financial donors. The Green party had experienced its own internal shake-up with a change in leadership and political strategy. Agriculture minister and former leadership candidate Corky Evans commented:

> In those days [during the 1996 general election] the Green party was a social democrat party, run by a social democrat named Stuart Parker. Then they had a coup, and Adriane Carr took over. It was kinda like what happened in the NDP, but on a much bigger scale. When Adriane Carr beat out Stuart Parker, she won only two ridings [out of 75], but there were school buses attached to them. I mean, he won all the other ridings, but she took enough delegates from them two ridings to become leader.[1]

Carr was a former New Democrat herself, and she went after the NDP with the vigour of an ex-smoker preaching about the ills of smoking. Two high-profile environmentalists, Carr's husband, Paul George, of the Western Canada Wilderness Committee and Colleen McCrory of the Kootenay-based Valhalla Wilderness Society joined Carr in her anti-NDP campaign. They, too, had formerly supported the NDP but now put all their resources into opposing the party.

Their non-profit, "non-partisan" environmental associations commented negatively about the NDP's environmental record, and both groups had a long wish list of environmental legislation and regulation that they wanted to see in place before the election.

Adriane Carr targeted Gordon Wilson's seat, and Colleen McCrory targeted Corky Evans. Corky Evans' political history with McCrory extended back to the time when both were in the NDP in the Kootenays. In the 1991 election, when it seemed certain that the NDP was about to take power from the Social Credit party, Evans recalled that McCrory approached him about a political strategy for Laska Creek, an environmentally sensitive logging area:

> She called me during the campaign and asked for a meeting right away. Then she said, "I'll get a huge number of environmentalists onside if you get an agreement not to log Laska Creek." I told her that I wouldn't do that, because I thought that actually logging that area was a good idea, and I told her why I thought so. She accused me of wanting to get loggers' votes, but I said it was simply a good decision. Then I'll never forget what she said next. She said she would still get votes for me if I would say that I supported logging during the campaign, then changed my mind after the next election. I said to her, "You're asking me to lie?" And she said, "Well, you're a politician, that's what you do, isn't it?" In all my years of municipal and provincial politics, it was the only time anyone ever asked me to lie. It was on my mind as she ran against me in the [2001] election. McCrory was on the inside of the party until we became government. Then she was on the outside criticizing us.

Ironically, while Carr and McCrory attacked the NDP government record on the environment as horrendous and negligent, the B.C. Liberals claimed that overly stringent environmental regulation was killing investment. By then, the IWA was also fed up with the NDP, since it perceived that the NDP was catering to the environmentalists by protecting 12 percent of B.C.'s land base in parks.

Despite internal dissent, the Dosanjh government, with the strong urging of MacPhail, tried to win over, or "win back," Green party voters, resulting in highly divisive policy decisions within the party and the caucus that separated the urban and rural MLAs. Perhaps the most publicized was the decision to ban grizzly bear hunting in B.C., an issue raised during the leadership forums. At that time the party had no official policy—generally urban members supported a ban, and rural members opposed it.

Environmentalists claimed that the number of grizzlies being killed by hunters was bringing the population to dangerously low levels. They mounted a multi-million dollar campaign of print, radio, television, and large billboard advertisements, calling on the government to ban grizzly hunting. In rural areas, many people saw this as yet another issue where misinformed "townies" were trying to dictate how rural people should conduct their affairs. Try telling someone that grizzlies are almost extinct when they are ambling in the children's schoolyard or down the neighbour's street. Also, rural people had already felt the impact of various land-use decisions, and they saw a limited-entry grizzly hunt as one way to keep hunting guides employed in a narrowing field of job opportunities.

Scientific opinion was divided on how endangered the grizzly was, because there were no reliable population counts. This meant that any decision, even one to maintain the status quo, was a political decision. The Dosanjh government made the political decision to ban all grizzly bear hunting, hoping for a public endorsement by the environmental movement. The endorsement never came. The decision divided the caucus since the interior and northern MLAs were opposed. Said Corky Evans:

> It was the stupidest thing that ever happened, just watching Ujjal manage that decision was painful. I watched Bill

> Goodacre, Jim Doyle, Erda Walsh, and other rural MLAs get up in caucus, over and over, and say, if you do that, you might as well write off every riding outside Surrey. Then you would look at some of the central team members and they wouldn't even look you in the eye, and you could see that they had already decided to do just that, because they had an election strategy that targeted only seven urban ridings as winnable, and they were making all their decisions based on that.

Evans, himself an MLA from Nelson–Creston, a seat in the interior, felt that the strategy was killing his re-election chances.

• • •

There was a growing panic in the party as the months after the leadership race ticked by, and the party continued to lag behind the Liberals by a large margin. The NDP was concerned that a new leader had not gained popularity; originally it had hoped for a repeat of the 1996 phenomenon when Clark brought a new leadership style and re-energized the party. That did not happen. Few people were joining, and in some of the 75 riding associations the NDP was having a difficult time mustering the most basic of organizational teams.

The Dosanjh team believed that running a campaign against Glen Clark would yield a positive response from the public. As a result, they denounced many of his controversial initiatives, particularly the fast-ferry program. Unfortunately, the strategy backfired.

Dosanjh's ferry minister, Joy MacPhail, was so effective at denouncing the new catamaran ferries due to their construction cost overruns that there was no one to speak in favour of any benefit they might have provided. The B.C. Liberals were only too happy to continue their public campaign against the catamarans. By the time MacPhail became minister of ferries, two of the fast cats were complete and a third was under construction. MacPhail implemented her instructions in a well-publicized manner. She halted work on the third ferry and initiated a review to determine if it should ever be completed. She pulled the two ferries in operation out of service, and when the review concluded that the third ferry should be completed, she authorized the work. On completion, she ordered that it be "shrink-wrapped."

Then she announced that these ferries, which both she and the opposition had declared a mistake and a boondoggle, were for sale. The announcement drew howls of derision from the opposition. None were sold during her tenure as minister of ferries, up until the general election of 2001, adding more fuel to the fire that they were worthless; and no one wanted them.

The spring legislative session, following closely on the leadership convention, also caused a few problems for the NDP. Dosanjh had an enormous task in quickly setting a legislative course. Finance Minister Paul Ramsey, who had taken over from Gordon Wilson when Wilson entered the leadership race, had been preparing a balanced budget and legislation for the session.

One of the highlights, publicized with considerable effort, was the "budget transparency" legislation, which Dosanjh and Ramsey announced would clean up the budgeting process. Unfortunately, this legislation played into the hands of the opposition Liberals, who had the fudge-it budget issue taken from them by the court-ruling in the HELP BC case and by the auditor-general's report. Both investigatons had concluded there was no wrongdoing in the 1996 budget process. Neither decision received much play in the media. However, the budget-transparency legislation allowed the Liberals to resurrect the fudge-it budget debate, even though the legislation dealt with issues that were, in some cases, decades old, and even though it flowed directly out of the recommendations of the auditor-general.

They Liberals jumped on the budget-transparency legislation as an admission by the NDP that they had perpetrated a fraud and were now making amends. The whole fudge-it budget issue was brought forward as a dynamic in the 2000 budget, and later in the 2001 election budget.

It was a difficult argument for Dosanjh to refute. If they had done nothing wrong, why were they forced to pass new legislation? What were they cleaning up? It appeared that Dosanjh was trying to make amends for a series of mistakes, and he seemed unable to counter this with a strong agenda of his own.

• • •

In the British parliamentary system, upon which our legislature is modeled, a government rules by its ability to command the majority of votes on most issues, particularly those considered "votes of confidence." If a government fails to receive a majority of votes on a piece of legislation or on part of its budget, then the speaker must accept a motion of non-confidence if one is moved. If the majority of votes favour a non-confidence motion against the governing party, the lieutenant-governor becomes involved in dissolving the "writ"—removing the government's authority to govern. Then the province is in an election. Because the NDP needed a majority of votes to pass its budget and its legislation, every MLA counted.

Glen Clark's attendance at the legislature was critical to the Dosanjh government. There were 75 MLAs in the house: 39 NDP, 34 Liberal, and 2 independents. The NDP had to offer up one of their own to be speaker and another as a committee chair. In order to win every vote in committee stage, and to pass legislation they had to have at least 36 votes. Helmut Giesbrecht, MLA for Skeena, and Ed Conroy, MLA for Rossland–Trail, had serious health issues, and sometimes had to be away from the legislature.

The NDP's narrow margin in the house allowed them to continue to govern. They had lost MLA Rick Kasper of Malahat–Juan de Fuca, who had crossed to sit as an independent MLA and was often voting with the Liberals. The NDP could not count on his vote.

The NDP caucus was divided. Hard feelings over the leadership race were still in play—some of it directed at party headquarters, some of it directed at the new team of political players surrounding Ujjal Dosanjh. Some of the hard feelings were directed at Dosanjh himself, since there were those who believed Dosanjh had, at best, profited from, and at worst helped engineer, Clark's downfall.

It had been a challenging time for Glen Clark, who was still an elected politician. He had moved from the premier's office to the political backbench, a place of relative obscurity for politicians. In his entire political career, Clark had never been obscure. His meteoric rise in the NDP as an opposition critic had been followed with prominent and powerful cabinet positions. As a member of the backbench, Clark had no ministerial power; as a politician under criminal investigation, he had little influence.

There was still one card in Clark's hand, and that was his vote as an MLA. He had the power to bring down the Dosanjh government simply by staying home.

One issue that almost brought the government down was the decision, led by Deputy Premier Joy MacPhail, to legislate members of the Canadian Union of Public Employees (CUPE) back to work. CUPE, one of the largest public sector unions, had gone on strike, demanding a new contract. The NDP decided to call an emergency sitting in the legislature on a Sunday to legislate them back to work.

Legislating CUPE back to work caused enormous internal fighting, because CUPE was one of the largest public sector unions and a base of traditional NDP support. The union had locals throughout the province that could be mobilized in the coming election campaign to help NDP candidates. CUPE had no reason to move from the NDP to the Campbell Liberals, whose policies were decidedly anti-public sector union.

CUPE had been active in the leadership race, and many members had publicly supported Gordon Wilson. This may have been a factor in the decision to legislate them back to work. Or perhaps it was done to demonstrate to the electorate an ability to deal harshly with union allies, in order to counter the B.C. Liberals' contention that the NDP was too cozy with unions. Regardless, many MLAs agonized over whether they would show up for the vote, and it took all the arm-twisting efforts of the party whip, Gerard Janssen, and other members, to make sure that there were enough votes to carry the day. It was not good public policy, and it did not generate a political win either within the party or with voters.

Glen Clark showed up and voted with the government. He continued to show up throughout the session, although he rarely sat in his seat except when he was called in for a vote. He made one speech toward the end of the session. Otherwise he kept very quiet and seldom offered an opinion, even internally, of the new leadership or its policy direction.

• • •

As an observer of many of the conversations amongst unhappy NDP MLAs, one story epitomizes the internal dynamic. It is regarding the election of the house speaker at the beginning of the legislative session. Independent MLA Jack Weisgerber, once a Social Credit cabinet minister and former leader of the B.C. Reform party, ran for the position. A respected MLA, Weisgerber was known to be fair-minded and was an experienced member of the legislature. Bill Hartley, a well-liked NDP MLA from Maple Ridge–Pitt Meadows, was also in the running. Hartley had already served as deputy speaker and had done a good job.

The rumours were flying within political circles that this was a race to watch. The Liberals and Independent Rick Kasper only needed two NDP MLAs to vote with them in a secret ballot in order to put Weisgerber in the chair, thus embarrassing the Dosanjh government by electing a right-wing speaker. However, when the votes were counted by the clerks, Hartley won and became the new speaker.

Afterwards I was at a reception with the NDP caucus. A group of them were in a heated discussion about the vote for speaker.

Several told me they had voted for Weisgerber, hoping to send a message to Dosanjh that he should not take their vote for granted. They were convinced that there were other NDP MLAs who had also voted for Weisgerber. The strategy had been to start the session with a story that some of the NDP MLAs were prepared to break ranks, if necessary, to capture part of the legislative agenda. They were mystified by the outcome of the vote. Regardless, they all had a good laugh and knew they would never know what really happened.

"Maybe a bunch of Liberals voted for Hartley," one joked.

"Just another day in B.C. politics," remarked another.

At the end of the session, the NDP's political fortunes had not improved. The party was still in financial difficulties after years of legal battles, a costly leadership race, and a strained membership. The public was no keener on the government than it had been a year previously. The clock was ticking toward the next election. When Clark was charged in the fall of 2000 with criminal breach of trust, it was just another cut to the party. The NDP had been hemorrhaging for years from so many cuts from so many sources that it was hard for its leaders to know where they could go to be safe from more damage.

Clark was on his own.

PART THREE

The Slow Wheels of Justice

12

The Allegations

"Forward, the Light Brigade!"
Was there a man dismay'd?
Not tho' the soldier knew
Someone had blunder'd:
Their's not to make reply,
Their's not to reason why,
Their's but to do and die …

When can their glory fade?
O the wild charge they made!
All the world wondered.
Honor the charge they made,
Honor the Light Brigade …

—Alfred Tennyson,
"The Charge of the Light Brigade"

Bill Smart was the Crown prosecutor who led the prosecution of Glen David Clark and Dimitrios Pilarinos. Clark and Pilarinos had been charged jointly and became "the co-accused." Smart was ably assisted by John Esson and other legal associates. Bill Smart was convincing in his role as defender of the democratic process, and he opened his case with an impassioned plea to protect the system.

I developed considerable respect for Mr. Smart, after reading several hundred pages of his opening statement. I have tried to extract those portions that convey his message. I have not included particular references to the local Burnaby aspect of the case, which did not weigh heavily in the final verdict. I also avoid the lengthy discussion of Katanos and the Greek–Canadian community connection, since the people discussed in this context were not criminally charged for their conduct.

What follows, then, is an edited version of Special Prosecutor Bill Smart's opening comments after three years of investigation into former premier Glen Clark and his dealings in the North Burnaby Inn casino licence application.[1]

> My Lady, I'm going to start by saying what has become patently obvious to all of us that I expect this will be a long and difficult trial ... Some may say, My Lady, that this case, that really this long difficult trial, significant expense all over a deck and a politician who is no longer in office ... doesn't warrant the time this case has taken and is going to take. The Crown says that it's about more than just a deck and it's about more than just a casino application which was potentially worth to the applicants in this case millions of dollars, over time potentially many millions of dollars. The Crown says what lies at the heart of this prosecution and any prosecution for these offences is integrity by our government and by those who govern us ...
>
> Political corruption is an insidious evil which can undermine the whole fabric of our democratic society.
>
> It is hardly necessary for me to expand on the importance of having a government which demonstrates integrity. Suffice it to say that our democratic system would have great difficulty functioning efficiently if its integrity was constantly in question ... I would merely add that the importance of preserving integrity in the government has arguably increased given the need to maintain the public's confidence in government in an age where it continues to play an ever increasing role in the quality of everyday people's lives. As the US Congress has stated about its own anti-corruption measures:

"The necessity for maintaining high ethical standards of behaviour in the Government becomes greater as its activities become more complex and bring it into closer and closer contact with the private sector of the Nation's economy ... It is quite accepted that criminal law has a role to play in this area. Protecting the integrity of government is crucial to the proper functioning of a democratic system. Criminal law has a historic and well-established role in helping to preserve that integrity."

In my view, given the heavy trust and responsibility taken on by the holding of a public office or employ, it is appropriate that government officials are correspondingly held to codes of conduct which, for an ordinary person, would be quite severe. For the public, who is the ultimate beneficiary of honest government, it is not so easy to sort out which benefits are legitimate and which are laden with a sinister motivation.

Moreover, it is inefficient for a government to be paralyzed by rumour and innuendo while an inquiry is made into the motivation behind a certain benefit or advantage conferred on an official. What Parliament is saying through this provision is that the damage sought to be prevented is actually done once the benefit is conferred, and not after an ex-post-facto analysis which demonstrates that no harm was intended. It is from the point of the conferral of the benefit forward that the appearance of integrity has been slighted.

The Crown says that political corruption, even small incidents, can have an extensive and insidious effect. It can have an effect on public confidence in government, on the morale of our public service and also on voluntary public obedience to our laws. After all, much like the justice system, what can be more important to our democratic society than public confidence in our government, in our public employees, in our public officials, and particularly our elected public officials who are elected to act in the best interest of the public who elected them?

This is a case in which the Crown says an effort was made by Mr. Pilarinos to corrupt the highest elected official in our province, our Premier. It was done in an effort to obtain a casino licence worth to Mr. Pilarinos millions of dollars.

And the Crown further says that that effort to corrupt was at least partially successful. Mr. Clark allowed himself to be compromised, whether reluctantly or not he accepted a benefit and he told no one about it until many months later. And he in, at times, a subtle manner attempted to assist Mr. Pilarinos's application to a successful result.

In many respects the Crown says the size or value of a benefit improperly given or received by a politician is irrelevant to the damage that such conduct can cause because it is the fact that there is corruption in government which matters, because corruption, the Crown says, is like a serious infection that can quickly spread and it's more likely to spread from the top down than from the bottom up; that is, from the highest officials down than it is to work its way from the perhaps less significant employees up.

If a contractor does $500 worth of free work on the chief building inspector in a municipality on his or her house, does it matter that it's a service rather than money, what effect would that conduct have on those who work for the chief building inspector and his department if they find out, what effect does it have on other contractors and persons doing business with city hall, what effect does it have on public confidence with city hall?

And in the present case the Crown says the benefit to Mr. Clark was substantially more than $500 in the example I've given, and the official Mr. Clark who received it was in a position to do substantially more.

The Crown's case against Mr. Clark is he not only improperly accepted a benefit but he attempted to assist a friend who provided that benefit, a friend who had no expertise in running a multi-million dollar business and no real expertise in operating a gaming business, to obtain a licence which I submit could have made Mr. Pilarinos a very wealthy man.

... the Crown's position is that Mr. Clark was both an official and a minister during the relevant time, but it may be argued otherwise and the Crown, therefore, has charged him with alternative offences in his capacity as a minister and an official ...

... this case concerns an application for a casino licence by a company of whom the principals were apparently Steven Ng and Dimitrios Pilarinos. The Crown says there was at least one other partner as I've already stated, a Paschos Katanas.

Mr. Pilarinos had a friend, Mr. Vrahnos, who by chance worked for the federal government. Mr. Pilarinos, the Crown says, obtained Mr. Vrahnos's assistance to review his application for this casino licence and that over many months while this application was pending before the government that is under consideration with other applications, Mr. Pilarinos had numerous conversations with Mr. Vrahnos about the application, about who was involved, about his relationship with Mr. Clark ... and about the assistance those individuals were providing him.

Mr. Ng was the owner of an establishment on East Hastings called the North Burnaby Inn, Mr. Katanas rented space in the North Burnaby Inn [NBI] and ran a social club there called the Lumbermen's Social Club, it had relatively recently moved to that establishment. I'm focusing on 1997, 1998. In fact, rather than being merely a social club, it was an illegal gambling establishment with all of the intended [attendant] problems and individuals associated with such establishments ...

(On) March 13, 1997, that was the date, My Lady, that the government announced a decision to lift a moratorium on new casino facilities, and the Lotteries Advisory Committee, which I'll [refer] to as LAC, was established as a temporary body to coordinate the implementation of gaming policy decisions. The committee was chaired by an individual experienced in gaming named Peter Clark and reported, the committee did, to the Minister of Employment and Investments ...

(On) June 20th, 1997, that was the date that a company, 545738 B.C. Ltd., was incorporated. The shareholders were Mr. Ng, the accused, Mr. Pilarinos and Mr. Katanas. On July 31st, 1997, the government announced what they called the Request for Proposals, often referred to by the initials "RFP." And there were four types of gaming facilities being considered, charitable-style casinos, destination casinos, charitable-style bingo halls and destination bingo halls.

The company that I've just referred you to [as] 545738 B.C. Ltd. applied for a charitable-style casino.

The following Government agencies are the key players in the conduct, management and regulation of the B.C. gaming industry:

the Lotteries Advisory Committee,
the British Columbia Lottery Corporation,
the British Columbia Gaming Commission and
the Gaming Audit and Investigation Office (GAIO)

GAIO is under the responsibility of the Ministry of Attorney General, has been recently created with the responsibility for conducting gaming audits, reviewing compliance procedures, carrying out background and security clearance investigations and consumer complaint investigations.

(And so there are) … really two bodies that were reviewing the application, one on sort of the business side, the government objectives, that is the Lotteries Advisory Committees, the Minister of Employment and Investment. The security aspect of it, background checks was by GAIO which is under the Ministry of the Attorney General.

… So as you can see, My Lady, that if successful, I have to highlight this, if an applicant is successful and if they are successful in operating their facility, potentially there is a significant amount of money to be made. And it appears, in my submission, I'm going to show you some documents later, that Mr. Pilarinos was optimistic that the casino that he was involved with would make a significant amount of money for him and his partners.

This application is for registration with GAIO. If registered, the GAIO will notify the Lottery Commission or Gaming Commission that the applicant company or person has been screened and registered as suitable …

… I've set out that on October 21, 1997, bearing in mind that it's the end of November, approximately the end of November when these applications have to be in, the company, I'll just call it Mr. Pilarinos's company, but it's his and Mr. Ng and the Crown says Mr. Katanas's, 545738 B.C. Ltd., registered as a casino proponent under the RFP system …

… The Crown will call two experienced quantity surveyors to give you their estimates on the dollar value of

Mr. Pilarinos's expertise, his labour, his time. And as one might expect there are going to be variations, it's like trying to estimate what it would cost for legal fees to do something, so it's an inexact science but I expect their evidence to be somewhere in the range of around $10,000.

You may well find that because of the variables it may be less than that, what is significant the Crown says, My Lady, is not just the dollar value as whether or not it created a sense of obligation. There is a benefit the Crown says, it's not an insignificant benefit, it's a number of thousands of dollars, and human nature being what it is, the Crown suggests it creates a sense of obligation and that's why it was done by Mr. Pilarinos.

... (On) October 8th, Mr. MacKinnon from the Gaming Policy Secretariat (office of the Minister of Employment and Investment Mike Farnworth) notified Mr. Letts from GAIO that the NBI application might receive approval in principle and that the GAIO investigation should therefore commence. So late in the day that process was now embarked on. There was a discussion in November of 1998 where Mr. Letts advised Mr. MacKinnon that his investigation, that is Letts or GAIO investigation, was not complete and it did not look good and he recommended that a decision be held off with respect to the NBI application.

That on or around December the 10th there was a meeting between the (NDP) MLA for this area in Burnaby, Mr. (Pietro) Calendino, and Mr. Farnworth during which Mr. Farnworth may have advised Mr. Calendino, you'll have different recollections of exactly what was said, he would be granting approval in principle to the NBI or the Luu/Pilarinos application, and that there may also have been a discussion with respect to the two applicants in Burnaby coordinating their efforts. Mr. Calendino thereafter spoke with, independently, My Lady, Mr. Ng and Mr. Luu to suggest, this is my words, that they get together and discuss perhaps combining their efforts.

Again around that same period of time, December 14th or 15th, Mr. Farnworth phoned Mayor Drummond to discuss the NBI application and Burnaby's position with respect to approval in principle was granted. Then on December 17th approval in principle is granted for four additional facilities, sorry, three additional facilities, one of which is Mr. Luu and Mr. Ng's application. Despite, as I say, the opposition and despite the fact the GAIO investigation is not complete. I should make it clear as approval in principle, unless the GAIO process resulted in a favourable result it would seem unlikely that the application would go ahead.

... I'm going to take you, My Lady, ahead, please, in terms of the chronology to ... one of the voir dires, that Mr. Vrahnos, having had apparently no response to the document he gave to the Liberal party, having heard that there was approval in principle, granted he prepared a document entitled How and Why the Premier Promotes the Casino Application of Some Very Questionable Characters. He took that to the *Vancouver Sun* and in fact met with a reporter Rick Ouston, and Mr. Ouston faxed that to Steven Letts at GAIO to ask for his comment about the content thereof. Mr. Letts brought it to the attention of Mr. Quantz then the assistant deputy attorney-general, the person in charge of criminal prosecutions in this province. There was, it turned out, already an RCMP investigation that had commenced as a result of the October 3rd letter that appears to have commenced around the time of December 17th, as you'll recall from the voir dire there's some debate about precisely when, but around that period of time.

So this document at Tab 28, the one given to the *Vancouver Sun,* faxed to the attorney general's office, brought to Mr. Quantz's attention is what he then was in discussions with the RCMP commercial crime section and which resulted in the appointment of a special prosecutor, Martin Taylor.

Now, this document, what I want to highlight about this document is a couple of matters. He sets out, as you can see, the various persons he calls the "players" which include Mr. Pilarinos, Mr. Ng, Mr. Katanas, the old man, being Mr. Young, Glen Clark. He sets out what he calls the "story" which relates what he says he's been told by Mr. Pilarinos, who the true partners are, who is involved.

... On the—and I should say, my lady, the other, another area of concern was the investigation by G.A.I.O., and there were meetings between G.A.I.O. investigators of Mr. Ng and Mr. Pilarinos and the documents being sent to those investigators. The Crown says meeting with Mr. Young was part of that to look after the municipal concerns. February the 8th, as you've heard, the RCMP, who had been trying to locate the author of the letter given to Mr. Ouston, and that was faxed to Steven Letts at G.A.I.O., and the author of the document given to Miss Barkey, the RCMP found him and interviewed him, and he provided more information to the police as to what he'd been told by Mr. Pilarinos. And as you'll recall, he told the police that in fact, he had a letter on his computer that he had been considering sending to the Premier, and had given a copy of that to the RCMP.

The police again, as you recall from our voir dire in relation to the intercept of private communications, then worked on assembling the information that they had gathered, put in an affidavit to present to Justice Dohm to apply for an authorization to intercept private communications, and that application was made and granted on February 14th, 1999. Unbeknownst to the police, Mr. Vrahnos, on February the 10th, faxed an anonymous letter to Mr. Clark's constituency office, using the name "Karmelita."

That office apparently sent the fax to a Mr. Wickstrom, who worked for Mr. Clark, who gave it to Adrian Dix, who provided it to Mr. Clark that evening ... The next day, February 11th, Mr. Clark and Mr. Dix summoned Mr. George Ford, who was the deputy minister to the Premier. They provided him with the "Karmelita" fax ...

The allegation, what's said here (The Karmelita fax reads):

Fact: You broke rules to help Pilarinos and Ng get a casino licence

Fact: You consider Pilarinos friend and supporter

Fact: Pilarinos did free construction work for you

Rumor: You have a piece of the action in the casino

Fact: Pilarinos and Ng are not the only partners. They have one more silent partner with a long criminal record. You have been used to accommodate the entrance of gangsters in the casino business in B.C.

Fact: The story is out. A lot of people have been indiscreet

Fact: The Liberals know the story

Fact: A special criminal investigation has targeted you, Pilarinos, Ng, and their gangster partners.

To save your reputation and your government:

(a) kill the casino application IMMEDIATELY

(b) "Clean" your home and all offices of any evidence IMMEDIATELY

(c) Careful how you use your telephones and faxes

(d) Destroy this piece of paper NOW—I risk my career to save your sorry ass.

You owe me big time you jerk
Remember the name "Karmelita."

> ... The other thing that the police didn't know is that Mr. Vrahnos also sent, and this is at tab 32, a letter to Mr. Pilarinos; and you can see the photocopy of the envelope, it appears to be by Express Post; it looks that the postmark is the 11th of February, '99. The return address in fact, I believe, is Mr. Pilarinos' in-laws. And that letter is not even a letter; just, it's a note that says:
>
> > (As read) This is no joke. The police is asking specific questions about your partnership with criminal elements in the gambling business. If you are involved, think of your family and jail. Get out right away. Do not trust anybody's telephone lines or cell phones. If you have any papers in your home, get rid of it right away. This is very serious, good luck, you will need it. Keep quiet about this warning, do not show this note to anybody. Destroy it now. (Not in a few minutes but right now this moment SOS)
>
> So in one sense, Mr. Vrahnos assisted the police investigation. On the other hand, he, one could say, obstructed.

This launched a lengthy and complicated trial with many twists and turns. There were many witnessses connected with the various aspects of the case. Numerous witnesses came from branches of government and the RCMP.

13

A Ringside Seat

... I've put my trust in you
Pushed as far as I can go
For all this, there's only one thing you should know
I tried so hard, and got so far
But in the end, it doesn't even matter
I had to fall to lose it all
But in the end
It doesn't even matter ...
—Linkin Park, "In the End"

"Order in court."

Everyone stood as the judge walked into the B.C. Supreme Court room in Vancouver, taking the bench to resume the second month of hearings in the criminal trial of former British Columbia premier Glen Clark. The judge would preside without a jury, since Clark and his lawyers had opted for trial by judge alone. In part, this decision was made because public opinion about Mr. Clark was, at best, uncertain at that time, and the defence believed a judge would be less influenced by news stories and public opinion.

I was still slightly winded from the climb up the stairs. The Clark case was on one of the top floors, and in some vain tribute to fitness I climbed each level of stairs to access it. It was such a visually stunning walk that it was worth the effort. The Vancouver Law Courts are an impressive architectural structure, and many of the courtrooms are on floors that are built to overlook an indoor courtyard. It is like a stacking of mezzanines, and you can look down from the top floors onto a large tiled area with seats and statues. The stairs from the courtyard were wide, running along the middle section of the long building, ascending in a graceful grey procession to the first landing, where they divided to direct the walker to the right or left in a smaller set of stairs. Overhead, above the top floor, a cascade of clear, light-green glass panes served as the roof and wall creating a giant atrium with a warm atmosphere of natural light and space. The architects' brilliance somehow extended to the acoustics, as there was almost no echo in the indoor courtyard as people walked across. Plants adorned each mezzanine level, and were present in any nook and cranny available. On a rainy day, waterfalls of rain ran gently across the glass and down the sloped roof in a mesmerizing parade.

The Clark trial was in a large courtroom, in the south corner of the sixth floor, at the end of the carpeted walkway. A security gate was set up near the entrance to the courtroom, and security guards were present near the gate, by the entry door, and inside the courtroom. The gate was not activated, and people were not searched; still I felt somewhat intimidated as I entered the hushed confines of the courtroom to take a seat at the back. From the back row, I had a good vantage point for the proceedings.

Six lawyers moved about in their long black robes to resume the ping-pong game with the witnesses. Today was a light match. Those due to testify were all RCMP officers involved in the surveillance of then-premier Glen Clark and his co-accused, Dimitrios Pilarinos. Records showed that 27 officers had played a role during the investigation, and this was the day their evidence was entered into the record. This roster of participants alone verified that significant RCMP resources had been allocated to a case originating from a tip about criminal activity involving the premier.

What magnitude of compelling evidence did they have to mount this level of investigation? To have so many RCMP officers involved in a criminal investigation is unusual. Assigning them to put the premier of the province under surveillance must have been based on a credible allegation of serious wrongdoing.

When the story broke in the local press, it called to mind the criminal investigation of former Saskatchewan cabinet minister Colin Thatcher, if only because both politicians had high-profile, dramatic and serious criminal allegations raised against them for issues that most people do not associate with our elected leaders. In Thatcher's case, he went to jail for murdering his ex-wife.

In Clark's case, the criminal charge was more nebulous. There were no dead bodies, no smoking guns, and no offshore accounts full of misappropriated funds. The magnitude of the alleged crime was not in the millions of dollars; it was not even six figures. The Crown's charge of corruption was based on allegations that Clark had used his political office as premier to receive a bargain on home renovations in exchange for assistance with the casino application of his neighbour Dimitrios Pilarinos.

There were several months of pre-trial hearings in the autumn of 2001 about the admissibility of evidence. Then the trial started on January 14, 2002, and through the next 136 days of proceedings, the courtroom drama unfolded in a series of strange scenes. For the attending press and regular spectators, the judge, the lawyers, and the accused seemed trapped in a macabre dance accompanied by fiddlers playing different tunes.

Glen Clark had to be present every day of the trial. This meant that his work at his private sector employment, Pattison Signs (a Jimmy Pattison company), would be fairly disjointed. Pattison was known to be a tough boss, and Clark had been hired as manager of the western division of the company and given the chance to prove himself. I wondered how he would manage this while sitting in a courtroom from Monday to Friday, 10 a.m. to 4 p.m. He had told me that he was often in the office by 7 a.m. and worked very late on weeknights and sometimes on weekends. Clark had originally scheduled his holiday time to coincide with the criminal trial, but it had run out during the preliminary hearings.

Glen Clark's new career as regional sales manager for Pattison Signs, was possibly the most unpredictable outcome of the entire NDP meltdown. A successful transition is a testament to Clark's resilience.

It must have been awkward for Clark at the office having to adjust his schedule around a criminal trial, knowing that all his employees were aware of where he was and why he was away for most of the day.

I watched Clark from the back of the courtroom as the trial progressed. If he felt stress, he did not show it. His behaviour was carefree, and he joked with the media during breaks. This attitude was a holdover from Clark's school days, when he was "a little guy" who was often picked on. Clark told me he learned early that it was best if you never let them know they were getting to you.

Even as his political team fractured and support for him deteriorated, he wore a "what, me worry?" look. Some would argue that this seeming lack of vulnerability was why he seldom had much public sympathy when he hit rough waters.

Clark once likened himself to the knight in Monty Python's *Quest for the Holy Grail,* when, in the midst of utter political chaos and calls for his resignation, he pronounced his political damage "only a flesh wound." But in politics, a criminal allegation is more than a flesh wound. In Clark's case, criminal allegations led to his beheading.

These criminal allegations came from the RCMP Special "O" Division's investigation, internally dubbed "Project Ezra," Ezra being a teacher in the Old Testament biblical times who insisted that God's law be followed. The time estimated for Project Ezra was 18,000 hours, not including government staff time and court time for hearings. The trial itself would add millions to the cost. The attorney-general's office had allocated a special prosecutor who required additional financial resources. The costs included chartering jets and hiring experts. Clark's legal costs were also covered by taxpayer dollars, and began the night of the raid on his home on March 2, 1999. The legal team of Gibbons and Fowler, one of the best in the province, worked for three-and-a-half years on the case, often incurring overtime. This investigation was an expensive exercise.

The investigation continued a disturbing trend in recent provincial political history. The investment in the criminal prosecution of Glen Clark was not the first time money had been put into investigating a premier or former premier. Bill Vander Zalm (Social Credit) also faced an investigation related to a property sale. Mike Harcourt (NDP) resigned over the criminal investigation of a bingo scandal. He was never cleared, but then he was never personally under investigation. The inquiry into the bingo controversy with the Nanaimo Commonwealth Holding Society went on for years, with witnesses and legal proceedings. Former NDP premier Dave Barrett was also under investigation in the bingo scandal for a matter of months, and then cleared.

It is one matter to be subjected to a criminal investigation and then be cleared of wrongdoing. If one is in politics, it is quite another to undo the damage in the public arena when the legal process receives widespread publicity. The follow-up seldom receives as much coverage as the original allegation.

• • •

So how did we come to be sitting in a Vancouver courtroom in 2002, picking through the pieces of the investigation into former premier Clark? Clark's trial followed his criminal charge, which followed the investigation, which came out of an anonymous allegation. The allegation was that the premier was being duped into using his political office to procure a casino licence for a friend, in exchange for renovations to his personal property.

As a stream of investigating officers took the stand, I wondered how much it cost to follow the premier around in 1999. What was the process to decide that this, more than anything else, was in the public's interest? How did the RCMP make sure enough resources were available? The more the trial revealed, the more questions came to mind. How do you keep this a secret from the premier's office? From the attorney-general's office? And if it was not a secret kept from the attorney-general's office, then when did this office first learn about it, and how was the best course of action decided?

While taking notes in the courtroom, my thoughts returned to the morning news. The media were all zoned in on the story of a Fraser Valley pig farm and the mass search for more than 50 women, some of whom had been missing for many years. I had to wonder what led the RCMP to make the investigation of the premier a higher priority than the search for the missing women. Someone or some extremely compelling evidence must have convinced them that delving into the allegations against Glen Clark was a good use of resources.

My attention returned to the questioning of the RCMP officer on the stand, Constable Stanley Drebot. He was the last of a number of RCMP officers who all faced similar lines of questioning. Despite his detailed notes, certain information the defence wished to have on record appeared to be missing from his records.

It was Valentine's Day, and I had spoken to this officer before the trial and found him to be very likeable. He had a pleasant, open face, and even on the stand his friendliness came across as he was questioned by one of Clark's lawyers, Richard Fowler. The witness acknowledged that he took notes and transcribed them later, as soon as possible, in his car. He was just doing his job, as he had been trained to do. It had been clear that all RCMP members were good at taking notes, and for the most part they demonstrated very clear memories.

The exchange between Drebot and Fowler brought to mind the Chip'n'Dale chipmunks: they were so polite to each other. Fowler was taking Drebot through his surveillance notes from an observation of Pilarinos. They were photocopied and apparently hard to read.

Asked Fowler, "The first thing that you appear to have written in quotation marks is, 'I'll send this off and it's done'; is that correct?"[1]

Drebot replied, "One moment, please. No, there's a line above it. I refer to Mr. Pilarinos as 'T1' on the notes, and Mr. Pilarinos says, 'It's a heritage house.'"

"But that doesn't appear to be in quotation marks, sir?"

"I just have a little squiggle there on the sides. I don't know if you saw that. The photocopy may well not have picked it up. I just have a little squiggly in here and a squiggly in there."

When Fowler was done, the defence lawyer for Dimitrios Pilarinos was up next with the same witness. Ian Donaldson was a bit of a cowboy in style, who tended to ride in tossing his questions like lassoes and hoping to rope something relevant. He was attractive, with dark, thick hair and a slightly dangerous look, as if he would be safe on his own in a dark alley at night.

Donaldson approached the witness aggressively and began firing questions at him about his initial briefing on the case. At first the witness answered as openly as he had answered Fowler. Later Drebot addressed his replies to the judge. Donaldson began by placing the witness at the beginning of his work on the case: "So your first day on this investigation, Project Ezra, was on or about the 13th of January; am I right about that?"

"Yes, that would be correct."

"And I take it you, together with other members of your team, were briefed before you started on the 13th?"

"Yes, that would be correct."

"Who briefed you?"

"I cannot recall at this time."

"I assume this is the only investigation in which you've ever been involved that involved one person as an object of surveillance who was the sitting premier of the province?"

"I beg your pardon?"

"This is the only case you've ever had that involved the premier of the province, right?"

"Yes, that is correct."

"Who briefed the Special "O" team? Who briefed you?"

"I cannot recall at this time, My Lady."

Donaldson looked intently at the witness, who was beginning to squirm as he pressed him for the name of the person directing the strategy in the RCMP investigation. He was looking for a specific name: "At these briefings—there was a briefing, though?"

"Yes. There usually is, yes."

"You received information from a person who was your leader ...? Is it normal that a person from the requesting agency would attend at that briefing?"

"No, it would not, My Lady."

Donaldson's frustration was palpable, and his body language was pushing the witness for information. He was looking for a name, one name, and he wanted the officer to say it. The friendly, open face of the witness was now flushed and stern. He seemed intimidated, even flustered.

"Do you have any notes or other writings at all that would assist you on recalling who was present at that briefing or what you were told?"

"No, I do not, My Lady."

"Is it a practice not to make notes at such a briefing meeting?"

"No. We'll scribble down notes ..."

"Did you?"

"... on pads and stuff, yes."

"Did you do that?"

"Yes, I'm certain I probably did."

"Okay. Where are those notes?"

"Those notes are destroyed at the end of every shift."

"You were part of a team?"

"That is correct."

"That is to say, there was a first, second, third, fourth team. There were various different teams of individuals who worked together?"

"Yes, individuals who worked together as a team, yes."

"From your perspective, who was the leader of this investigation within Special "O"?"

"I don't know if there is a specific leader of the investigation within the Special "O"."

Donaldson continued to push as tension rose in the courtroom. Finally Judge Bennett must have felt some compassion for the witness. She broke into the line of questioning.

"... You're asking for information from three years ago. Surely there's a better way of getting this information than from this officer?"

Donaldson approached the bench, his body language signalling resignation. "We have made requests of Crown counsel to obtain this information. It has not been forthcoming. I don't accept that it doesn't exist, and Crown counsel hasn't said it doesn't exist."

Judge Bennett looked from Donaldson to the lawyers for the prosecution. "Well, it must exist. I mean ..."

Donaldson shook his head and replied, "No, no ..."

Bennett prompted the Crown lawyers. "Mr. Esson?"

John Esson jumped to his feet. He was a slight, unassuming lawyer with a shy, sincere face. He was notable for his short, tightly curled light-brown hair and his quiet voice. I thought he would fit in well with Christopher Robin playing in the 100 Acre Wood.

Before he could reply, Donaldson, still wound up, piped in. "I'm not faulting Mr. Esson, My Lady, please understand."

Judge Bennett gave a half smile. "I'm not going to yell at Mr. Esson, that's all right, Mr. Donaldson, you don't have to step in and say anything."

Esson added quietly, "He can step in and save me."

Esson may have felt uncomfortable, because he couldn't produce the documents that should have been available months previously.

Bennett turned serious. "What's the problem of getting this bit of information? I mean, to ask this officer to cast his mind back three years to try and remember ..."

Esson replied before she had time to finish; he sounded uncomfortable with his reply. "No, I agree. I've been trying to get this information. I haven't got it in any form that would be useful to pass on to my friend in any certain form yet. I'm still endeavouring to do that. I've ..." He did not finish his sentence, just shrugged.

Bennett must have sensed his discomfort. She seemed almost angry. "Tell them I've told you to get it. Maybe that will help."

Esson seemed relieved: "It probably will help."

Drebot was soon excused and was visibly relieved.

Donaldson appeared annoyed to have his line of questioning cut short without receiving the name he sought.

What was the significance of the name? How could so many Mounties not recall who had been driving the investigation only three years earlier? Even to the casual observer, the forgetfulness seemed suspicious. Donaldson was looking for the name of the RCMP officer who had initiated the investigation, who had followed up on the anonymous tip, who was politically active, who had maintained the will to investigate the premier, and who apparently devised the strategy directing the investigation.

By this stage of the trial, every media observer knew the name Donaldson was seeking, the name he wanted to hear from the mouth of the RCMP officer. Defence lawyers had repeatedly tried to have RCMP witnesses establish the separate trails of the Special "O" investigation leading to Premier Clark. Their collective pre-trial research showed that every trail led to one name:

Staff Sergeant Peter Montague.

• • •

Criminal charges and courtroom drama aside, most of the Clark trial dealt with the minutiae of paperwork, conversations, and home renovations as the legal teams presented their cases. How much does a deck cost? This question, and the variety of answers to it, had to be explored at some length in the Clark trial. This happened in the early stage of the trial, and although it was short on drama, it was important to try to follow the financial and legal twists of the courtroom. I took notes and observed people during one of these sessions, relieved when lunch arrived and I could take a break from my scribbling. An inability to take shorthand is a distinct disadvantage in the courtroom, I mused as I packed up my notebook.

"It's really boring today, eh?" Clark asked me, "too many numbers." He came across as if he was responsible for our enjoyment at his trial, welcoming us to the show, worrying about the entertainment value of the day's events, hoping we hadn't been bored.

"Actually, it's quite interesting," I smiled reassuringly, putting away my notebook. "Although the numbers could make your head spin, it's pretty important to nail them down, and Fowler is doing it well."

"It's all bullshit. What a goddamn waste of money." Former IWA president Jack Munro grumbled his way out of the courtroom with his trademark style. Munro had been a fixture in B.C. politics, especially in the 1980s when he had taken on the large forest companies on behalf of the unionized forestry workers. He was a big bear of a man with a booming voice, gruff demeanour, and heart of gold. He was retired, and he would occasionally show up to provide moral support for Clark. "You gonna grab some lunch?" he asked Clark.

"Yeah, sure, and I think Judi's going to join us," Clark replied, referring to our earlier discussion.

"I'll only join you if Jack agrees not to swear," I replied, teasing.

"I promise not to swear if you promise not to talk," was Munro's quick reply.

Clark laughed loudly, and we walked toward the law-courts dining room. I couldn't help but think what an incongruous trio we made: larger-than-life labour activist and socialist ideologue Jack Munro, always-cheery former socialist premier-turned-hardened-capitalist Clark, and me, a federal Liberal still idealistic enough to write about Clark's trial, hoping it might make a difference. It was a true B.C. moment.

During lunch, we avoided talk of the trial, as the two men spoke of union activists, ideology, and motorcycle rides. Both passionate motorbike riders, they compared notes. Jack Munro bought lunch, which is pretty good for a socialist, or at least that's what I told him.

It was the day that the Crown had produced its second, and more credible, witness to testify to the benefit given to Clark by Dimitrios Pilarinos. The Crown's case was that Clark had received discounted renovations on his East Vancouver house and his recreational cabin near Penticton. The renovations centred around a sundeck on each property, plus renovation work on the East Vancouver house.

The Crown had two expert witnesses who provided estimates of what they believed the work on both projects was worth. There was a significant difference between these estimates and what the Clark family had paid. Based on the difference between the estimates and the amount paid, the Crown determined that a benefit of roughly $10,000 had been provided to Premier Clark. This, combined with an allegation that Clark had interfered to assist Pilarinos in his casino licence application, was at the heart of the criminal trial.

It was critical to the prosecution that they provide evidence of a $10,000 benefit to Glen Clark, and it was equally critical to the defence that this evidence be called into question and the original estimates reduced.

The first witness for the prosecution who had provided a construction estimate was Derek Sanft. He had not done well in cross-examination, as it turned out his math was seriously flawed. Clark had told me that he felt sorry watching him on the stand as his report crumbled for the world to see. Just a small portion of the volley between Clark's lawyer Richard Fowler and Sanft provides an insight into what happened in his days on the witness stand. Fowler began.[2]

"So you have a 15 percent mark-up on the labour, and then another 10 percent on the whole; is that correct?"

"10 percent on the bottom line, yes."

"See, if you look over at page 17 under the heading 'reconciliation' you say, 'add labour to reflect true labour costs for the project, 10,800?'"

"Yes."

"Which is your labour estimate, plus 15 percent overhead and seven percent GST; is that correct?"

"Yes."

"And then you add overhead and mark-up and GST of $2,675?"

"Yes."

"And the $2,675 is the overhead and mark-up on your invoice costs and labour?"

"Yes."

"At 10 percent and seven percent?"

"Yes."

"There seems to be some problem with the numbers there, would you agree with me?"

"Yes, probably the—we allowed the seven percent on the GST on the $9,800."

"You wouldn't recommend to a client that they pay the government seven percent twice, would you?"

"No, we wouldn't."

"And I'm sure you probably wouldn't recommend a 15 percent overhead and then another 10 percent overhead on the same item, would you?"

"No."

"Because if you do that it tends to inflate the price a little bit, would you agree with me?"

"Yes, I would."

At the end of his testimony, there was very little credibility left in his quote, which meant there was little basis to determine a benefit to Clark from this evidence. The Crown's second expert witness, a professional contractor named Evan Stregger, had to stand up to cross-examination in order to salvage the Crown's claim that Clark had received a significant benefit. It was up to Clark's defence lawyers to pick apart the quote given by Stregger.

Special Prosecutor Bill Smart began with his examination of Stregger, entering general details into the trial record. Smart, who had begun the trial with an articulate speech about political corruption and a financial benefit to former Premier Clark, knew that a good part of his case rested on Stregger's shoulders.

Bill Smart had a thoughtful look as he examined his witness. His short dark brown hair, always meticulously combed, had a peppering of grey that gave him a mature look. Smart was slim, with a serious, handsome narrow face, and the kind of pale skin that comes from spending too much time in libraries or offices.

Smart clearly took his job seriously. As a Crown prosecutor, when he said it was important to the people of B.C. that the Crown prosecute a premier for corruption, he clearly meant it. He did not have the pained, slightly mean look of Kenneth Starr, the U.S. prosecutor who went after President Bill Clinton. One would more likely cast him as the defence lawyer in *To Kill a Mockingbird* than as someone with a political agenda.

Smart walked Stregger through a mundane list of construction materials, perhaps in an attempt to make him feel at ease, perhaps to give the court the impression that here was a contractor who was very comfortable with his quote. He made sure that the judge understood that in addition to the contractor's quote there was an opportunity to add cost later, if necessary, to keep the quote high. Smart was anticipating that the defence team would pick holes in the estimate, and he wanted to make sure that even if Stregger's estimate was reduced, there was room to add on later.

Richard Fowler (left), the detail man, and his highly regarded partner David Gibbons, used a courtroom style that worked.

It was crucial that Smart be left with a significant quote from Stregger after the cross-examination. Unless the Crown could demonstrate that Clark received a benefit, the Crown could not allege political corruption.

After Smart, Richard Fowler took over. Fowler, of Gibbons Fowler, was one of Glen Clark's two senior lawyers. The other, noted defence lawyer David Gibbons, was the lead in the case and was the pit bull. Fowler was the detail person.

Fowler was well-named. Both his features and gestures were a little like a bird. He tended to glide across the courtroom in his legal robes, from his notes to the witnesses, to coax answers from them. His slight build, John Lennon glasses, and narrow face gave him an owlish academic look, and he talked with his hands in a quiet, understated manner that seemed to put witnesses at ease. Fowler had enough of an English accent to add to the "university-researcher" image, and his clipped voice politely delivering his analytic questions gave an air of efficiency and method to his technique. He would wait for the answers, his body language drawing out each move. His manner would bore anyone not paying attention to his line of questioning, but this was misleading.

Fowler would make a good chess player.

As he walked across the courtroom, his collar-length dark blond hair followed the rhythm of his stride, adding to the impression of Fowler drifting toward the witnesses. He swooped back and forth, questioning Stregger.

Stregger appeared relaxed. The contractor had provided testimony in other cases and was comfortable speaking in public. In his mid-fifties, Stregger was credible, nicely dressed, and presented well in the courtroom. His manner was respectful of Fowler's questioning; he was experienced, and he knew to answer with as few words as possible. Fowler began with the quote Stregger had provided to the RCMP about the value of the renovations to the Clark property.

Fowler: "Now, I'm presuming that you have no data in regards the work habits of Mr. Pilarinos, am I correct?"[3]

Stregger: "That's entirely correct."

"You've never met him?"

"No."

"Never seen him work?"

"No, I have not."

"You don't know whether he's a fast worker, a slow worker, an efficient worker or an inefficient worker, is that correct?"

"That's correct."

"You don't know whether he takes three coffee breaks in the morning or none at all, do you?"

"No, I don't."

"Of course I presume in terms of valuing the labour component of either of the two jobs that you analyzed, knowing something of his work habits would've been helpful to you, isn't that correct?"

Stregger was not prepared to concede this point at all. "It would not necessarily change the value, no."

"Well, sir, if he were able to complete a task in half the amount of time that you estimated it would take, wouldn't that affect the value that you would attribute to it?"

There was a pause. "It would adjust the value, yes, somewhat."

"Downwards?"

Stregger replied, reluctantly, "Yes."

"As I understand it, you rely on your historical cost data to determine the man hours per unit for the descriptions in either of your reports, is that correct?"

"That and my own opinion of the work specifically relating to this, these projects, so it's not a simple mathematical take a figure, plug it into the estimate, ignore the actual work that's been done."

"Do you have Exhibit 39 in front of you? That's the report that you wrote about Mr. Clark's cabin in Penticton … For example, for what you describe as pier blocks, your man hours per unit is thirty-five hundredths of an hour? Approximately 20 minutes per block?"

"That's correct."

"… Do you have data that specifically deals with pier blocks such as this?"

Stregger shrugged. "A minimal amount ..."

As the questions became more specific, Stregger's discomfort increased, and he seemed reluctant to answer. A pier block is a cement footing that is placed under the deck. Twenty minutes is a pretty specific number to assign to this task, and the contractor may have sensed that Fowler was about to challenge it.

"Well, what's the size of the range? Is it plus or minus ten percent? Plus or minus twenty percent? Thirty percent? Or what is it?"

"I would say plus or minus *five* percent."

"How do you know that?"

Stregger squared his shoulders. "Based on my experience of past estimates, on other projects, other work."

Fowler continued to push him. "Okay. So if a task such as installing a pier block were to take ten minutes, that would be plus or minus fifty percent ... Well outside of your expected error rate, is that correct?"

Stregger hesitated. "Yes."

The tension grew. Fowler moved another chess piece to try to tie Stregger up in knots.

"So if somebody, hypothetically, were able to install one of these concrete blocks in ten minutes as opposed to twenty minutes, I suggest to you that that shows that either your cost data is not particularly accurate or that you have insufficient experience in determining this. Would you agree with that?"

Stregger became defensive. "I'd suggest that their assumptions *were probably incorrect*."

"So can I take from that that you would prefer to rely on your experience than on the evidence of somebody who completed a task?"

Stregger was not giving any ground. "Before I would rely on the evidence of someone who completed the task, I would want their full description of *what is included* in that task."

Fowler moved on to another detail in the home renovations, this one concerning the gas fireplace.

"So your total for those three items is about twelve and a half hours, would you agree with me?"

"Approximately, yes."

"Do you know the person who installed the gas fireplace that you saw in the bedroom?"

"No, I do not."

"Never asked him how long it took him?"

"No."

"Well ... it took him about an hour and three quarters, with 15 minutes of assistance from Mr. Pilarinos ... Your estimate is more," Fowler paused, he seemed stern, "about *ten hours* more."

• • •

Fowler moved to the report on the Penticton cabin, which had detailed estimates of market costs for the work. He was moving in for the grand finale. His technique was now like a magician, working up to pulling the rabbit out of the hat. He was leading Stregger through the evidence, asking him to agree on the points, moving on to the next trick. His pace began to pick up as he worked through the questions.

"When you wrote this report on June the 3rd, 1999 you didn't have access to any receipts or anything like that, is that correct?"

"That's correct."

"Did you ask for the receipts?"

"No, I did not. "

Fowler seemed puzzled. "Why not?"

Another shrug from Stregger. "I was asked to provide a value for the work as I saw it on site."

"But, sir, you'd agree with me that if receipts are available, it's preferable to rely on receipts rather than doing an estimate, wouldn't you agree with me?"

"If they're available, yes."

"Well, did you ask if they were available?"

Stregger looked confused. "I don't recall."

Fowler swept closer, leaned toward the witness slightly. "You don't recall whether you asked whether they were available? Is that your evidence, sir?"

Was that a touch of panic? A struggle to remember? "I don't believe they were. I was made aware that receipts were available later …"

"Did you ever ask the …?"

Judge Bennett, following each move intently, intervened to provide Stregger with a little breathing room. "Let him finish his answer, please Mr. Fowler."

Stregger took a moment. "I don't recall that I ever asked specifically if receipts were available."

Fowler had relaxed a bit, and moved away from the witness box, and now suggested his questions very logically. "You would agree with me, sir, that if they are available, it's preferable to rely on them, correct?"

"Yes, I would."

"So as an expert I would presume that as part of your due diligence before you embark on a task, you would inquire as to what documents are available, wouldn't you?"

Stregger responded tentatively. "Yes, and I believe I was told there were no documents available."

"And do you recall who told you that?"

"It was either Corporal Stein or Sergeant Zinetti."

"The two people that effectively retained you in April of 1999, is that correct?"

"Correct."

Fowler, apparently satisfied with this answer, switched to another topic. This is when he lobbed a hand grenade, having worked Stregger into a position of extreme discomfort.

"You wrote an article entitled 'Value of the Work—Actual Cost v. Estimated Value,' didn't you?"

What could he say? He answered truthfully. "Yes, I did."

"And in your article you write the following in the first paragraph, 'The expert for the defendants measured the work and prepared a hypothetical estimate of the value of the repair costs. In a settlement conference the judge said to this expert, "An estimate based on hypothetical value is not applicable as the work has been completed and the invoices, time sheets and contracts have been produced." Your opinion, based on hypothetical costs, is not relevant.' Do you recall writing that?"

"Yes, I do."

"And you go on in your article and state the following: 'As I had based my opinion on actual costs, quantities and methods, whereas the other experts had relied on sample areas and hypothetical costs, when we met to resolve the differences, the other expert recognized that he could not precisely show what the contractor had done wrong or possibly overcharged. On almost all issues, joint agreement was reached at the value set out in my original report.' And that was a report based on actual costs, is that correct?"

"... And then you state at the concluding paragraph in your article, 'It is my experience that where actual costs are available the expert is best to analyze those costs rather than produce a hypothetical estimate. While reviewing invoices, etc. is a tedious and most often more costly approach I have found that cases can be proven and disproved by the documents. Disproving a claim based on a claimant's own documents is far superior to presenting a hypothetical analysis.' That remains your opinion, isn't that correct?"

"Yes, it is."

Fowler was no longer very friendly. "So in that that is your experience as a quantity surveyor and an expert witness in other cases, I suggest to you that you should've asked and didn't ask to see the receipts, isn't that correct?"

Stregger's demeanour changed at this point. He seemed deflated, bested by Fowler. "I don't recall specifically asking to see receipts. I do recall that I was told no documents were available, and that I was to base a value on the work as I saw it at the time of inspection."

Fowler's cross-examination of Stregger continued in a dazzling display of mathematics and meticulous analysis of the documents. Ironically the Penticton deck built by Clark, Pilarinos, and friends was so inadequate to the building code that it had to be rebuilt.

What became clear in the balance of the questioning was that Fowler had done his homework. In fact, at one point he appeared more familiar with the B.C. Building Code than the witness, citing requirements and pointing to deficiencies visible in the photographs.

Fowler and Stregger engaged in a relatively heated argument over how long it took to unload a truck full of lumber. Stregger had quoted eight hours, and Fowler was after him on the quote, suggesting that one hour was more accurate. Stregger kept insisting that Fowler's suggestions were "hypothetical," until it became a contest of wills.

Whenever there were numbers involved, Fowler's carpentry math was accurate to the decimal place, and when there was a conflict, his math won out. Fowler's understated style is probably the only reason the judge did not call for a "time out," since Fowler seemed to know when to back off and give Stregger some room to recover.

One interesting point raised in the questioning was that the quote for the materials was based on prices in Penticton, which were higher due to the smaller market, but the quote also included the cost for "cartage" which is the transportation of the materials from Burnaby to Penticton. If they were purchased in Penticton at the higher rates, then why were they driven from Burnaby? A small point, but the whole exercise seemed to be that values were built up in this manner from many small points that were, at best, questionable.

Fowler sought the answer to this, and Stregger was no longer resisting the questions. The questions and answers played out in a quick, rhythmic fashion:

"... but you don't know how the lumber got to Penticton, do you?"

"No, I don't."

"Right. You don't know how it was unloaded out of the truck before the construction started, do you?"

"No, I don't."

"You don't know how many people helped?"

"No."

"You don't know how many families were staying in Penticton to assist with this construction, do you?"

"No."

"Who asked you to include the 800 and some dollars for cartage, do you recall that?

"I believe that was [RCMP officer] John Taylor."

• • •

At the end of Fowler's questions, the second quote was not on solid ground. It would be up to the judge to weigh the numbers, but it was generally conceded that the Crown's contention that there was a $10,000 benefit had not held up to scrutiny.

If Clark had been peddling influence as premier, it was critically important to determine its value. Fowler had planted the seed that these numbers could have been conjured up to form the basis for the charges. A determination of Clark's innocence or guilt meant that the macabre dance would play out based on a series of carpenter's quotes.

14

The Source

The Crown's case against former B.C. premier Glen Clark—which has included allegations of political interference, cover-ups and criminal gang involvement—has wrapped up after more than eight months of pre-trial arguments and testimony …

At the height of the investigation, RCMP commercial crimes investigators were monitoring 22 channels to intercept phone calls and conversations.

Clark's telephone was not wiretapped, but he and Pilarinos were under surveillance for up to 16 hours a day. At one point, police had a microphone hidden in the alley behind Clark's home.

… Clark's lawyers have suggested there was a link between one of the lead investigators in the case and Clark's political enemies, pointing out that then-opposition leader Gordon Campbell had asked Staff Sgt. Peter Montague to run as a Liberal candidate in a 1997 byelection.

The defence also attacked the informant whose allegations prompted the entire investigation.

… On the stand, Vrahnos said he didn't believe that Clark was knowingly involved, but he worried that the criminal underworld had infiltrated the province's gaming industry.

"I was very concerned about gangsters, who already, according to Mr. Pilarinos, were involved in illegal gambling, in loansharking and in money laundering, entering the legitimate industry of gambling using the office of the premier of the province," Vrahnos testified.

—Canadian Press, May 7, 2002

Who was the source of the original allegation against Glen Clark? What did he hope to accomplish in making the allegation? Where did he receive his information?

The who, what, where, and how of Clark's downward spiral into a criminal charge began with a man named Dimitri Vrahnos (a.k.a. Dimitris Vrahknos), whose source of information was his friend Dimitrios Pilarinos. While assisting Pilarinos in his application for a casino licence, Vrahnos heard about interaction with Premier Clark.

Clearly, what Vrahnos heard concerned him enough that he wanted someone to follow up. Vrahnos circulated anonymous allegations listing his concerns, chief among them that Premier Clark was being duped by the casino applicants, who were connected to "questionable characters." Some of these questionable characters were alleged to have connections to organized crime. Vrahnos believed that one of the applicants, Dimitrios Pilarinos, a neighbour and casual friend of Clark, was conducting renovations on the Clark house free of charge in exchange for Clark's help on his casino licence application.

Vrahnos sent an anonymous letter to the constituency office of Gordon Campbell, then leader of the opposition. Vrahnos was worried that this was not going to be effective, so he sent a similar letter to the news department of the *Vancouver Sun.* The *Sun* did some digging on the allegations, and then they passed the file on to the provincial Gaming and Audit Investigation Office.

Campbell's office passed the allegations on to the RCMP. Three RCMP officers were key to the investigation: Inspector Bill Ard, Staff Sergeant Peter Montague, and Corporal John Taylor.

• • •

Who was Vrahnos? Vrahnos was a Revenue Canada employee when he brought forward his allegations against Clark. And he was an immigrant from Greece with strong connections in Vancouver's close-knit Greek community. He was a friend of Dimitrios Pilarinos and, according to evidence presented during the trial, Vrahnos had a falling out with the staff of the North Burnaby Inn one evening when he was out socializing. Vrahnos then had a falling out with the Burnaby RCMP when he did not feel they followed up on his complaint against the North Burnaby Inn.

I observed Vrahnos as a witness in the Clark case. He spoke in English with a Greek accent. He was clean-cut and well-dressed in casual, unpretentious clothes. Vrahnos spent several days on the witness stand. Sometimes he became flustered if it seemed that he was contradicting previous evidence presented either at, or before, the trial. He appeared to be concerned that his testimony be taken seriously and would sometimes become argumentative if the questioning seemed unflattering.

That said, he did not come across as an insincere man, and although he seemed judgmental and contradictory, he did not sound unintelligent. Sometimes he was clearly embarrassed by the questioning. Other times he seemed confused about when events had occurred, or what the details were concerning the casino application. When he became confused, and the defence suggested he was being dishonest or malicious, Vrahnos became belligerent, and he appeared to have more difficulty with his English. The overall impression was that this man wanted to make a good impression.

As a young man in Greece, Vrahnos had led a politically active life against a government and police force that he perceived as corrupt. This activity landed him in jail twice. He entered Canada by jumping ship when he was only nineteen years old, then lived and attended university under a false name as an illegal immigrant. He became a Canadian citizen in 1977, following an immigrant amnesty declaration.[1]

Vrahnos' testimony described an interesting series of events leading to his allegations:

> There were rumours within Vancouver's Greek community that then-B.C. premier Glen Clark was

helping a friend obtain a tentative casino licence, a key Crown witness told Clark's breach-of-trust trial Wednesday …

"The way it was presented, the premier was in Mr. [Dimitrios] Pilarinos's pocket, or the premier was doing something improper helping Mr. Pilarinos with his application," Vrahnos told the court.

Vrahnos said Pilarinos himself told him that the premier had made suggestions about the application and had set up a meeting with someone in Victoria. He also said Pilarinos and his business partner, Steve Ng, had hired a lawyer that Clark had suggested.

Vrahnos said he did not believe what he had heard and went to Pilarinos about it.

"What I said was that this kind of rumours were wrong," Vrahnos said. "I was offended that the premier's name was used in that manner."

Any slim chance the casino application had could be quashed by such rumours, he said he told Pilarinos and his wife.

"So what I suggested was that they tell [anybody] who wants to gossip and defame the premier that this particular application has been rejected and from then on they do their business in confidence and not tell people about it," Vrahnos said.

He testified that he didn't want to know about the casino proposal.

But he has told the court that Pilarinos showed him the proposal several times and asked his advice.

Justice Elizabeth Bennett, who is hearing the case without a jury, has heard that Vrahnos eventually went to the constituency office of then-Liberal opposition leader Gordon Campbell in August 1998 with allegations about Clark's role in the casino application.

> Those allegations made their way to the police and prompted an investigation that included a search of the premier's house in March 1999.[2]

Under the prosecution's questioning, Vrahnos said Pilarinos had offered Glen Clark and his children shares in the casino if the application was successful. According to Vrahnos' testimony, Pilarinos told him Clark rejected the shares, saying, "That's not why I do it." Vrahnos said that Pilarinos had been bragging in the Greek community about his friend Clark who was going to help him with his casino application. The prosecution painted a picture of a shady deal evolving between Pilarinos and Clark, dutifully brought out by Vrahnos.

> After the RCMP investigation began, in a strange turn of events, Vrahnos tried to warn Clark and Pilarinos, separately, about the investigation. This was presented as evidence, referred to as the Karmelita fax:
>
> The court was also given copies of a fax Mr. Vrahnos sent to Mr. Clark, while he was still premier, warning him that police were beginning to make inquiries into the matter.
>
> The fax, sent just after Mr. Vrahnos was interviewed by police for the first time, warned Mr. Clark to be careful on the phone and to get rid of all evidence of the casino licence application …
>
> He signed the fax "Karmelita."
>
> A day later, he sent another anonymous, warning fax to Mr. Pilarinos.[3]

The defence lawyers challenged Vrahnos' testimony, his comments, his credibility, and his motives. They raised the spectre of a vendetta against the North Burnaby Inn and its owner, and they introduced evidence of jealousy against Pilarinos. Pilarinos' lawyer, Ian Donaldson, was particularly cutting, perhaps in part because his client had once considered Vrahnos a friend, or perhaps because all of Vrahnos' information was, allegedly, from his client, Pilarinos.

> The informant whose allegations led to charges against former B.C. premier Glen Clark was lying, says the lawyer for Clark's co-accused ... And he didn't want to be "outed" for telling police these stories, Donaldson suggested.
>
> "You were trying to be everything to everybody, weren't you?" Donaldson asked Vrahnos. "You were prepared to lie on all fronts to advance your own ends."
>
> "I disagree with you," Vrahnos answered ...
>
> During Vrahnos' eighth day on the witness stand, Donaldson asked about letters Vrahnos sent to Clark and Pilarinos warning them of the police investigation.
>
> "Why were you lying to the police about that?" he asked.
>
> "I'd probably be in trouble, I thought, with the police because I interfered with their investigation," Vrahnos testified.
>
> He said he thought he needed the police for protection.
>
> The defence says Vrahnos had no interest in the truth but only in getting revenge on Paschos Katanas, a man he believed to be a silent partner in the casino venture.
>
> Vrahnos has repeatedly denied that hatred for Katanas is behind the allegations but has admitted he didn't like Katanas.
>
> Vrahnos rejected the suggestion that he was jealous over the casino proposal.
>
> "Did you ever suggest to Pilarinos that this business might have been something that you would have been interested in?" Donaldson asked.
>
> "Did you resent him in any way for leaving you out?"
>
> "No,"Vrahnos answered.

> "Did you resent him for apparently preferring Katanas to you … ?" Donaldson asked.
>
> "No."
>
> Vrahnos said if at first he was reluctant to believe the premier was involved, he changed his opinion of Clark after he sent him the warning letter.
>
> The so-called Karmelita fax warned the former New Democrat leader to kill the casino application, clean his home and office of any evidence and to be careful how he used his telephone and fax machine.
>
> "You have been used to accommodate the entrance of gangsters in the casino business in B.C.," Vrahnos wrote in the letter.
>
> "I expected that the premier would have gone public with it, that he would have alerted the police," Vrahnos testified Monday.
>
> Instead, Clark turned the letter over to a senior bureaucrat in his office and the Pilarinos casino application was effectively derailed.
>
> Pilarinos stared intently at his former friend, at times shaking his head at Vrahnos' answers.[4]

Once the defence lawyers were finished with him, Vrahnos' personal life was an open book, including a number of indiscretions like a practical joke that backfired when he "mooned" (showed his backside to) a group of children by mistake. They also brought forward evidence of a medical condition involving anti-depressants that was serious enough to warrant a leave of absence from work.

The cross-examination was hard to watch sometimes. The level of personal disclosure is a by-product of the adversarial court system, and the defence lawyers were masters at making sure that all the possibly relevant details were part of their case. The senior defence lawyer did the best job of examining the credibility of the information that Vrahnos provided to the police. David Gibbons led Vrahnos through a series of questions in a logical manner. First, he addressed the machismo of Greek men in the coffee shop:[5]

> "... And these men ... involve themselves in this macho discussion about who has the most influence, and inevitably, as it turns out, usually, none of them do; correct?"
>
> "I agree with you."
>
> "Yes. When you heard of the gossip at Minerva's restaurant, cafe-deli, you became upset because it appeared to you to be just more of the same? ... And in this new country that you'd come to, you especially didn't think it was appropriate?"
>
> "I agree with that."
>
> "And you told that to Pilarinos, and I believe his wife?"
>
> "Correct."
>
> "And of course, there's no way of you knowing at Minerva's restaurant whether any of it was true or not?"
>
> "I agree with you."
>
> "And I think you've ... said virtually the same thing under oath at your examination for discovery?"
>
> "Yes."
>
> "... And he [Pilarinos] continued to tell you these things about various people ... and you became quite concerned about all of this ... did you not? It culminated in you writing letters, or documents, perhaps, they're better called, some of them, to various people: the Liberal Party, the *Vancouver Sun,* Mr. Clark's constituency office, and Mr. Pilarinos?"

Gibbons turned to an exhibit that was a copy of the document that Vrahnos sent to the *Vancouver Sun.*

> "... under the heading, you call it 'The story'... this is the story that you were told by Pilarinos ... And you

write it out as best you could recall, I assume ... Not knowing whether or not it's true or not, because you ... weren't there, correct?"

"Yes."

"... And then if you look through that document, you'll see there in your story you discuss, first of all, in the first paragraph, you'll see that first paragraph under the word 'story,' where you say: 'The Premier suggested that Pilarinos apply for a charity casino licence.'"

"Correct ... I got three versions of the same story, yes."

"... Okay. So you had three different versions coming from Mr. Pilarinos about this?"

"Correct."

"And you're like everyone else, I suppose, when somebody tells you three different versions of something, you tend not to believe them; correct?"

"I tend to believe that it cannot be three, all three of them accurate ... All I can say is that I believed that there was discussion of what I was told, there was discussion that, to approach the premier or having approached the premier for a, for a licence of some kind ... I wasn't there, I didn't know, I didn't know what was happening."

"That would have had to have been verified for you before you would have accepted that?

"Absolutely, I agree with you."

Later in the examination, David Gibbons moved to the original estimate provided to the RCMP of the "benefit" in renovations received by Clark. Gibbons asked:

"You say in this document that the work was done for free ... A hundred thousand dollars worth of it, you say in this document?"

> "No. The $100,000 I referred to is the value of the work ... not that Pilarinos did $100,000 worth of work."

Gibbons turned to the exhibit of Vrahnos' allegations made against Clark:

> "Let's just see what you say here, okay ... 'The Premier's personal benefit ... has been so far the free construction work in his Vancouver and Okanagan residences (valued at over $100,000)'... I suggest to you that must have surprised you, the fact that it was paid for and not done for free?"
>
> "The surprise to me was the value of the work, which in the news reports was reported as being $15,000 or $16,000 or that kind of amount ... it wasn't clear from the newspapers what that implied, or where that belong. I couldn't tell by reading in the newspapers ... what was happening ..."
>
> "Did you see, you didn't see the building permit, for example ... that outlined what they thought the value would be?"
>
> "No, I did not ..."
>
> "All right. But were you led to believe by Pilarinos that everything had been done for free?"
>
> "Yes."
>
> "... So you're telling the judge here that what Pilarinos told you was that he did a hundred, over $100,000 worth of his labour?"
>
> "No ... The $100,000 I referred to was the entire work, the value of the work as I understood it to be ... the $100,000 is my own estimate ... Mr. Pilarinos did not tell me that it was $100,000. What he did tell me was that it was major renovation work. He extended the house. There was exterior work done. There was the roof

done with skylights ... There was bathroom, kitchen renovation involved, and exterior work and a deck in the main residence. What he did say was, 'I made it like new,' referring to the premier's house. And then, as far as the summer residence is concerned, he said that he was there—I believe he was there for two or three weeks, and he says that he worked his—off, working the whole time."

"He worked his ass off, he said?"

"Yeah. That's what he said."

"Don't worry about that word, we use that word fairly regularly in here ... What I'm troubled with is ... you say that it was free construction work. You don't say in this statement here that what you're talking about is his labour?"

"I agree with you. I don't say that, it's not very clear, yes."

"What you meant was, his labour was free?"

"Right."

"And you don't make that clear in here?"

"Right."

"And that the whole, the value of the whole construction project, as I understand your evidence now, including his labour and everything else, was over $100,000?"

"Correct."

It is worth noting that the building permit valued the work at $10,000 dollars. Then Gibbons asked Vrahnos questions about the transcripts from the pre-trial examinations, to emphasize that Vrahnos passed on information to both the RCMP and the *Vancouver Sun*. Vrahnos explicitly told them that the information was second-hand, the source was Pilarinos, and all information would have to be verified independently.

> "… I told them I didn't know whether the story is true or not … And I made it very, very clear at the time that this is secondhand information … And it has to be investigated and either verified or not. My objective was to have this story—this information investigated …"

Campbell's constituency office followed up on Vrahnos' anonymous letter. Campbell's assistant, Rachel Barkey, met with Vrahnos on more than one occasion in the late summer of 1998, interviewing him on the points raised in his letter. Her account of what happened once she obtained this information was provided during questioning by defence lawyer David Gibbons.[6]

> "Any notes that I made in regards to my discussions [about the information from Vrahnos] with caucus research were right here in terms of my second page of notes where I said I spoke—called Adam [Leamy, Liberal caucus research] and spoke to Adam."
>
> Gibbons asked, "When did you give these notes over to the police?"
>
> "I would have given these notes on January 11th [1999]."
>
> "So you made them in August [1998], you kept them until January 11th?"
>
> "Yes."

This may seem like an unusual process, however Ms. Barkey was working on the notes with Liberal caucus research, who in turn were consulting with the official opposition critic to the attorney-general, Geoff Plant (now attorney-general) and Liberal lawyer Clark Roberts. The document that was eventually used to generate interest in an investigation was compiled after considerable discussion between the offices. Barkey explained to Gibbons:

"… I had a conversation with Adam Leamy … And this is the document that he put together."

"This is Adam Leamy's document?"

"Correct."

"You spoke to Leamy over the telephone?"

"Yes."

"He then prepares this summary of what you told him?"

"Yes."

"He sent it back to you?"

"Yes."

"And when you get it you make handwritten notes on it?"

"Correct."

"And the handwritten notes are all yours?"

"Correct …"

"Did you fax your document that you made notes on back to Mr. Leamy?"

'Yes, I did, the Summary of a Story Told by a Third Party."

"Yeah, he sent it to you, you made notes on it, you sent it back to him?"

"Correct."

"Did Mr. Leamy tell you that he spoke to Mr. Plant and Mr. Roberts?"

"No."

"Did he tell you that he wanted to speak to them?"

"Yes."

"That was in August of 1998? ..."

"Yes."

"All right. When did you first speak to Mr. Campbell about these matters?"

"It was September [1998] … I have September 8th as the date that I spoke to Mr. Campbell about it."

Rachel Barkey spoke to Gordon Campbell about the Vrahnos allegations almost six months before the raid on Glen Clark's house.

• • •

On the matter of Staff Sargeant Peter Montague's involvement, Gibbons tried to press Rachel Barkey on the politics of the case:

> "All right. So on January the 8th [1999], for example, at 4 p.m. you became aware that Peter Montague was one of the investigators of the case?"
>
> "I made that note, yes."
>
> "Yeah. And since then you have had discussions with him about the case?"
>
> "Yes."
>
> "And you knew that he was one of the senior investigators?"
>
> "Yes."
>
> "Now, of course that did not displease you, did it?'
>
> "I don't understand what you said."
>
> "You were pleased with that?"
>
> "No, I didn't know Mr. Montague."
>
> "You didn't know him at all?"
>
> "No."
>
> "You knew of him?"
>
> "I knew of him."
>
> "Yes. We were told by way of disclosure from the Crown and through Mr. Montague that on the 1st of June, 1997 he met with Gordon Campbell and was asked to run as a Liberal, you were aware of that?"
>
> "I was made aware of that, yes."
>
> "Yeah. Did you organize that meeting?"
>
> "No."

"Now, you were the office administrative person in that bielection?"

"Yes, sir."

"Yeah. You knew that Peter Montague was somebody that had been involved in politics in White Rock/ Surrey?"

"I knew that he had been approached to be a candidate."

"You knew more than that about him, you knew he was involved in a municipal election effort on behalf of McCallum?"

"No, sir, I did not know that."

"You didn't know that?"

"No."

"What you did know is he was a Liberal, they wanted him to run, Gordon Campbell met with him just prior to this investigation, he thought about it and decided not to for whatever reason?"

At this point, Gibbons was interrupted by Bill Smart, "Those are a lot of propositions in one question."

Gibbons was not upset by the interruption, "They are all true, aren't they?"

"No," answered Barkey.

"What is untrue about it?"

"I knew that he had been approached as a candidate."

"You knew he decided not to?"

"I knew he declined, yes."

"For one reason or another?"

"Yes."

"Did you talk to him about it?"

"No."

"Then you were later informed that he was actually going to be one of the senior investigators on this case?"

"Yes."

"And of course you discussed that with caucus research, didn't you?"

"I do not—yes, I would have discussed it with Adam Leamy."

"Of course you would have, you were all titillated and excited with the fact that you got one of your own leading the investigation into the Premier of this province, ma'am?"

"Sir, the name was familiar to me, I did not start working on the White Rock bi-election until July [1997] which is why I made a note of it because we were discussing who I would meet with once the investigation was brought to my attention."

"That's your answer to my question, is it?"

"I was not titillated, no."

"Certainly caucus research was?"

"I can't speak of any knowledge of that."

"They told you they were pleased about the fact they had Peter Montague investigating this case?"

"No, they did not."

• • •

Although Vrahnos had insisted on anonymity in exchange for the information he gave to Barkey, after the last interview, Barkey wrote down Vrahnos' licence plate number and passed it on to the RCMP. The RCMP tracked Vrahnos down and then visited him at his home to expand their investigation.

Staff Sergeant Peter Montague was the chief investigating officer in the case. Montague, a politically astute officer, a known supporter of the Campbell Liberals, and one with experience in communications campaigns, was not called to the stand by the prosecution in the Clark trial, even though he was the chief investigating officer.

Montague was one of the officers on Vrahnos' doorstep when they confronted him to seek more information. Vrahnos testified that he was surprised and frightened to see the officers at his home.

Inspector Bill Ard, a tall, friendly looking RCMP officer, spent a few days in the witness box answering questions about the case, particularly about Montague's involvement in the investigation. He presented a sincere, guileless face to the courtroom. He was an experienced witness who remained unruffled in the face of some relatively aggressive questioning. Clark's defence lawyers asked Ard about the politics of the case and whether or not Montague's participation affected the direction of the investigation.

> "Were you aware then of contacts that (Staff Sgt. Peter) Montague had with the Liberal party?" Clark's lawyer, David Gibbons asked.
>
> "I believe I was at that time, yes," said Ard.
>
> Ard said he spoke to Montague about his Liberal connections. According to Ard, Montague was asked at least twice about running under the party banner ...
>
> "Didn't it strike you that it might not be such a good idea to have somebody with political interests like Montague examining key witnesses in this case? Didn't that strike you as a concern?" Gibbons asked Ard.
>
> "Yes, it was," the RCMP officer responded.
>
> "Yeah, because, of course, his approach might not be as professional as yours because he has mixed interests, perhaps?" Gibbons suggested.
>
> "I was more concerned about the perception than Peter Montague's professionalism."[7]

Although the RCMP appeared motivated to investigate Vrahnos' allegations, the investigation sputtered along, and was almost abandoned on one occasion, when an internal RCMP memo was written up stating that there was little basis to proceed. One officer recommended that the file be passed to the provincial Gaming and Audit Investigation Office. However, after the provincial government announced that the North Burnaby Inn was on the list of approvals in principle for casino licences, there was renewed interest in the investigation. This renewed interest was advocated by Staff Sergeant Montague. The North Burnaby Inn was already under investigation by the RCMP in another matter, a fact known to the B.C. attorney-general's office, and the rules of casino licensing dictated that any facility under investigation was not eligible for consideration for a gambling licence. How could approval in principle have been awarded? Did this back up the allegation that Glen Clark was using his political office to assist his neighbour's application in exchange for home renovations? The RCMP ramped up the investigation.

For the RCMP, the approval in principle of the North Burnaby Inn had all the appearances of corruption. Didn't this back up everything Vrahnos had been alleging? Vrahnos himself appeared to be a citizen doing the right thing. He had nothing personal to gain out of the exercise. But by the time Vrahnos left the witness stand, there did not seem to be a solid foundation to the Crown's case, unless there was independent evidence that the premier had interfered in the casino licence application. This evidence could only come from the bureaucrats or Mike Farnworth, the minister responsible for gaming.

15

Muddy Waters

Direct intervention by former premier Glen Clark helped keep a friend's application for a lucrative casino licence from being turned down, the cabinet minister in charge of gaming at the time testified Wednesday.

In a startling revelation, Michael Farnworth told Mr. Clark's breach-of-trust trial that he had wanted to reject the application, in part because of concern over the appearance of granting a licence to "a friend of the premier."

But after a private discussion with Mr. Clark, Mr. Farnworth said that he reconsidered the matter.

Five months later, Mr. Farnworth granted approval in principle to the application made by Dimitrios Pilarinos, who had given the former premier a good deal on renovations to his house and family cottage.

Ever since the Casinogate controversy became public three years ago when the RCMP raided his home, Mr. Clark has maintained that he had nothing to do with the application and took steps to insulate himself from any involvement.

Mr. Farnworth said, however, that during his meeting with Mr. Clark, the former premier asked him what was wrong with the Pilarinos application and offered a solution to a problem mentioned by Mr. Farnworth.

Mr. Farnworth said Mr. Clark then rejected his recommendation that a number of Lower Mainland casino applications, including that of Mr. Pilarinos, be turned down. He

> *recalled the former premier telling him: "We need another casino for the Lower Mainland. You need to take another look at this."*
>
> *Asked by Crown prosecutor Bill Smart whether he would have given conditional approval to Mr. Pilarinos's application if he had not had the conversation with Mr. Clark, Mr. Farnworth replied: "My recommendation was not to do that, give approval."*
>
> —*Globe and Mail,* March 28, 2002

Testimony from Glen Clark's former minister, Mike Farnworth, and from staff in Farnworth's former Ministry of Employment and Investment, was initially very damaging to Clark's case.

When the police raided Clark's home on the night of March 2, 1999, an enormous news story erupted over the North Burnaby Inn casino application. Mike Farnworth was on holiday at the time, and he returned early to face an onslaught of media attention. During the RCMP investigation, Farnworth was questioned several times. These sessions were the subject of controversy during the trial.

Farnworth was a key witness for the prosecution, and as he waited to be called to the stand, he seemed composed but nervous. Farnworth was tall and well-built, and almost bald, with a short fringe of light hair. He exercised regularly and dressed well. He had been considered a junior minister in the Clark government, since he was one of the youngest and newest members of cabinet. Farnworth had been elected to the B.C. legislature in 1991 when the Harcourt government came to power, but remained in the backbenches. He was a skilled public speaker with a good sense of humour, although he always came across to me as a little shy.

The first time I met Mike Farnworth was on the opening day of the legislature in March 1992. It was an historic day for the Harcourt NDP since it had won a majority government, and the outgoing Social Credit government had been decimated. The new official Liberal opposition, under the leadership of Gordon Wilson (Powell River–Sunshine Coast), consisted of seventeen novice provincial politicians.

As a witness, former gaming minister Farnworth was eager to help.

The world felt fresh, the legislature was abuzz with younger members than ever before, and it was a time of renewal and possibilities. Many of us were championing a political idealism that had been absent from B.C. provincial politics for some time. I put Mike Farnworth in this category of young, enthusiastic idealist.

I was an elected member, representing Okanagan East (Kelowna) and had given birth to my third child three days prior to the House opening. Not wanting to miss the opening, I flew to Victoria for the day with tiny Tanita, and with the help of a friend managed to keep her fed and happy while all of us, as newly elected members, took our seats for the Speech from the Throne.

After the excitement of the day, the speech was long, the room was hot, the seats were comfortable, and I noticed MLAs drifting off to sleep. I fought the heavy fatigue and tried to focus on the speech as I scanned the faces of the new government across the floor.

When the Speech from the Throne ended and the lieutenant-governor departed, it was as though a switch had been thrown. A loud buzz began amongst the 75 MLAs and their guests, and there was much backslapping and grinning. An informal handshaking session broke out on the floor of the legislature, something I had not seen before and have not seen since. New MLAs from both sides of the house crossed the plush red carpet to meet each other.

I was too tired and a little overwhelmed and did not move. As the first MLA to give birth while holding office, I found myself shaking hands with so many NDP MLAs that I lost track of names and faces. It was a blur of friendliness through a haze of post-partum drowsiness.

Suddenly an eager, friendly face broke through the haze to grab my hand and pump it with vigour. A soft but assertive voice said, "Congratulations on the baby. I think that's just great! I'm Mike Farnworth, from Coquitlam. You and I have something in common—we're both Generation-X MLAs. I think we might be the only ones. Even though we're on opposite sides, I wish you well."

"Nice to meet you," I fumbled out, and added, "Actually, Gary Farrell-Collins is Generation X, too," I remember saying, "so I guess that makes three." I was 27 at the time, and Gary and Mike were a little older than me.

As I sat in the courtroom a decade later watching Mike Farnworth, I thought that it must be very difficult for him to prepare to testify against his former leader and boss. If it was difficult, he did not show it, but then he seemed to smile more when under stress, as if a permanent grin had been tattooed to his face.

I remembered that there were many people who questioned Glen Clark's wisdom when he put Mike Farnworth in such a turbulent ministry. I also remembered how vigorously Clark defended Farnworth's abilities. Would the world be any different if Dan Miller had remained "minister of gambling"? Miller, who succeeded Clark as premier of the province, was an experienced politician who was ferociously loyal to Clark. Would it have mattered?

The first days of Farnworth's testimony did not go well for Clark's defence. The Canadian Press, on March 27, 2002, stated:

> A casino proposal by a friend of former premier Glen Clark was not a particularly good proposal and was not going to be recommended for approval, the former gaming minister testified Wednesday in B.C. Supreme Court.

Mike Farnworth said the casino application by Dimitrios Pilarinos did not score well and he was concerned about Pilarinos' friendship with his boss.

"I was also concerned from the political optics point of view with the fact that one of the applicants was a friend of the premier," Farnworth said, his voice dropping to a whisper as he testified.

The former New Democrat cabinet member said he was not going to recommend that cabinet grant approval in principle to the proposal for a charity casino at the North Burnaby Inn.

But the application was granted approval in principle at a cabinet meeting in July 1998.

Farnworth was so concerned about Clark's friendship that he met with the then-premier's closest confidant, his primary secretary Adrian Dix, to discuss the matter.

"I said, you know, it doesn't look good. This has the potential for problems," Farnworth said. "In politics, it's called optics ..."

Clark didn't tell Farnworth who his friend was or which application he was involved with, he said.

Farnworth did find out who Pilarinos was, however, in part because Pilarinos presented a business card of the premier to gaming ministry staff at one point.

Clark met with Farnworth in the days before he was given the plum job of employment and investment minister.

The portfolio included responsibility for gaming, which the then-NDP government was trying to expand.

Farnworth said he was surprised by the high-profile appointment, in which he replaced veteran MLA Dan Miller as minister.

Farnworth said Clark briefed him on his portfolio, explaining what was going on in each.

"He said, 'If you fuck up, I'll fire you,'" he said.

> It was unclear how Farnworth interpreted that warning at the time.
>
> Of 13 casino and bingo applications in the Greater Vancouver area, Farnworth only recommended approval of two.
>
> He said government objectives and the nature of the proposals were considered in his recommendations, but the score was of tantamount importance.
>
> "I picked, by and large, with the exception of one, the high scores," Farnworth testified.
>
> The North Burnaby Inn proposal scored only 46 percent according to criteria set out by gaming experts.
>
> Others, some with scores as high as 70 percent, were not recommended for approval.

When the defence had a chance to explore other lines of questioning, a slightly different perspective emerged regarding the investigation. On April 9, 2002, the *Times Colonist* reported:

> ... The NDP minister responsible for gaming in 1998, Farnworth agreed with suggestions by Clark's lawyer that RCMP Staff-Sgt. Peter Montague seemed bent on receiving a certain answer concerning Clark's guilt in the matter.
>
> "Officer Montague especially had a theory about how this whole thing went on?" David Gibbons asked, referring to a police interview Farnworth had two months after the Mounties raided the premier's home in 1999.
>
> "Yes," replied Farnworth.
>
> "A conspiracy to get a casino for Mr. Clark's friend in Burnaby?" continued Gibbons.
>
> "Yes," the witness replied.
>
> "Montague tried to get you to buy in?" asked Gibbons.
>
> "Yes, he asked the same question over and over," replied Farnworth. "The answer was always, 'No.'"

Montague, a member of the RCMP commercial crime squad, is key to Clark's defence. Defence lawyers are expected to argue the officer crossed the line because of his association with the B.C. Liberals, who were in opposition in 1998 and 1999 but now rule the province with a massive majority.

Farnworth said Montague appeared unsatisfied with his answer that the decision to delegate the authority to make decisions whether to grant approval in principle to a number of casino applications was Farnworth's, not Clark's ...

"Montague told you you were being set up from the beginning?" suggested Gibbons.

"Yes," replied Farnworth.

"He said you were a victim?" asked the defence lawyer.

"Yes," said the witness.

Farnworth said he told the police that Clark had wanted a new casino, but he didn't say which one.

The former minister of employment and investment also explained his rationale for granting conditional approval to the NBI group:

The government needed to find new revenue because a downturn in Asian economies had cut into anticipated revenue.

The Lower Mainland was the intended target of a provincewide request for new casino and bingo proposals because of its huge population.

Farnworth said he would have approved two more worthy proposals by Indian bands in Delta and Richmond, but they didn't have the support of the municipal governments.

That left Burnaby, which was open to new gaming.

Although the NBI application scored low—88 out of a possible 190 points—it was considerably higher than the only other application, so Farnworth approved it.

> "At the end of the request-for-applications process, if all the government had to show for it is a new casino in Penticton and none in the Lower Mainland, it's a bust," said Farnworth.
>
> He also said he would not have approved the NBI application if he had been made aware by investigators in the Gaming and Audit Investigation Office of their concerns that organized crime was connected to it.
>
> The RCMP asked the GAIO investigators not to tell anyone about their organized crime suspicions, Farnworth confirmed.

On the last day of his testimony, I saw Farnworth run his hand along his forehead and over his head, his brow wrinkled, a tense look on his face as he prepared to answer questions.

Gibbons for the defence was sparring with Prosecutor Smart over the details of Farnworth's evidence. Smart wanted to return to the role of the Gaming and Audit Investigation Office and the RCMP, and was asking Farnworth about his diary. Although the questions were technical and may or may not have been crucial to the case, I noticed with interest that Farnworth was trying really hard to provide answers and be helpful.

"I very much remember this particular meeting ..." one of his answers to Smart began.

I noted the irony. I had witnessed RCMP officer after RCMP officer take the stand to answer questions from the defence about the investigation. Whenever the lawyers tried to blaze a trail to Montague, they encountered witnesses who failed to remember details of their surveillance, had no notes because they were destroyed, or were unable to produce records to answer the questions. Montague's colleagues had, intentionally or not, created a protective wall of silence for him. An image of U.S. president Ronald Reagan answering questions at the Iran–Contra hearings flashed through my mind, when he frequently said, "I don't remember," and that was an acceptable answer.

So here was one of Clark's former ministers bending over backwards to assure the court that he could re-create meetings from three years earlier. He was so helpful; it was in his nature. There would be no Reagan-like defence of "I can't remember" in Clark's case.

The lawyers became so assertive that the judge had to ask Farnworth to leave while she sorted out the examination process. Farnworth left and could be seen pacing the corridor while the machinations of justice continued inside.

This is where Madam Justice Elizabeth Bennett really earned her pay. She was refereeing two talented lawyers in a high-stakes game. Smart was trying to backtrack over the evidence Farnworth had given regarding Montague. Smart wanted to re-create a timeline that could disprove Gibbons' strategy that implicated Montague's interrogation of Farnworth during the investigation. Gibbons was calling foul on the process.

The judge had to walk a tightrope between giving latitude and providing possible grounds for appeal to either side in the eventual outcome. In this instance, the judge gave latitude to Smart, except where Gibbons was able to cite law. In the parry and thrust of the courtroom, there was skilled legal manoeuvring on all sides. It turned out Smart had a lengthy series of questions.

The one fact that was clear in this exchange in front of the judge was that she had a thorough understanding of the structures of government related to gaming and legislative process, and she had an impressive memory of the series of events as laid out in the documents. I knew from my own experience that some judges did not read their briefing materials thoroughly, or that they sought assistance from the lawyers in "reminding" them of evidence. This judge was not in that category.

Gibbons appeared to carry the legal debate on this occasion.

Farnworth's testimony about the casino approval process, the motivation for a Lower Mainland casino, and the points system, was similar in content to that of the witnesses from government staff who spoke about how the approvals had occurred.

Much of this evidence provided strong support to the prosecution during the examination, and strong support to the defence in cross-examination. Rather than advance either side of the case, it muddied the waters.

The prosecution wrapped up its case after months of evidence. It was now time for the defence.

16

Sworn Testimony

Clark, in his third day on the witness stand, told the court he resigned in August 1999 because of the "unrelenting" media coverage that went on for months ...

After police "raided" his home, it was a difficult for him and his family, he recalled.

"They [the media] staked out my home in such a fashion that my children couldn't get to school," Clark told B.C. Supreme Court Justice Elizabeth Bennett ...

—*Vancouver Sun,* June 6, 2002

In a surprise move, the defence put Glen Clark and Dale Clark on the witness stand to tell their version of what happened. Glen Clark began his testimony answering questions from his lawyer David Gibbons, and finally, after more than three years of brief comments about the case, Glen Clark had a chance to talk openly.

> Asked point-blank by defence lawyer David Gibbons whether he helped his onetime friend and neighbour Dimitrios Pilarinos obtain a casino licence, Mr. Clark replied: "No."
>
> He gave the same one-word replies when Mr. Gibbons also asked him whether he ever accepted free labour from Mr. Pilarinos, whether he helped Mr. Pilarinos have the proposed casino site moved to avoid zoning problems, and whether he influenced former gambling minister Mike Farnworth in his handling of the application.

> Mr. Clark resigned as premier in August, 1999, after it became known that he was under criminal investigation in the matter.
>
> He testified that he believed his resignation was inevitable once the RCMP staged its dramatic, nighttime raid on his home that March, with television cameras there to capture the event.
>
> The publicity was too intense to ride out, Mr. Clark explained.
>
> Yet, while they were inside his house, police barely did any searching at all, he said. After they left, his wife found the material they appeared to be interested in and that was turned over to police the next day [in the early morning hours].
>
> Mr. Clark said he expected to be exonerated and the controversy cleared up in a few days or weeks, at the most. "At least then the party would be stronger, without a cloud over them ..."[1]

In Clark's evidence he tried to put the controversy in the context of his professional life as premier. He told the court that he "ran the government," while his wife Dale handled the renovations. He claimed he was busy with the affairs of government and was hardly aware of the arrangements to add 100 square feet onto their second floor. And he spent most of his time in Victoria during the construction period. While the renovations to his home were underway, he was extremely busy with the Nisga'a Treaty settlement, the SkyTrain extension initiative, the fast ferry cost overruns, and numerous political issues. This included legal matters such as the lawsuit against the party on the 1996 election budget controversy.

His evidence on the motivation for expanded gambling included the need for government revenue to support health care and education.

When it came time for the cross-examination of Clark by Special Prosecutor Bill Smart, the former premier became angry and flustered at the questioning that implied he had been dishonest in his dealings on the Pilarinos file.

> Smart suggested the real reason Clark resigned was because a court document outlining allegations of criminal wrongdoing against Clark was going to be released to the public …
>
> "Mr. Clark, you resigned when the public was going to become aware of the fact you were under investigation. That's why you resigned, isn't it?" Smart said.
>
> "Police told me I was not under investigation," Clark said. "Inspector [Bill] Ard told me that evening that I was not the subject of the investigation. Because I'm innocent, Mr. Smart, I assumed, naively perhaps, that in a matter of days, this matter would be resolved and then I could have resigned in an orderly fashion."
>
> "Mr. Clark," Smart said, "your lawyer, Mr. Gibbons, was told on March 10 [1999] by Insp. Ard that you were under investigation and he was hearing on the radio otherwise. Do you not remember that?"
>
> "I'm not aware of that," replied Clark, his face reddening. "He said to me privately, Mr. Ard, that I was not the subject of the investigation."
>
> "So right up until August [1999], when you were advised by the attorney-general, you didn't know you were under investigation?" Smart asked.
>
> "That's correct," Clark said. "I remember vividly because I had a meeting with the attorney-general, who told me he was going to have a press conference to announce I was the subject of an investigation.
>
> "We had a caucus discussion about that—a rather heated one—in which I said, 'Well, if that's the case, then of course I will resign,' which I did."

> Smart suggested to Clark he knew he was under investigation for months and he was hanging on, hoping the matter would blow over so he wouldn't need to resign.
>
> "No," Clark said, laughing. "Mr. Smart, believe me, hanging on in the circumstances I was in was not an enviable position. I was doing it because, first of all, my caucus asked me to, and secondly, the unshakable conviction of my innocence and the unfairness of this ..."
>
> Smart reminded Clark he earlier testified he had instructed his staff, after the police search of his home, to fully co-operate with police and provide full disclosure. The prosecutor suggested Clark initially exercised his right to remain silent and didn't give a police statement until June 8, 1999.
>
> Gibbons objected, pointing out that Clark never exercised his right to silence but allowed himself to be openly questioned by the conflict commissioner, the police, the media and the public.
>
> Clark testified his police interview was delayed because he refused to be interviewed by one of the police investigators—Montague—"because he was partisan and biased. He had been asked to run for the Liberal party."[2]

This line of questioning gained no admissions from Clark that he had acted inappropriately other than Clark's acknowledgement that he could have said more about his relationship with Pilarinos. Clark said that his staff were in a state of deep shock, and he expended considerable time trying to move everyone back on to the government's agenda.

Regarding Pilarinos, Clark told the court that Pilarinos kept bugging him about his casino application, and Clark kept putting him off.

Glen Clark, the former NDP premier, cast himself at his trial yesterday as the victim of an overzealous neighbour and friend who kept dogging him for details on the progress of the man's bid to secure a casino licence ...

In cross-examination, Mr. Smart noted Mr. Clark bullishly took on the Americans over salmon policy and the federal Liberal government over issues related to Nanoose Bay, a Vancouver-Island testing area for anti-submarine warfare technology.

Why, wondered Mr. Smart, couldn't Mr. Clark get Mr. Pilarinos, a building contractor, to leave him alone?

Mr. Clark said he was trying to be considerate, as usual, to a constituent in the East Vancouver riding he had represented for 13 years by 1999.

"I try very hard not to alienate people," Mr. Clark told Justice Elizabeth Bennett, who is hearing the case without a jury.

"I never lock my constituency door in spite of people protesting. I try to be very open and very careful in my dealings with my constituents and I was, in this case, as best as I could."

Mr. Pilarinos is also a family friend. Mr. Clark, who has two children, has said he met Mr. Pilarinos through a pre-school where his wife and Mr. Pilarinos' wife were executives. The families were part of a group of neighbours who met for pot-luck dinners.

"He actually followed me to another friend of ours [when] we were having dinner, and interrupted. You're right. He was bugging me about it. I had no advice to give him," said Mr. Clark, who took the stand in his defence this week. "I had no idea what the strategy was and that's what I told him."

> Mr. Clark said he urged Mr. Pilarinos to write a letter to Michael Farnworth, then B.C.'s gaming minister …
>
> The former premier also told the court he occasionally found Mr. Pilarinos' queries "aggravating," suggesting he phoned often to ask about the casino licence.
>
> Mr. Clark said he found the questions vexing because they intruded on a home life he tried to keep separate from his busy schedule as premier.
>
> "Mr. Clark, you're not a politician who gets pushed around," said Mr. Smart in cross-examination. "Surely you could say, 'This is my personal time.'"
>
> Mr. Clark said he made the point. "I was less and less polite. A lot of time he didn't phone. He just came by [my house]."[3]

It was during the cross-examination dealing with the payments to Pilarinos that Clark stumbled in his evidence, regarding the payments for labour on the renovations.

> In his fourth day on the witness stand, Clark admitted there was no payment for Pilarinos's work.
>
> Clark said he questioned Pilarinos about the cost, which he felt was "a bit light."
>
> Clark said Pilarinos was adamant that all Clark owed for the project—which included a new roof on his home, a second-floor balcony and a bedroom renovation that included a gas fireplace and hardwood floor—was $11,200.
>
> Pilarinos would accept no more, according to Clark.
>
> "Finally, I relented and I paid him that amount," he testified ...
>
> Clark said he had many discussions with Pilarinos about how the project had to be "on the up and up."
>
> Clark said he never connected the renovation project to Pilarinos's casino application, which was under

> consideration by the government even as Pilarinos picked out tile for the Clark home.
>
> He said he was concerned that the proper taxes be paid and that he not take advantage of his friend.
>
> "Did you say Mr. Pilarinos, I'm the premier of the province, your application is before the government right now, Minister Farnworth is considering it ... I can't accept something from you. Did you say that to him?"
>
> Clark denied he ever spoke to the then-gaming minister about the charity casino proposed by Pilarinos and his business partner.
>
> Mike Farnworth must have been confused when he testified that Clark asked what was wrong with the North Burnaby Inn proposal and suggested management could be hired to improve it.
>
> "We didn't have that discussion in any way, shape or form in this fashion," Clark said. "We had a general discussion."[4]

The admission that Clark may have knowingly received a benefit provided an opening for the prosecution. However, this would have to be linked to an attempt to advance Pilarinos' casino application in order for a criminal offence to have occurred. Whether or not the prosecution had been successful in drawing this link through evidence from Farnworth and other witnesses could only be determined by the judge.

On the eighth day of Clark's testimony, he faced a series of questions levelled at him by Bill Smart that contained accusations and implied criticism of Clark's judgement. Clark showed signs of anger and impatience with the prosecutor as he responded to the questions. Whether Smart deliberately provoked Clark's temper or not, it is clear that the answers to the questions were at the heart of the case. Smart suggested that Clark had not been forthright about his relationship with Pilarinos and that this meant he was withholding information from the public.

Clark fought back by trying to put his relationship with the media in context, citing the cozy relationship between the police and the media as an issue for him.

> "… Remember, the *Vancouver Sun* had seven full-time reporters working in a locked room for weeks before this [story broke]," Clark testified. "So they were pretty well ahead of the curve on the investigation, obviously working with police."
>
> But Smart pointed out to Clark that it was the *Sun,* not Clark, that first disclosed that Pilarinos had done renovations on Clark's east Vancouver home in 1998 while Pilarinos had a casino licence application under government consideration.
>
> Smart said that fact had been omitted by Clark in a public statement he made March 4, 1999, a day after police executed a search warrant on Clark's home.
>
> "Well, it was a difficult time," replied Clark, sighing. "I wanted to give a minimalist statement in the hopes that it could be cleared up very quickly …
>
> Clark recalled he initially decided to resign right away, but after an emotional March 8 meeting of the NDP caucus, he reluctantly decided to stay on. "I didn't want to give in to the unfair allegations," he said.
>
> Smart suggested that Clark didn't tell the caucus about giving Pilarinos a hunting knife as a gift for doing the renovations.
>
> "What's your point, Mr. Smart?" Clark shot back. "That I could have handled this better? You're absolutely right. But it was a very difficult time. A time of great stress and difficulty and I was doing the best I could."
>
> … Smart said no one was challenging the fact that

> Clark was very busy while premier. But he suggested that Clark made errors in judgment, including having a discussion with Mike Farnworth, the minister in charge of gaming in 1998, about Pilarinos' application in July 1998, before a cabinet meeting at which casinos were on the agenda.
>
> Clark denied he raised Pilarinos' casino application at that meeting. "There was no error in judgment at that meeting [with Farnworth]," he said. "It was a meeting about the Penticton Indian band [casino application]."
>
> Smart suggested Clark made a second error in judgment when he ultimately accepted free labour from Pilarinos for the renovations done on Clark's home.
>
> "I certainly tried not to accept any free labour," Clark testified. "My wife was involved in it and we both tried to pay for everything ..."
>
> "But ultimately you didn't pay him," Smart suggested.
>
> "Ultimately, he refused to accept more money," Clark replied. "I was worried about that."[5]

The floor was now wide open for Dale Clark, the "mastermind" of the renovations, to take the stand. Dale is not the kind of person who enjoys the spotlight. She is not short on opinions and has no problem carving out her own identity, however she is not a politician. This means that public speaking in a highly charged environment is not easy for her. The courtroom where her husband was facing criminal charges was such an environment, especially since she testified after her husband's closing comments, and he had become quite agitated with Smart's final questions.

Nevertheless, Dale took the stand to add her pieces to the puzzle. Dale Clark is petite, with a soft light-brown bob of hair, and a welcoming face. Since she had been cited as the person overseeing the renovations, she was asked about the series of decisions that led to the renovation work. Her testimony was a new story in this old controversy.

The normally publicity-shy wife of former premier Glen Clark entered the witness box yesterday to offer a more innocent explanation for the infamous home renovations by a neighbour who had applied for a provincial casino licence …

Dale Clark, a school teacher for more than 20 years, said in B.C. Supreme Court yesterday that she had wanted her cousin to do renovations after a leaky roof had caused some damage to their house, but her cousin was busy.

Their neighbours in East Vancouver were often talking about renovations they wanted to do in their older homes, she said. Mr. Pilarinos, who had done work in other homes in the neighbourhood, drew up plans and obtained a building permit for the work at their house without their knowledge, she added.

Although she felt Mr. Pilarinos had been presumptuous, she and her husband decided after a while to extend their credit line and get him to do the work.

Mr. Pilarinos initially estimated the work would cost about $3,000 and take three days. However, the building permit estimated the work at $10,000, she said, and the renovations took about 2 weeks.

She also set out details about the payments for the work. She wrote a first cheque for $3,000 "to cover the cost of labour, materials et cetera," she said.

She wrote a second cheque for $5,000 after she thought the $3,000 had been used up, she added …

Ms. Clark also told the court that she occasionally overheard her husband and Mr. Pilarinos in conversations about a casino application. Mr. Pilarinos would be talking and her husband would either just nod or look distracted, she said.

She also recalled that she overheard Mr. Clark tell Mr. Pilarinos that he did not know what the approval process

> was for a casino licence. "He would say, 'you just have to go through the process,'" Ms. Clark said.[6]

Dale Clark had not given any media interviews since the RCMP visited her home in March 1999, so when she took the stand the public heard, for the first time, about her perspective on that dramatic night.

> "My heart is just pounding," Mrs. Clark admitted, before taking the witness stand in defence of her husband ...
>
> She also gave an emotional description of the night three RCMP officers arrived at the family home in 1999 to search the house.
>
> "The first thought was that Glen had been killed in a plane crash," she said. "I remember standing there thinking which of these lucky guys gets to tell me."
>
> Instead, they handed her a search warrant. "It was a bit of a relief," she said. "I looked at the manila envelope but my hands were shaking so hard [it was difficult to read]."
>
> The officers waited in the front room, while she frantically made telephone calls trying to locate Mr. Clark, who was in Cabinet offices. After he arrived home, Mrs. Clark gathered up some receipts related to the renovations, which she turned over to the police.
>
> For the embattled Mr. Clark, who earlier in the day had struggled to remain composed during cross-examination, the appearance of his wife in court was an emotional moment.
>
> Throughout his 13-year political career—and during this long trial, which began last September—Mr. Clark has tried to maintain a firewall around his personal life. That wall collapsed yesterday when Mrs. Clark walked into the courtroom after taking several deep breaths to steady herself.

Mr. Clark said outside court he was worried that if she became emotional, he would too. But Mrs. Clark testified calmly and at times even managed to laugh about her inability to recall details from years ago.

Mrs. Clark has always avoided the public stage. Her privacy, she has said, was a way to cushion the family from the high-pressure political life he was leading.

While her husband was premier, Mrs. Clark made only two notable public appearances. She christened a new ferry at a launch ceremony and shortly before Mr. Clark resigned, because of the police investigation, she attended an NDP convention. During that meeting, Mr. Clark gestured toward her in the stands, and thanked her for always being there for him. She got a thunderous standing ovation—and he left the stage in tears.[7]

The closing arguments lasted a week, including the rebuttal. Estimates of the cost of the criminal investigation and the following trial were in the millions of dollars.

17

The Last Day of Testimony

Former British Columbia premier Glen Clark owes a would-be casino owner $1,300 for renovations to his family's cabin, a building expert testified in B.C. Supreme Court on Friday.

According to Evan Stregger, a professional construction cost estimator, a deck built on the cabin near Penticton, B.C., was worth $4,875.

After taking into account invoices and receipts supplied to RCMP by Mr. Clark's lawyers and assuming that Mr. Clark and Dimitrios Pilarinos shared the work equally, $1,311 is outstanding, Mr. Stregger said.

"The total man-hours for deck construction is 64.35 hours and you've broken that down to … just over four days for two men working eight hours a day?" asked special prosecutor Bill Smart.

"Correct," answered Mr. Stregger.

Mr. Pilarinos would have contributed labour worth $727 under Fair Wage Act rates enacted by the New Democrat government under Mr. Clark, according to Mr. Stregger.

The rest of his contribution came in the form of equipment and materials that he supplied and does not appear to be reimbursed for, according to the Crown.

—*Globe and Mail,* February 1, 2002

The criminal trial of former premier Glen Clark ran months longer than anyone anticipated. The pre-trial hearings began in the early fall of 2001, and they ran for weeks, with legal wrangling on different issues. The defence tried to have wiretapped evidence disallowed, introducing evidence of partisan political influence. The major media companies made applications to try to have cameras and broadcast recording devices allowed in the courtroom. In the end, neither of these applications were successful. The jostling and jockeying of the lawyers settled down before Christmas as all parties prepared for the trial, which opened in mid-January.

The trial ended on June 28, 2002, more than three years after the night of the raid on Clark's house. It was a gloomy day for June, with the promise of rain looming over the city as my cab negotiated the traffic to the courthouse. I had flown in from Powell River that morning to catch the last day of the trial, and the thick unseasonable clouds were clinging to the mountains and cooling the day.

The courtroom was relatively crowded. Attendance had been slowly growing as the media stories filtered out over the months. Most of the people attending were members of the public interested in the proceedings; some of them were former political supporters of Clark. Ian Waddell, Gerard Janssen, and Gordon Wilson were the only former elected colleagues of Clark to attend the courtroom in a show of support.

The buzz in the courtroom was friendly on this last day, and I noted the difference in feeling—a stark contrast to the tense environment of the beginning of the trial, with the forced laughter and polite, strained smiles. On this last day, some members of the media were talking quite openly to Clark, and snippets of conversation about work and holidays floated around the room as we waited for Judge Bennett's appearance. It reminded me of the last day of school—regardless of whether it had been a good or bad year, everyone knew they were about to be dismissed from class.

Clark looked tired but somehow more relaxed. I noted that he was dressed well, in an electric blue shirt, matching tie, and smart suit; his new-found entrepreneurial pursuits were obviously rubbing off on his wardrobe. He presented quite a contrast to his years in office where his clothes were more suited to a labour-leaning, socialist ideology. Noting the change, I was amused to think he would likely be offended if I remarked on it.

On the last day of a criminal case, the defence had a chance to present a rebuttal to the prosecution's closing statements, and David Gibbons was preparing to make his final comments. It had been a week of closings, beginning with Pilarinos' lawyer, Ian Donaldson, providing a concise summary of his case. After Bill Smart's passionate defence of the Crown's case, Clark's lawyers had to sharpen their pencils.

The Crown's case was that Premier Glen Clark received $10,000 in home renovations, for which he did not pay. In exchange for this benefit, he used his office as premier to assist Dimitrios Pilarinos, his friend and the general contractor who did the home renovations, in obtaining approval in principle for a casino licence.

In order to prove this case, the Crown, under the direction of Bill Smart, had to:

- demonstrate the value of work that was not paid.
- provide evidence of interference by Premier Clark in the awarding of approval in principle on a casino licence.
- convince the judge that the two actions were linked.

The Crown engaged expert witnesses in obtaining valuations, and both of them were challenged in cross-examination until the original $10,000 was substantially reduced. Regardless, it would still be a problem for Clark if he had knowingly not paid for the full cost of his renovations and, in return for this benefit, had pulled strings on behalf of Pilarinos and the North Burnaby Inn.

The judge looked less tired than previously. Madam Justice Elizabeth Bennett appeared to be in her late 30s. She was attractive, with an almost-shoulder length cut of thick dark hair. And she had a dimple when she smiled, which was rare. Her dark eyes followed everything in the trial, and her forehead often creased in a thoughtful frown as she processed the information presented to her. Her patience had been obvious in many instances, and her written presentations on rulings throughout the trial were thorough, intellectual, and full of legal references.

Everyone expected Gibbons to close with one of his trademark scathing speeches, a vehement defence of this client, a lambasting of the Crown. Instead, he provided an articulate, thoughtful, methodical rendering of his case in a very persuasive presentation. It was like a scholarly chat with the judge, and the rest of us in the courtroom were just lucky to be present to hear this summary of the previous months' proceedings.

It was very impressive.

Judge Bennett had to be looking forward to the end of the trial, but she gave no indication of her feelings, remaining as stern as ever. She was very careful and very good at her job. She looked like she could clean up in a poker match. At one point, Gibbons made a joke, and everyone laughed, including Bennett. She looked so much younger when she smiled, and very playful. It was as if a mask had slipped, but it had slipped briefly, and she resumed her professional air. Sometimes there was a hint that she had a good sense of humour, but clearly she liked to have a controlled, professional atmosphere in the courtroom. Too much humour, or too much posturing, was discouraged by the occasional comment from the judge's seat. Otherwise, she rarely interrupted.

Gibbons began:

> Basically, My Lady, the Crown here has asked you to convict Mr. Clark on statements made out of court, not in the presence of the accused, and argue to the court that these statements are necessary and reliable. Now, this of course is opposed to Mr. Clark's evidence under oath which was cross-examined for days, and it was evidence that did not change from the first statement he made to the police to when he gave evidence here in court.
>
> … the hearsay evidence that the Crown asks you to rely on does not meet with the principled approach in Starr, My Lady, and you have very succinctly outlined that in your ruling, in your previous ruling, and I won't read that to you, but I ask you merely to consider the evidence that

> the Crown asks you to rely on, these out-of-court statements, and see if it meets the test.
>
> The Crown implies that Clark deliberately and deceitfully withheld information … in other words, what he told people and what he did not tell people was carefully orchestrated to further Clark's and Pilarinos' agenda … None of this accords with all of the evidence; none of it accords with the fact that Clark had an overwhelming agenda as premier and hardly enough time to think for himself, let alone plan such a charade. I mean, just remember the evidence from these people. He didn't put any restrictions on their—he said, go and do proper investigations, do whatever you want to do. And every single one of these people called by government said that what Clark asked them to do was appropriate … none of Mr. Clark's actions were clandestine or secretive. None of the people involved in these matters, such as Farnworth and Ford, were instructed to do anything untoward or inappropriate.
>
> … The Crown has resorted to a conspiracy theory based on subtleties, indirect actions and oblique motives. In other words, the Crown's theory is speculation based on supposition and built on innuendo.
>
> … This really does underscore the court's concern about the unfairness of using hearsay evidence like this to convict an accused. When you look at this and try to decide what they're talking about, it's impossible to be sure. And you don't have to be absolutely sure, My Lady; you have to be nearly certain. The Crown has a high onus, a high test to meet.[1]

The courtroom was silent except when Judge Bennett interrupted him with a comment.

"We used to say '*morally certain*,' but—" she said quietly, almost to herself.

David Gibbons stopped, "Beg pardon, milady?"

She smiled, and responded louder this time, "I said, we used to say *'morally certain.'*" She shrugged, almost dismissively. "I think it's now 'sure.'"

Gibbons chuckled and replied, "Yes!" He shook his head. "Yes, I used to say all *sorts* of things to the jury, My Lady, that I'm not allowed to say anymore, My Lady."

A rumble of laughter moved through the courtroom. The laughter broke the tension, then the room returned to silence as Gibbons continued through the list of the Crown's case. He concluded with:

> The Crown's analysis of the evidence cannot be accepted because it takes events we know occurred and works backwards to posit reasons why these events must have occurred. In other words, the Crown's theory uses speculation to support fallacious, circular reasoning. For example, the Crown suggests Pilarinos must have been receiving advice from Clark or he would not have continued to go and see him. Firstly, that argument assumes that every time Pilarinos went to see Clark, they discussed the casino application. That point aside, Pilarinos' persistence is just as consistent with a desperate person who saw the casino application as one big break, trying to do anything to succeed ...
>
> ... The evidence just didn't turn out here the way, and I'm using the word "Crown" in the largest sense, including the investigating police and others, the way they thought it would ...

During Gibbons' address, Bill Smart sat back in his chair, hunched over his material, his head on his hand. He did not look up.

The trial ended at lunchtime after a minor diversion by Ian Donaldson, refereed by the judge, when it came to light that he had not been paid for his services. Bennett was careful to stickhandle this development in a manner that would not jeopardize the case that had just concluded. You could have heard a pin drop as Donaldson presented his material to her in as delicate a way as possible. After all the months of cowboy behaviour, Donaldson demonstrated that he was actually a man of considerable integrity by waiting until the very end to bring to light the lack of payment by the government for his defence services. "I have put the interests of my client, the public, and the ministration of justice to the forefront," he explained to the judge. He could not afford to wait much longer for a resolution.

When this was over, with the discussion and decision on Donaldson's situation deferred, Judge Bennett announced that she would deliver the verdict on August 29. Then everyone stood as she left, and we all began to file out of the courtroom. That is when I noticed that Dale Clark was standing quietly at the back of the courtroom. She was on a summer teaching schedule, and she had been sitting in the back row of the courtroom, near the door and a couple of seats behind me.

"Hey Dale, how are you?" I said to her, smiling, "You must be relieved."

"Oh, I don't know, ask me on August 29th," she replied with a nervous but friendly smile. She was nicely dressed and stood writing for Glen.

"Well, I'm relieved for you, then, and really glad it's finally over."

As she agreed, Glen walked up and gave her a hug and kiss as we all moved toward the door. We decided to grab some lunch together and catch up on things, and we headed to the stairs, Glen and Dale holding hands. A media representative approached Glen on the way out and asked if he would mind walking out the north exit, and perhaps answer a few questions.

"Sure, why not?" Glen answered, always eager to please. I offered to wait until it was over and join them later, but both of them shrugged and said I should walk with them.

"Don't you think people are going to wonder what the heck I'm doing with you?" I asked.

"Who cares?" Dale answered with a laugh. "Maybe you should hold Glen's other hand and really give them something to wonder about."

We all laughed and walked out together through the magnificent glass structure that was the Vancouver law courts, past Lady Justice with her blindfold, and Glen faced the media scrum on the terrace. The questions were about the trial, the emotional impact, the possible verdict, and once Glen had danced around these, a killer question came from one of the reporters.

"Now that this is behind you, do you think you might get back into politics?"

I groaned, while Dale turned to me with a mischievous grin. "Who do you think would be more scared if he said yes, the NDP or the Liberals?" We both laughed.

• • •

Lunch was very pleasant, seated on the covered outdoor terrace of Joe Forte's while the rain fell down in sheets around us. The conversation wandered past the trial—*we are all hoping for the best*—to our families, *how the children are growing up*—to summer holiday plans—*we really have to make time to meet.* Glen's job was a challenge he enjoyed, but the free enterprise focus was different from his past experience, and he was adjusting to it.

We spoke of the last week of the trial, with Glen wondering about Gibbons' low-key style in his final comments. I told him I thought it worked really well; it was a good note to end on.

Glen was still upset about the prosecutor's closing arguments. We had talked about this earlier; Glen said he felt physically sick when he heard Bill Smart arguing that he was a liar and guilty of fraud and breach of trust. "It was by far the worst thing I've had to go through in this case," he said. "I don't know why it affected me so badly, but sitting there listening to him really made me feel sick." He sounded so sad about it.

"Glen, maybe it was because after all of these months of sitting in the same courtroom with Smart, after all your testimony, you hoped that you had convinced him that you were innocent. Then after all that you were still hearing him say you were guilty, and you thought, 'hey buddy, don't you know me at all by now?'"

He looked down. "You're absolutely right. I guess that after all the evidence, I hoped he would have learned something about me. But clearly he still felt I was some kind of dishonest weasel. He kept calling me a liar, and he even went after Dale's testimony. The stuff he was saying, it was *awful*."

"Of course, he represents the government, and the government's position is that you are guilty, so he has to do his job."

"I guess, but he even *handed out copies* of his statement. It was pretty damning; I think he convinced a lot of people." He paused, shrugged. "My lawyers didn't hand out any statements."

I felt badly for him. "I'm not a lawyer, Glen, but it seems like the side that thinks it's losing is going to try harder. Smart must have thought he needed the statements—maybe that's a good sign."

Clark changed the subject, which was typical of his personality. He would seldom dwell on anything negative for any length of time, and he also did not like to talk about himself much.

While we were at the restaurant, Glen ran into an old friend, who hugged him like a lost brother. As well, a former political ally offered Glen his support. During this time Glen was friendly, upbeat, and full of comments about what was going on in British Columbia. Glen raved to Dale and me about the former political ally, calling him a political master, a potential future leader of the NDP. Glen was also enthusiastic about his old friend, saying he was a great salesman, describing their old times.

It was hard to believe that this was a man who had just finished several months of a criminal trial. Although the trial was finally over, the unknown verdict was going to hang over him for two months.

"August 29th will be the hardest day of my life," he said at one point, uncharacteristically revealing a sore spot.

"No," I replied, "August 28th will be."

He laughed, "Yeah, probably."

• • •

After lunch, I ran through the rain to the Vancouver library, and from there hailed a cab to the airport, as I was planning to be back in my own office that afternoon. The rain was warm and there was no wind, but I still felt like a sorry case as the cab pulled up.

"Where to?" asked the friendly cabbie.

"The south terminal please," I said, shaking rain off my hands, wiping it off my sleeves.

We chatted about everything and nothing on the drive out, and it turned out the cab driver followed politics. Since the Clark trial had been in the news over the past weeks, and since cab drivers often have a pretty good idea of the general public's view of current events, I thought I would ask him his opinion of what was going on.

"What really burns me," the driver said, "is that we're paying for that crook's legal bills. I hope the case drags on, because there must be a limit to what we have to pay, and then Clark would have to pay his own bills. I hope they bankrupt him, and then throw him in jail for a long time for what he did to this province."

I was surprised that he was obviously so angry about what had happened, but I did not want to interrupt. "I mean, here's the guy lying about whether or not he was friends with the Greek guy, then he gets a free deck out of it, and his buddy gets a casino licence. Plus, look at this province, the economy is a big mess and it's all Clark's fault. I hope he rots behind bars. The guy's a lying crook."

I thought back to lunch at Joe Forte's, and the juxtaposition of this image and the driver's image had a dreamlike quality. Then the cab driver recognized me and asked me why I wanted to know. I told him I was writing about the Clark years and was tracking the opinions of people, to keep in touch with public opinion. He seemed satisfied, and we continued a friendly conversation to the airport.

The cab driver's opinion was consistent with what I had been hearing constantly prior to the start of the trial. Before the trial it was hard to find anyone who didn't think Clark was guilty of something. I had noticed that some people's minds had changed somewhat because of the reporting of the trial. Clearly, some people continued to feel that Clark had been a wrecking ball of a premier with criminal inclinations, even after the publicity from the trial.

18

The Verdict

Alas, how soon the hours are over,
Counted us out to play the lover!—
And how much narrower is the stage,
Allotted us to play the sage!
But when we play the fool, how wide
The theatre expands! beside,
How long the audience sits before us!
How many prompters! what a chorus!

—Walter Savage Landor,
"The Play"

On August 29, 2002, Madame Justice Elizabeth Bennett handed down her verdict in the case of Glen David Clark and his co-accused, Dimitrios Pilarinos.

We had left for the courthouse early that morning, anticipating a large turn-out. All the Vancouver morning radio programs and newspapers had made reference to the decision being handed down later that morning. By the time we arrived at around 9 a.m., there was already a line-up of journalists and members of the public. It was a challenging day for us, since my husband's uncle had passed away. Gordon was to deliver the eulogy at the funeral that afternoon. Our daughter Christina Wilson was with us, and as we waited in line we could overhear the conversations, everyone wondering what was going to happen. Behind the barrier the curious gathered, hoping for a seat. So many people were anticipated that the trial had moved to the larger Courtroom 55.

It was hot and stuffy in the lineup in the waiting room, and the tree-like plants at eye-level created a jungle-like atmosphere. To hold a conversation with someone you had to weave in and out, around the pots and bench seats.

The media were all wondering how long it would take. There was loud murmuring speculation about what the judge would decide. Someone mentioned that the judge's verdict was 150 pages long, and this caused a buzz of interest. Would she read the whole thing? Her previous decisions in the Clark case had been lengthy, but she had only announced them and referred people to the written reasons.

Everyone agreed that she wouldn't read the whole thing—it would take too long. She would probably go over the key points and then just announce the verdict. People were predicting a one-hour hearing.

Suddenly one voice was loudly cutting in to the various conversations. It was Jack Munro, someone who had turned up many times to show support for Clark. He called out, "At ten to ten there's a meeting for all media people on the sixth floor in ten minutes."

There was silence while Munro bellowed this out, followed by a rumble of laughter.

"Why don't you go up there first, Jack, and let us know what's going on," was the reply from one of the reporters.

People returned to their conversations, everyone wondering how long the hearing would last. Christina laughed and said, "If I were the judge, I would make my verdict last until ten minutes after the media deadline, just to make them squirm." She was joking, but as it turned out, the hearing went well beyond the noon deadline for most major news. The rumour of a long verdict was correct.

When the doors to the courtroom opened, the security guards allowed people in to take their seats. One of Glen's former staff members saved a seat for Dale Clark, at the front near the door. When Dale arrived, she was greeted with hugs from a small group of friends. She looked fresh, but stressed. Gerard Janssen, the former caucus whip and MLA for Alberni, arrived with former government staff member Sharon Prescott. The courtroom filled up quickly, and it was clear that many people, including some media, would not have seats. Reporters spilled over into adjacent seats reserved for the court, and some of them stood along the walls. Dozens of people were turned away.

When Glen Clark arrived, his legal team looked confident, and Clark was sporting a new haircut and a nice suit. The place was filled with the energy of a big day, when everyone knows that something significant is about to happen.

The judge entered and took her seat. The courtroom went instantly silent as she began to read. It was her moment, her turn after so many weeks of testimony. She began her verdict with an overview of the facts, which was long, precise, and very thorough. She was clear and did not rush.

We knew we were in for a long session. At first, the courtroom was absolutely silent. David Gibbons sat forward with his head down, while Bill Smart was sitting back, looking at the judge. Judge Bennett read to a captivated audience for almost two-and-a-half hours, with few people leaving. Some reporters ran out to file noon stories, then returned quickly.

Judge Bennett showed her sense of humour while dealing with the allegation of a benefit on the Penticton cabin:

> … The deck ultimately had to be ripped down because it was not safe. Therefore, at the end of the day, there was no actual benefit to Mr. Clark or his family. Although Mr. Pilarinos did the bulk of the work on the deck, the Clarks and the Morrisons (friends who were also staying with the Clarks), also helped to build the deck. The value of Mr. Pilarinos' work was not significant. The value of the lumber he provided was also not substantial, particularly given the Clarks paid close to $1,000.00 for material for the deck. The Pilarinos family was invited to the cabin by Mrs. Clark, stayed with the Clarks for over a week and

> paid no rent. It is fair to say that the work on the deck was, in some ways, a reciprocal arrangement for the Pilarinos' vacation at the lake. Everyone worked or helped out when they visited the Clarks' cabin.[1]

Judge Bennett paused then, and as she read out the next line, you could hear the irony in her tone, "This is a common occurrence that no doubt occurs at thousands of cottages and cabins across the country." She shrugged, and looked up briefly, "For some reason, people buy cabins so they can work on them." The courtroom erupted into laughter, then immediately went silent again. "Mr. Clark said that if visitors did not help out, they were not invited back. I conclude that the work performed at the cabin and the used lumber provided do not constitute a 'benefit.'"

There was a ripple of relief through the audience, a feeling of silent assent, then the tension level rose as Judge Bennett turned to the first verdict:

> [207] The Crown must also prove beyond a reasonable doubt, not only that a benefit was conferred, but that the benefit was conferred to an official (Mr. Clark) as consideration for cooperation, assistance or the exercise of influence in connection with the granting of the casino licence.
>
> [208] The testimony of Mr. Vrahnos, the correspondence between Mr. Ng and Mr. Pilarinos and the wiretap evidence overwhelmingly support the conclusion that Mr. Pilarinos conferred the benefit on Mr. Clark with the ulterior motive of obtaining Mr. Clark's assistance in obtaining the casino licence. He told Mr. Vrahnos that Mr. Clark was doing things for him, that Mr. Clark had come through for him, that he had done renovations for Mr. Clark for free because Mr. Clark was helping him, and that he did free work for other people so that it would

> not look bad for Mr. Clark. The work was done close in time to when the application was under consideration. He tore up the cheque given to him by Mrs. Clark. He did not charge the Clarks for his work and that is reflected in the bill that he provided to them. I have considered the conversation between Mr. Pilarinos and Mr. Young in the Blue Button Club. However, this statement does not raise a reasonable doubt in the face of the other evidence.
> [209] The evidence demonstrates beyond a reasonable doubt that between December 1, 1997 and October 1, 1998, Mr. Pilarinos intentionally conferred a benefit on Mr. Clark with the intention that the benefit would be consideration for Mr. Clark's assistance or the exercise of influence in the granting of the casino licence.
> [210] I find Mr. Pilarinos guilty of Count 1.

The room was a confusion of small sounds. What did this mean for Clark if the judge had ruled that a benefit had been conferred? Bennett quickly went through the counts against Pilarinos, and one after the other, pronounced him guilty, except for Counts 3 and 4, which were based on the allegation that Pilarinos had tried to bribe Clark with offers of shares in the casino.

> [214] These allegations are founded on the evidence of Mr. Vrahnos that Mr. Pilarinos offered Mr. Clark a 15% share in the casino, but that Mr. Clark refused the offer. Mr. Clark denied that Mr. Pilarinos offered him 15% of the casino. Although I accept the evidence of Mr. Vrahnos that Mr. Pilarinos said this to him, I find that Mr. Clark's evidence raises a reasonable doubt on whether Mr. Pilarinos actually made this offer to Mr. Clark. See *R. v. D. (W.), supra.*
> [215] Therefore, I find Mr. Pilarinos not guilty of Counts 3 and 4.

When the judge finished with Pilarinos, he had been found guilty on Counts 1, 2, 5, 6, 7, and 8. In effect, he was guilty of conferring a benefit on an official with the intent to receive preferential treatment. Judge Bennett deferred her decision on the breach of trust charge until she had rendered her verdict on Clark.

When she turned her attention to Clark, people shifted forward in their seats. The place was packed, and it felt like we were all holding our breath for the decision.

> [268] In cross-examination of Mr. Clark, the Crown pointed out that Mr. Clark was no shrinking violet and during his term of office as Premier was prepared to take aggressive stands on a number of issues, including against the Federal government and the American government. The Crown argued that it was ludicrous to believe that Mr. Clark could not convince Mr. Pilarinos to accept payment for his labour. However, people often act differently in their professional as opposed to their personal life.
> [269] Mr. Clark paid what he thought was full value for the renovations. Mr. Pilarinos refused to accept payment and insisted that he had been overpaid. The estimate for the renovation, both from Mr. Pilarinos and on the building permit was $10,000.00 and this supports Mr. Clark's assertion that it appeared that Mr. Pilarinos had been paid.
> [270] I have not overlooked Mr. Clark's evidence that when faced with Mr. Pilarinos' hand-written bill, he knew there was no money for Mr. Pilarinos' labour. It is important to carefully review Mr. Clark's evidence on this point, because it is not as cut and dried as the Crown submits. I add that I accept this aspect of Mr. Clark's evidence.
> [271] Mr. Clark testified that this was a five-minute conversation with Mr. Pilarinos. Mr. Clark told Mr. Pilarinos that it did not appear that there was anything

there for him. Mr. Clark was concerned about exploiting his friendship with Mr. Pilarinos, as Mr. Pilarinos had a reputation for helping neighbours. While it did not appear from the list that Mr. Pilarinos had billed for his time, Mr. Pilarinos was adamant that was all that was owed. He refused to accept any more money. Mr. Clark testified that eventually he relented and wrote a cheque for the amount requested by Mr. Pilarinos. He accepted Mr. Pilarinos' word regarding what he owed.

[272] Mr. Clark did not know the value of Mr. Pilarinos' work. He was not there during most of the renovation. Similarly, Mrs. Clark was at work during the day. For all Mr. Clark knew, Mr. Pilarinos could have spent a few hours calling sub-contractors and dropping by the site. He gave Mr. Pilarinos a unique gift valued at a few hundred dollars.

[273] It was not unreasonable for Mr. Clark to accept the assertions of Mr. Pilarinos that he had been paid, especially given the original estimate for the project.

[274] A month of evidence in this trial resulted in widely disparate estimates from experts regarding the value of the renovation. One could not expect Mr. Clark, who had little experience in the area, to know that he owed Mr. Pilarinos more money or how much.

[275] In light of this evidence, I am not satisfied beyond a reasonable doubt that Mr. Clark consciously accepted what he knew was (or was wilfully blind or reckless with respect to) a benefit from Mr. Pilarinos.

[276] There is no question Mr. Clark exercised poor judgment in hiring Mr. Pilarinos to do renovation work for him when Mr. Pilarinos had an application for a casino licence before the government. However, there is nothing in his conduct that crosses the line from an act of folly to behaviour calling for a criminal sanction.

[277] I find that Mr. Clark is not guilty of Count 11.

There was a large, collective sigh of relief when the words "not guilty" were read. A few smatters of applause began, then suddenly it was as if they all thought "what the heck," and then the whole courtroom broke out in loud applause and even a little cheering.

A security guard who had been present throughout the trial was standing by the wall, and he looked to the audience with an expression of puzzled surprise. "*Or*-der!" he said. It was almost a reprimand.

Judge Bennett looked up with annoyance, as if the whole lot of spectators were students who had been acting up. I shrank back in my seat and had an impulse to yell out "It wasn't me," and that made me want to laugh. She said sternly, clearly unimpressed, "There'll be no more of that." A man ran quickly out the door, and about ten seconds later, with the courtroom quiet again, we heard a loud cheer from the hallway.

Judge Bennett returned to her judgement.

> [278] The fact that Mr. Pilarinos has been convicted of conferring a benefit on Mr. Clark, while Mr. Clark has been acquitted of accepting that very same benefit is not an anomalous result in the circumstances of this case. I have found that Mr. Pilarinos knowingly gave Mr. Clark the benefit of his free labour for the purpose of obtaining Mr. Clark's influence or assistance with respect to his casino application. Mr. Pilarinos was aware of the value of his work on the renovation. I have also found that Mr. Clark did not accept that benefit within the meaning of the law since he was under the impression that he had fully compensated Mr. Pilarinos. Mr. Clark did not know the value of Mr. Pilarinos' work on the renovation. The different states of mind of Mr. Pilarinos and Mr. Clark with respect to the benefit explain the different outcomes.

Bennett turned to the charge of breach of trust, and cited legal precedent.

> To count as a real crime an act must be morally wrong. But this, as we said earlier, is but a necessary condition and not a sufficient one. Not all wrongful acts should qualify as real crimes. The real criminal law should be confined to wrongful acts seriously threatening and infringing fundamental social values.
>
> The purpose of the criminal law is to sanction serious violations, which derogate from fundamental social values. The making of a personal profit from the exercise of a public office is certainly one of these. However, the criminal law need not sanction a mere technical breach of conduct, an act of administrative indiscipline or administrative fault, even if deliberate. The sanction of these comes within the domaine [sic] of administrative law, perhaps even civil (private) law. If it were otherwise, the criminal law would be constantly on the look-out for comportment which is of course reprehensible, undoubtedly blameworthy, obviously irregular, but which has nothing criminal about it. It would be necessary to sanction the police officer who had received specific orders to intercept all vehicles exceeding the speed limit fixed by regulation and who proceeds to make selective arrests. It would be necessary to condemn as criminal the civil servant who, according to the regulations, is required to receive members of the public in the order in which they arrive and who despite this, gives preference to and precedence to an older person, etc.

She went on to find Clark not guilty on this count:

> [289] When Mr. Clark spoke to Mr. Farnworth in July, he had paid Mr. Pilarinos full value for the renovation. No further conversations occurred between Mr. Clark and Mr. Farnworth regarding the Lower Mainland casinos

> until after Mr. Farnworth granted approval-in-principle to the North Burnaby Inn. There is no evidence that Mr. Clark knew that Mr. Farnworth would not grant approval-in-principle if he knew Mr. Pilarinos performed the renovations. Indeed, Mr. Clark thought the matter had to be returned to Cabinet for approval. I do not see how the failure of Mr. Clark to tell Mr. Farnworth that Mr. Pilarinos was not paid for his work on the renovation, in these circumstances, breached a duty imposed on Mr. Clark in connection with his office.
>
> [290] More importantly, there is no benefit accruing to Mr. Clark as defined in *R. v. Perreault, supra,* as a result of not disclosing to Mr. Farnworth that Mr. Pilarinos did not accept payment for his part of the renovations. If a benefit did accrue, indirectly to Mr. Pilarinos, a third party, there is no evidence Mr. Clark was aware of this as he thought the proposal had to be returned to the Cabinet.
>
> [291] I conclude that the Crown has not proved that this conduct amounted to a breach of trust.

Earlier in the day, Judge Bennett had dealt with the questions raised during the trial regarding Staff Sergeant Montague, and this led to controversy after the ruling was announced.

> [177] Before leaving the overview of the facts, I wish to make this observation: during the trial, repeated allegations of misconduct were made against Staff Sergeant Peter Montague. The defence theory was, in part, that Staff Sergeant Montague drove this investigation for political motives as he had been approached by the provincial Liberal party to run as a candidate. At the outset of the trial, the defence said it wanted to cross-examine Staff Sergeant Montague. Later in the proceedings, the Crown

> said that he would produce Staff Sergeant Montague for cross-examination. The defence advised that they did not want him called as a witness. The Crown had no other reason to call him and he did not testify. At the end of the trial, the defence again raised the fact that Staff Sergeant Montague had not been called and had to be reminded that it was their decision that he not testify. I find this conduct by the defence, of making serious allegations regarding matters that go directly to the professional character of a person and then refusing to take any steps to back up the allegations, unacceptable. The defence is given wide latitude in terms of mounting the defence of an accused person, and for good reason. However, it must stop short of allegations of professional misconduct which it is not prepared to substantiate.

This commentary was reported in the media as if Judge Bennett was chastising the defence team for raising the spectre of political motivations concerning Staff Sergeant Peter Montague. However, she was actually criticizing the defence team's tactics. What she said about the substance of the questions raised concerning Montague was quite different:

> [178] I find that there was no evidence in this trial that substantiated any of the allegations made against Staff Sergeant Montague. *Whether there was in fact substance to the allegations cannot be determined* because of the defence's decision not to cross-examine Staff Sergeant Montague. (Emphasis added.)

It is true that many people wanted to know what was really going on, and whether or not there was substance to the allegations. Afterward, many commentators on radio programs and political programs wondered why David Gibbons did not put Peter Montague on the stand after introducing him as such a strong element of the trial. The only person who can answer that question is David Gibbons.

• • •

Careful with his words both during the trial and afterwards, David Gibbons Q.C., had no second thoughts about his performance. Why would he? He won.

David Gibbons' law office is in the beautiful Marine Building near the Pan Pacific Hotel, and his personal office with shelves full of books has a corner view. Gibbons gives off the impression that if he travelled back in time a few hundred years he would still do well as an English barrister. He has ruddy cheeks and owlish looks that give him a wise but mischievous appearance. Imagining him as a boy, I think he probably managed to wriggle out of many a tight spot with a shrug and an offhand comment. At the same time, it is very difficult to tell what he is thinking or planning to say next.

Throughout the trial, there were discussions about whether or not the prosecution was going to put the chief investigating officer, Staff Sergeant Peter Montague, on the stand. Tactically, this would work for the defence, because if Montague was the Crown's witness, the defence could cross-examine him. When the prosecution did not call him, they offered him to the defence as a witness. The defence did not want him as a witness.

I asked Gibbons why he did not put Montague on the stand for questioning.

"Because I felt that I didn't have to call him after the evidence of the other Crown witnesses was complete. And in addition to that, very, very rarely does the defence call the chief investigating officer. Remember, their evidence is going to be from the point of view of the Crown."[2]

How often does the prosecution not call the chief investigating officer?

"Not often. Probably, they have their own reasons for not calling him, and I don't know what they were—but I was surprised that they didn't call him." Gibbons paused, then added, "Although there's nothing wrong with not calling him. It's their choice."

What about the judge's criticism of the tactics of the defence in not questioning Montague?

"It would not be fair to comment on that, because the judge would not be able to respond to my comments. I cannot comment on that outside of the courtroom."

If you had known that you would be criticized for raising the allegations about Montague when he was not going to be called as a witness, would you have done anything differently?

"I would not have changed my approach to the trial at all."

• • •

In the days following the verdict, Glen Clark was feeling pretty good. In addition to the relief of knowing the outcome and finally bringing to an end the years of criminal allegations, he was receiving congratulations from many people. Prime Minister Jean Chretien took time from his work at the Johannesburg Summit on Sustainable Development to telephone Clark. Chretien was very considerate of Clark and had been concerned for his family ever since the police raid on his home. Clark received congratulatory phone calls from the federal minister of natural resources Herb Dhaliwal and Alliance MP John Reynolds, and a letter from former Ontario premier Mike Harris.

In addition, Clark said that people were stopping him on the street to tell him how happy they were. They all said they knew he was innocent all along.

"I wonder what they would have said if I had been convicted," Clark joked to me, laughing. "Where have they been for the past three years?"

PART FOUR

And Yet We Wonder

19

Questions Remain

Gloucester: These late eclipses in the sun and moon portend
no good to us: though the wisdom of nature can
reason it thus and thus, yet nature finds itself
scourged by the sequent effects ... in
cities, mutinies; in countries, discord; in
palaces, treason; ... We have seen the best of our time:
machinations, hollowness, treachery, and all
ruinous disorders, follow us disquietly to our
graves. Find out this villain, Edmund; it shall
lose thee nothing; do it carefully. And the
noble and true-hearted Kent banished! his
offence, honesty! 'Tis strange.

William Shakespeare, *King Lear*

Questions remain about the nature of the Clark investigation. What was the role of the RCMP? What happened within the NDP to leave Clark so vulnerable? And what was the role of the current government and political establishment in B.C?

Andy Ivens, an experienced reporter for the Vancouver *Province,* covered the Clark trial and followed the story closely. Ivens said, "I think it is the most important case I can remember regarding our democracy. The police have to protect the public and they have to protect the premier. The cameras at Clark's on the night of the raid—it looks like a political move—how did it happen?"[1] Ivens noted that corruption is a serious charge to make against a premier:

> The allegation that the RCMP could do what the voters couldn't is chilling. The bills for the investigation and the trial must be staggering. If they convict [Clark] on half a load of lumber—it seems like small potatoes for a sitting premier.
>
> I mean, there are corrupt politicians, and they often go unpunished. Why so eager to get Clark?

Ivens also pointed to the timelines involved, which seemed extremely long considering the stakes involved for everyone. "Look at the length of the process. What happened there?"

Ivens discussed the critical element that led to the wiretap authorization by Associate Chief Justice Dohm:

> The choice to withhold information seemed to be setting a trap for [gaming minister Mike] Farnworth. If I were a cynical cop and assumed that Clark was guilty, I would be looking for Farnworth to provide approval in principle for the NBI application. The RCMP would not have received the wiretap authorization without the approval in principle.

After the Clark verdict was announced, former Social Credit premier Bill Vander Zalm and former NDP premier Dave Barrett both, separately, called for a public inquiry into the role of the RCMP. Barrett elaborated:

> The Clark case is a shocking case. I called for a public inquiry into the relationship between the press and the police. In many jurisdictions, if there is collusion or the appearance of collusion between the media and the RCMP, the case will not be tried. There will be no

> criminal case whatsoever if there is any contact between the media and the police during the arrest process.
>
> A hell of a lot is at stake, once that relationship [close ties between the media and the RCMP] occurs, all bets are off ... it is dangerous for a free democratic society because it means the police are in the position of dictating the agenda in the public arena.
>
> If the press are dependent on the police for a story, they will mitigate any stories that might be negative to the police.[2]

Ivens summed up our need for vigilance: "Think of this: in Canada, the RCMP is the FBI, the CIA, the town cop, and the palace guard. We respect them, and they've earned it, but they have so much power. What happens if they act inappropriately?"[3]

• • •

And what was going on in the NDP? The NDP party membership was tired after two terms of almost continuous scandal; party members had resigned over internal issues such as the leadership race in 1999. At the end of the final term, there were few ideas that appealed to the imagination of voters. The election campaign's apologetic tone did little to restore NDP credibility.

The NDP was almost wiped out in the 2001 provincial election. When the smoke cleared from all of the political controversy, and the election was held, British Columbia was left with a ruling party of B.C. Liberals with 77 of the 79 seats, and an opposition of two NDP MLAs.

Some NDP members thought this defeat was predictable. Fred Steele and Ken Charlish were two long-time NDP members who launched a campaign against party headquarters over the handling of new party memberships during the leadership campaign of 1999. Fred Steele said he was worried about the party's strength during and after that campaign, especially concerning the new memberships taken out.

> There were three-month old children; there were dead people ... The party imploded, because huge chunks of provincial Liberals were signed up—they hijacked the party; they just cared about power. They didn't care about the province of British Columbia, or the party. When you end up tracing memberships down to seventeen people using the same address with one cell-phone number, you've got a problem.[4]

When asked about the NDP's credibility today with some of its former members, Steele said:

> Slowly some people are coming back to the party because of the current government, but I maintain that the people who administered the party through the last election should have all resigned. You had guys down there campaigning for Ujjal, openly, when they were supposed to be administering the party. They are all still there.
>
> When you run a campaign where the premier [Dosanjh] of the province comes out and surrenders half way through, you've got a problem. Where were his advisors? They were the same ones who pulled all the skullduggery during the leadership campaign. This was ... a basic question of honesty and basic morality—there was no moral direction ... The executive was lost.

The NDP has often been referred to as a coalition of diverse interests. Prior to the election of the NDP government in 1991, these interests were working together on specific issues. Corky Evans, former cabinet minister and leadership candidate, commented:

> ... in about 1985 ... at the regional conference in Creston, when people like Colleen McCrory were still in the party, and logging activists from the IWA were in the party, the motion went on the floor to take 12 percent of B.C.'s land base and put it aside for wilderness, to be consistent with Gro Harlem Bruntland's report on sustainability. You know the wonder is that it passed and became part of Harcourt's platform. And the NDP carried it through and put it in place, the first jurisdiction in North America to do it. And this was when we were this unwieldy coalition of loggers and greenies and rural people and city folk.
>
> So when people look back on our years of government, they tend to see only the negative. I think that shouldn't be the story. Instead the story should be that our government was a good thing—it was all about how we hung together long enough to make this a reality.[5]

This coalition of interests broke down before the election of 2001. As well, many campaign workers were worn down by the constant attacks. The Green party's strength comes from disaffected New Democrats. The role of the Green party in joining the Liberals' attacks on the NDP was to further erode part of the traditional base of NDP support. The urban focus of the NDP in the 2001 election campaign left rural voters without a populist option; their choice was the urban B.C. Liberals or the urban NDP.

• • •

As for the current government and political establishment's philosophy at work, former premier Dave Barrett is not short on opinions:

> The current government is an amalgam of Socreds; some have even been cabinet ministers in previous Social

Seen here in their respective "premier" eras, both Dave Barrett (left) and Bill Vander Zalm have experienced the three-pronged assault of media, legal investigation, and their own party members—as if fighting the opposition wasn't enough.

> Credit governments. They are not really Liberals; they just call themselves this—this shell game has been going on since the turn of the century. You have to understand the context for this—there is immense wealth in this province. The power balance has always been in the realm of the very wealthy.[6]

Former premier Vander Zalm has similar opinions:

> I have always said there is a small group with enormous influence, and if you're not in with that group, you will probably be on the outs not long after. I don't want to put names on it, but I certainly don't have friends on Howe Street.
>
> I have said many times, a lot of the decisions that we see coming out of the present government, that don't

> make a lot of sense in a number of ways, are probably coming directly from Howe Street—they have another agenda, and it probably goes beyond the next two elections.[7]

Anyone who has spent time in B.C.'s corridors of power might quickly conclude that the reference to Howe Street does not include everyone on Howe Street, but is more specifically alluding to Peter Brown of Canaccord, and a small circle of powerful financiers who are active politically. If "he who pays the piper calls the tune," an investigative journalist would do well to check the financial backing of the B.C. Liberals and cross-reference this with their policy decisions.

20

Beyond the Headlines

The fundamental purpose of news dissemination in a democracy is to enable people to know what is happening, and to understand events so that they may form their own conclusions.

—Canadian Association of Broadcasters,
Code of Ethics, Article 6

Some people have been angry with the media for the attacks against Glen Clark and previous premiers. Since the media in general base stories on the information in front of them, how fair are these attacks? And what are the pressures on the reporters?

When the subject is provincial politics, a "wire service" story is often a source for the regional media, and that source is usually the press gallery in Victoria. The press gallery operates a little like an elite club of reporters, and from my observation there is an "inner club" that stays the same from year to year, and a larger, somewhat transitory group. With centralization of media ownership in recent years, an ever-decreasing circle of reporters is competing to be first with a story. Often the major media chains are represented by just one reporter, who may be responsible for content in several newspapers, radio, and television. So the reporter has the unrealistic task of following everything the government does, finding a story that meets the objective of the news editor, staying ahead of the heavy competition, and meeting the deadlines. The task is unrealistic, and of necessity, the reporter becomes increasingly reliant on "sources" within the government and the opposition—perhaps even the ever-quoted "party insiders."

In my time working for radio and television, I have attended sessions with consultants brought in to teach us how to find a "good" story. All the consultants were from the United States, and their job was to coach reporters and news readers in what "sells," that is, what captures the public interest. On a few bothersome occasions, we were told the public is not interested in politics—government is boring, so we were not to file stories or cover what government does. We were told to report on scandal, and because scandal sells, the only political stories we should file should be scandal-related. We were told that a sex scandal or a scandal involving corruption, especially if money is involved, was important news. The importance of the story was related to the power of the person involved. From these perspectives, it is not hard to understand that with limited resources and encouragement to find scandal, press gallery reporters are keen to receive information about politicians that is negative.

Another dynamic at play in the press gallery is what I refer to as "reverse cynicism," a condition whereby the reporters adamantly refuse to believe that politicians are planning scandals in advance, or working together to bring someone down for political advantage. I cannot explain why reverse cynicism exists, because it is the opposite of what one would expect. But it is there, especially with the editorial writers including Vaughn Palmer (*Vancouver Sun*), Mike Smyth (Vancouver *Province*), and reporters like Keith Baldrey (BCTV and Global TV). They scoff at the suggestion that the person feeding them information could have an ulterior motive such as the advancement of his or her political career. Perhaps this blindness insulates them from the consequences of stories fed to them by their "sources."

When the verdict came out in the Clark trial, I had many people say to me, why didn't the media figure this out a long time ago? I told them that the media responsible for political stories was the press gallery in Victoria, and they almost never talk about political conspiracies or motives. People are stunned when they hear this.

One person said, "I thought they were supposed to look for conspiracies?" To underscore that point, Mike Smyth was on CKNW radio talking to the host on the afternoon of the Clark verdict, and again he said, "I don't believe in conspiracy theories."

What is unusual is that the entire Clark episode originated in Gordon Campbell's constituency office with an anonymous allegation.[1] Whereas most anonymous allegations are ignored, this one was advanced by an RCMP officer who considered running for Campbell as a candidate. These are the facts that we know without any digging at all. The attorney-general provided special resources for an investigation and began organizing his own leadership campaign. He apparently held onto the investigation information for several months and then publicized its existence, prompting Clark's resignation. Then the attorney-general ran for leader and, after some questionable practices in the race, won the leadership. All of these actions paved the way for a landslide victory for Campbell.

What would it have taken to prompt the press gallery to look further into the story?

• • •

Glen Clark was not the first B.C. premier to fall victim to a cabal of ambitious colleagues or opponents. On the other end of the political spectrum, another charismatic politician swept to power on a populist wave to head up the Social Credit party, which had governed British Columbia for decades. Bill Vander Zalm emerged from the business sector to lead the Socreds to victory, but he ended his days ignominiously due to a series of allegations that were later found to be baseless.

The media circus began with an allegation that Vander Zalm was using the office of premier to assist the private sale of Fantasy Gardens, an amusement park in Richmond. This created an explosion of controversy and, according to Vander Zalm, had all the elements necessary for a great story:

> The media liked it when protesters showed up at Fantasy Gardens—it made great pictures and was easily accessible from the Lower Mainland. There were lots of reporters in the Lower Mainland.[2]

The press gallery had a field day with it, as did the NDP opposition, led by Mike Harcourt, who called for an inquiry. Ted Hughes, deputy minister to the attorney-general, conducted an inquiry to determine whether or not there had been a breach of any rules. Bill Vander Zalm recollected:

> Ted Hughes said there was the appearance of conflict of interest—and I had said that if it looked like there was a problem, I would resign. I was getting tired of it all; it was pretty hard to take. Perhaps it wasn't the best time to make such an important decision, but that was my decision.
>
> The cabinet under Rita Johnston decided that they wanted to keep the issue out of the election, and the way to do this was to charge me with breach of trust. That was the rationale—keep it out of the election campaign. At that time they still believed they could be re-elected, and they thought it would look good if they had me charged because it would show them to be impartial. Plus, they could say they couldn't comment because it was before the courts.

The effort of representing himself in the inquiry and defending himself in court cost Bill Vander Zalm over half a million dollars out of his own pocket. Vander Zalm did not know what it cost the province to follow up on the allegations.

People who followed the reporting heard about realtor Fay Leung, who made for a great story because she wore large, outlandish hats and made colourful statements that kept the reporters happy. According to Vander Zalm, a judge found Fay Leung to be a dishonest manipulator. In addition, two well-respected legal minds investigated all the allegations against Vander Zalm in great detail. Both Mel Smith and Nathan Nemetz concluded that there was no evidence to support the allegations of improper conduct or conflict of interest.

Vander Zalm also makes a distinction between the press gallery and the media in general:

> The media are all looking for a story, and on a slow day they will take anything. Then a competitor will pick up the story and try to add an element, then it gains momentum.
>
> The media in this province has played a major role in what's happened to the governance of the province. In my case, not only was it harmful to myself and my family, but the whole event, the publicity was bad for the province. Not only did it cost us economically, but people were watching, wondering what is happening in the province, wondering whether they should invest here.

Vander Zalm thinks that the reporters in the press gallery have slim pickings when it comes to "juicy stories," and this means they may make small stories bigger:

> There is a far greater danger with people in the press gallery fabricating a story or sensationalizing something than there is for someone in the general media—because their [the press gallery's] shopping list is much more confined, they don't have as much to go with. Because they have much less to choose from, they will take some little thing and make something much bigger.

How accurate are the stories?

> It's hard to tell—how does the public know if it's real or fabricated? Most people have no way of checking, so it gets

> by, and then is quoted in other articles. It becomes like fact—it's difficult to judge the accuracy of the stories.
>
> If you hear something often enough you begin to take for granted that it is a fact. In the *Globe and Mail* they referred to me as "disgraced former premier"; it colours people's perception of me. The controversy lasts for weeks and weeks on the front page, then the clearing is a one-day story that often doesn't even make the front of the paper.

One would think that a former NDP premier would have a different perspective on the media, but Dave Barrett, the fiery former leader who is never shy to speak out, has similar views. Dave Barrett has spent 55 years observing politics in British Columbia, which means he has seen many governments come and go. What does Barrett see as the role of the press?

> I was in politics for about 24 continuous years and saw a dramatic change in the relationship between politicians and the media. When I was first elected, into opposition, being in the provincial press gallery was a professional goal ... Some of the most highly skilled journalists were there ... There were many, many skilled people who were in the gallery during this period; they did a lot of research, and they did a lot of drinking.
>
> The press gallery room was a mess, but it was a sacred mess; no one was allowed to clean out anything. There was an ease of relationship between members and the press gallery ... They [the reporters] were after facts, not gossip, and I enter that point now, because the biggest difference is that a significant amount of journalism today is gossip journalism, called "gotcha politics" by noted former journalist George Bain.
>
> I call it gossip politics.[3]

Barrett believes this evolution from digging out facts to writing up stories has changed the working dynamic for many politicians.

> Press gallery reporters did excellent background research on stories. When a policy was announced, they gave detailed background and research. Editorials were not just a bland appeal to one point of view ...

Barrett has observed a different political machinery today, with communications staff and speech writers and an industry of political handlers.

> There was none of the spin-doctoring that you see today—it was more issue-based stories, the idea of having a government spokesperson just was not there. The ministers spoke for themselves; the idea of public-relations hacks was not there.

Barrett is also concerned about the focus of some reporters in the press gallery.

> The only ones who stay are what I call the gossip columnists. They make sure their stories are written with a vituperative account of the event, covering their own rear ends with their editors.
>
> They only have "nostril nose" stories, you know, they stick a microphone up your nose and ask you a question—the whole process is meaningless.
>
> Generally speaking, the reporters asking the question don't understand the question or the answer; they don't have the background. They haven't spent the time in the precincts to have any depth on the issue, and they don't have time to prepare the research for the story. Part of this is technology—the 24-hour news cycle, the importance of

> television in delivering the news—the approach has changed due to the nature of distributing news and the electronic medium. There were always highly skilled journalists, celebrities, but they evolved through peer recognition based on their skill and experience.
>
> Today you have newsreaders who become stars—you are the star for reading, not for collecting, or editing; this is bizarre. To some extent this has happened in politics; politicians have become readers instead of orators or politicians—formerly, you weren't allowed to read speeches, the most you could have were some notes.

In my experience, the majority of the press gallery reporters and editorial writers are educated and have an interest in fairness. However, they are guided by the editorial direction of their news companies, and the overarching drive to be competitive with the other news outlets. The media has been a powerful element in democracy since its creation. To what extent do we rely on the media in forming our opinions and making our choices? As voters in elections and consumers of the media's products, how responsible are we for its message?

Does the media lead us in forming our opinions, or does it reflect what we want to see?

21

Reflecting on Glen Clark

> *... Endanger them to observe their fears. Be tranquil to observe if they become lax. Move to observe if they have doubts. Mount a surprise attack and observe their discipline.*
>
> *Mount a sudden strike on their doubts ... Take advantage of their failure to avoid harm. Obstruct their strategy. Seize their thoughts. Capitalize on their fears.*
>
> —The Methods of the Ssu-Ma

You have to hand it to the ancient Chinese military strategists. They knew how to set out a strategy that would take advantage of certain predictable aspects of human nature. To a large extent, this is what the Campbell Liberals did in the years leading up to the 2001 election, although I would also add that they flattered the weak-minded, inflated the value of those who could weaken their opponents, and mastered the "divide and conquer" routine. Having said that, many members of the NDP were susceptible to this strategy, and this left them vulnerable to political decimation. Solidarity was a concept selectively applied. So what can be taken away from this exercise of poking around the entrails of the Clark years?

One perspective comes from former "insider" Adrian Dix, who was a senior aide to Glen Clark during Clark's years in cabinet. He also became Clark's part-time roommate in Victoria, as they purchased an apartment together. Glen would stay there overnight when the legislature was in session.

Dix ended up in the middle of the casino controversy, in large measure over the Karmelita fax, and a scandal over a memo-to-file that Dix created after the fact in an attempt to protect Clark. Notwithstanding his error in judgement, Dix is respected for his political perspective. He was featured as a political expert on several media outlets after the 2001 election campaign.

He knew Clark as well as anyone did during Clark's years in Victoria. Dix claimed that Clark was a private person, who kept to himself, and he valued his family and his private life above everything else. Dix noted that Clark seemed to feel violated after the police searched his house, and he tried to spend as much time at home as possible.

What is interesting about the North Burnaby Inn scandal, according to Dix, is that political scandals usually occur around the office or in a business environment. A politician's house is not usually a public place. This aspect of the controversy made it very hard to deal with, as opposed to a controversy over political patronage or ferry construction cost overruns.

Dix noted that Clark was unusual in the NDP, especially if you compared him to the other recent NDP premiers, Harcourt and Dosanjh, who represented poor ridings but lived in wealthy ones. Clark lived in his riding. In fact, Clark had never lived far from his current home for any length of time. This had influenced his choices in life. To the voters in his riding he was their friend, neighbour, MLA, cabinet minister, and premier. Remaining connected to your community can be a source of admiration or criticism, depending on your perspective. Clark could take part in community events and try to be a "regular person" when he was at home. He could also be criticized for not viewing himself as important when he was the premier of the province.

To some extent, Clark was a throwback to the working class populism of the NDP, which ended with the Barrett leadership. After Barrett, the party moved toward an institution of middle-class intellectuals, and the balance of power shifted, leading to a party of professional politicians and paid political operatives. According to Dix:

> Glen's vision of the NDP became a minority position, an old-labour vision of class politics ... this made the 1996 election a kind of political miracle. The NDP was removed from the issues of the interior of B.C. during the Harcourt years, and Glen ran a populist campaign and recaptured the hearts of many of the workers in the interior.[1]

In truth, according to Dix, the party turned to Glen only in desperation. "Everyone expected the NDP to be humiliated in the election." And there was no real organizational base to back Clark up when he did win. So when the Media turned against Clark, the party had "no organization, no grass-roots base, no community spirit."

Dix had this observation of the B.C. NDP and B.C. politics in general: "There is a mean-spiritedness to B.C. politics that is not confined to "the other party"—the political system in B.C. is remarkably lacking in generosity and appreciation to the people in it."

What about Clark's legacy?

> Politically he didn't do very well, but he did great as premier—he's an idea guy. Just look at education—the participation rate in education has increased dramatically. Against the advice of everyone in the NDP, and I mean everybody, he instituted a tuition freeze—and many people benefited. He invested in the economy during the recession to stave off unemployment. Over time, this will be recognized more.

• • •

Few people outside the political arena stop to think what do you do with an ex-politician? What about a premier who is in his forties, has a wife and two children, and is facing criminal charges? Who will hire him? There was a ripple of controversy when the answer to that question was Jimmy Pattison, one of British Columbia's best-known citizens and an icon of entrepreneurial success. Pattison and Clark share a few things in common—they are both from East Vancouver; they both work hard; they have strong personalities and are self-made people. And they both like to win. Pattison recognized these traits in Clark, and despite the controversy, hired him. Pattison said:

> Every area has its own political stories. I don't know whether we in B.C. are much different, although I guess we've had a few more difficulties at the top position, with a Bill Bennett issue, a Bill Vander Zalm issue, and then a Glen Clark issue.[2]

Why did Pattison hire Glen Clark?

> I always liked Glen Clark as an individual; he was always a hard worker. And he is quick and bright, and he had come up the hard way. He is an energetic guy, with lots of drive; we like people like that. He obviously is a leader, or he wouldn't have got to where he got to—these were good qualities for our company.

As Pattison talked about Clark, he sounded very definite that Clark was a good choice for his company. He acknowledged that at first there was considerable negative feedback from their customers when they heard that he had hired Clark. "We understood that there might be political baggage; we anticipated that. We planned for it, but once we made the decision to hire him, the decision was made,

Pattison attends the reception after the swearing-in of the Clark government, following the surprise 1996 election victory.

... It was a surprise to a lot of our people that he joined the company. But once Glen got involved, well, he can tell his story better than anybody," Pattison laughed as he said this.

When asked if there were repercussions to hiring Clark, Pattison refered to the tragedy of the terrorist attack in New York on September 11, 2001, which had a huge impact on the business community. And he pointed out that many priorities shifted as more important issues surfaced.

> You have to remember that before nine-eleven came along, there was a lot of negative feeling by a lot of people

> about Glen Clark. We anticipated that this would occur, and we had some fallout, but we expected it. We had no internal problems [with staff], but we did have some external fallout ... from some of our customers, lots of it, for awhile. Then it all went away, as time goes by ...

Pattison noted that the change was dramatic enough that he heard from customers directly, shortly after the verdict was announced in the Clark trial.

> In fact, I had a call from one of the people who was one of the toughest people on Glen Clark and the NDP—couldn't believe that I had hired him, really negative. Today he called to say how happy he was to see him get off. So that's how it turns around.

Jimmy Pattison is a successful man known as a critical thinker who weighs decisions carefully before making them. He is also extremely careful in an interview to say exactly what he wants you to hear; his comments are precise. For that reason, he deserves the last word in the story of Glen Clark, because perhaps if enough people had taken the same approach, British Columbia's political history would have been quite different.

What about the criminal charges? Weren't you concerned that you were hiring someone who was accused of some serious crimes?

> I did not believe that Glen Clark would do the things he had been charged with.
>
> I believed in him enough that I didn't think he would do the things he was accused of.

22

My Opinion

> *It is said that one who knows the enemy and knows himself will not be endangered in a hundred engagements. One who does not know the enemy but knows himself will sometimes be victorious, sometimes meet with defeat. One who knows neither the enemy nor himself will invariably be defeated in every engagement.*
>
> —The Art of War, Sun-Tzu

The Art of War underscores the need to have some understanding of what you are up against if you want to be successful. This applies to almost anything in life. It particularly applies to politics in B.C., which is a blood sport.

I wrote this book because I believe it is important to have a record of what was happening during a critical part of B.C.'s political history, from a perspective that moved beyond the headlines. This book demonstrates what we are up against in the world of B.C. politics. It also leaves many unanswered questions about certain key institutions in our democracy: the role of the RCMP, the slow process of justice, and the impact of the media on the democratic process.

Should the RCMP be impartial as individuals, like many government workers and the judiciary? I am uncomfortable with police officers who take phone calls from communications offices of government ministers before responding to the media, as reportedly happened in October 2002 in the case of a shooting in Kamloops. I feel nervous when I hear that a stream of police cars carried officers to participate in the NPA's candidate selection meeting in Vancouver, as noted on CBC Radio in October 2002.

When criminal allegations lead to a serious fall from a position of power, and the process of hearing these allegations takes three years, is this really justice? The shadow of a criminal investigation is difficult for a private person; how much more difficult is it for a person in a public position?

Can the media be trusted to weigh the impact of their stories on the democratic process in cases such as the raid on the Clark house in March 1999? Or is there a need for a media watchdog with some teeth? How could you have a media watchdog that could enforce media restraints without risking censorship? Was the issue the manner of reporting or the fact that the event was reported at all? To what extent should the media be held accountable for covering the scandals as a top story for several days or weeks, while the decision, if it runs contrary to the allegation, is given short shrift as a low-priority story?

To what extent are we too trusting of our institutions? Does this trust help create the problem in the first place? If we, as consumers of the media and voters in the elections, were more skeptical of the reports, would this temper the reporting?

In the cutthroat arena of B.C. politics, do parties that turn on their leaders to rid themselves of potential baggage help their opponents more than they help themselves? A party that turns its back on its own members when under attack by a bully is playing into that agenda. An audience that applauds when the bully scores a hit is also in part responsible for the outcome. And so the blood sport continues.

I have never voted for Glen Clark, and it's no secret that I am a right-wing centrist. There are many things about the NDP that I really, really don't care for, because I am a strong supporter of individual rights, and the NDP is more interested in collective interests. Ideology aside, what happened in British Columbia to pave the way for Gordon Campbell and Gary Collins to run the province is a nasty episode that cannot lead to good government. One example worth examining in a little more detail to demonstrate the strategy behind this successful quest for power is what is referred to as "Hydrogate."

In the scandal over BC Hydro that was dumped on Glen Clark just before his swearing-in, Gary Farrell-Collins said there was a "secret deal" for "NDP friends and insiders." The controversy led to a series of actions that hurt the careers and personal lives of John Laxton and John Sheehan. Yet it is important to know that in September 1995, roughly five months before Farrell-Collins raised this issue, the Liberals had received the documents from BC Hydro describing the public share offering. For five months they sat on these documents, knowing that anyone from anywhere could buy shares in this very public exercise. Then Farrell-Collins raised an alarm with a story he had to know was fictitious.

What happened to Laxton and Sheehan? As a result of this story Laxton and Sheehan saw their careers with the government disintegrate in a matter of weeks over the political fallout. I don't think this would have bothered Farrell-Collins; he would have considered them collateral damage in his attempts to get to Clark. Some people will say "who cares?" All's fair in love and politics, to paraphrase American strategist James Carville. History is written by the victors, etc.

In the BC Hydro case alone, the RCMP spent three years investigating Laxton. Just from an economic point of view, there should have been concerns. In B.C. how much money has been spent on false allegations? How much for court costs, RCMP resources, special prosecutors, auditor-general investigations, and conflict-of-interest reports when you add up all the allegations, investigations, and controversies from 1996 to 2002?

• • •

As this book goes to print, the Campbell Liberal government has been in power for about a year and a half. Their landslide victory was a result of many factors, including the promise to cut taxes and provide fiscal responsibility—including balanced budgets. They also promised no cuts to health care and education—all fundamental to "A New Era" election platform. Let's take a brief look at their record since May 2001.

The tax cuts promised by the B.C. Liberals were delivered; however, a freeze in health care and education spending created stress and increased pressure on both systems. Also, the civil service was cut back dramatically, meaning that not only civil service jobs were lost but many government programs were cut. Cuts in day care, pharmacare, and special services for the blind and for the disadvantaged caused hardship for those on limited or fixed incomes, especially seniors, students, welfare recipients, and the disabled. Many unexpected program cuts were also announced. Some programs were scrapped altogether, especially those that were championed by the Clark government, including the freeze in tuition fees, BC Hydro rates, car insurance rates, and ferry fares. Other government agencies, particularly those concerning the environment, such as Fisheries Renewal BC and Forest Renewal BC, were disbanded, with resulting job losses.

There were also increases in user fees in many areas, including health-care services and health premium rate hikes. For many British Columbians, especially those in low and middle-income brackets, this meant less disposable income.

In November 2002, the gain for the general public was not yet evident in "A New Era."

• • •

Like his boss, current Finance Minister Gary (Farrell) Collins made comments while in opposition that he has to live with today. In 1996, Farrell-Collins responded to the announcement that the Clark government could not deliver on the balanced budget, as promised in the election campaign. He told the *Vancouver Sun,* in an article on May 31, 1996,

> ... Clark's pre-election budget was always meant to win votes, not provide good fiscal management.
>
> "If he's going to now rejig his budget that 28 days ago was the best thing to happen to British Columbia—I

> think it shows exactly the kind of integrity the man has," Farrell-Collins said. "The only thing that needs wriggle room is a snake."

Five years later, Collins had his own concerns about "wriggle room," adjusting his budget several times, even amending it by half a billion dollars within a six-week period. Although Collins tried to point the finger at the outgoing NDP government, in fact the NDP had left the B.C. Liberals with a surplus budget that had followed two audited balanced budgets. Pre-election budget promises and the realities of governing had come home to roost for Collins. Although the B.C. Liberals believed their tax cuts would lead to an increase in spending and would stimulate economic growth, a year and a half after the election, the growth had not materialized. The *Vancouver Sun* commented on November 23, 2001:

> B.C. may already be in recession, Finance Minister Gary Collins said Wednesday while releasing a gloomy economic forecast for the coming year.
>
> Collins revised his growth estimate for 2002 down to 0.6 per cent, down more than three percentage points from the forecast of 3.8 per cent that he made less than four months ago.
>
> He also cut his forecast for the current year to 0.9 per cent, down from 2.2 per cent in July …
>
> A drop of three percentage points could mean reduced revenue of $600 million to $900 million …
>
> In July, Collins announced the deficit for the current year would be $1.5 billion. Six weeks later, he revised that number upward to almost $2 billion.
>
> In the quarterly report released Thursday, Collins raised the estimate for the deficit another $55 million to just over $2 billion …
>
> This year's deficit of $2.036 billion will be the largest

> since the first year the NDP took office.
>
> Without a one-time credit of about $1.4 billion relating to pension changes, the actual deficit would be more than $3.4 billion.

After the first year of the Campbell Liberals, B.C. went from a surplus budget to an extremely high deficit. Perhaps the first year was beginner's luck. So how did they do in year two? On September 14, 2002, the *Vancouver Sun* reported that the government "posted an $800 million dollar deficit in the first quarter this year and now projects the full-year deficit of $4.02 billion ... B.C. will have about $30.6 billion in taxpayer-supported debt by March 31, 2003."

The tax cuts that contributed to much of the Campbell government's revenue problem were supposed to stimulate economic growth, yet B.C. lagged behind the rest of the country. Economic growth in Canada was pegged at around 3.8 percent, while B.C.'s was less than 1.5 percent. The tax cuts failed to generate growth.[1]

Bill Tieleman, a political commentator who worked with the NDP during its time in office, wrote the following analysis:

> Only in British Columbia would a finance minister—while giving a report that shows the province has the largest deficit in its history and the worst economic performance in the country—have the nerve to say: "The quarterly report shows clearly that our efforts to restore prosperity are beginning to pay off."
>
> ... Take the projected $385-million reduction in the province's deficit, which will now be a phenomenal $4.02 billion for the year, says the finance ministry's first-quarter report. (It covers government revenues and expenditures for the period April 1, 2002 through June 30, 2002, and makes new estimates for the full year.)
>
> ... Underlying all this bad financial news is the fact that the centrepiece of the B.C. Liberal economic strategy,

> the $2 billion annual tax cut for individuals and businesses, has failed on all counts. Instead of enjoying a greatly stimulated economy, B.C. can't even match the growth of Prince Edward Island or Saskatchewan.
>
> And thanks in large part to the $2-billion-a-year tax cut, the province will have a total debt of $39 billion by next March, with overall debt projected to increase by $10 billion in the Liberals' first term. The interest payments on the public debt in this budget year alone were estimated at $1.9 billion in the February budget's "consolidated revenue fund, expense by standard object."[2]

After the first two budgets from the Campbell government, the deficit and debt were at the highest levels in B.C.'s history. Yikes. These were the guys who ran on *fiscal responsibility.*

But wait, there's more.

• • •

In light of the Clark trial, it is reasonable to expect that cabinet ministers would become more careful about perceived conflicts of interest or inappropriate conduct. However, in the summer of 2002, B.C. Liberals were promoting a private fundraiser with a B.C. Liberal cabinet minister. The controversy arose when it was alleged that the guest of honour was billed as a "minister," and access to him was an enticement to attend the reception. Although one *can* assume that perhaps the person organizing the fundraiser was unaware that this was an inappropriate action, the minister himself could be liable for political or legal repercussions.

Will there be an RCMP investigation? Should there be? Would there have been an investigation if the government had been less popular? If it had been an NDP minister?

Consider this section below, cited by Madame Justice Bennett in her ruling on Clark, referring to the Criminal Code of Canada:

> The government's business must be free from any suggestion of "under-the-table" rewards or benefits made to those who conduct business on behalf of the government by those who stand to gain from those dealings ... That integrity is compromised not only by bribery and corruption in their crassest forms, but by other insidious arrangements ...
>
> Quote from Judge Lyon: "... the appearance of objective, uncorrupted impartiality must be of the highest importance. This indeed is an ethic which has been given the full support of the criminal law in the section that I have made reference to, and the reason for that, I think, is obvious because the appearance of justice is equally important as justice itself. And the appearance of honesty and integrity in dealings by Government employees particularly where large sums of public money is involved must be at all costs preserved lest the failure to do so could result in de facto corruption, one perhaps sliding imperceptibly into the other."[3]

In this case, unlike the Clark case, there was direct evidence that the minister was complicit in trying to obtain a benefit or advantage, because he had committed to attend the private dinner. Whether the benefit would be determined to be direct or indirect could be placed in front of a judge, if someone was worried about the integrity of government.

Is anyone *really* worried about the integrity of government? Or is this concern selective? Will anyone ever take the RCMP to task for their choices and methods, or will we be too intimated by their power?

In a democracy, we are all in it together. The problem with the current voter attitude of "they are all crooks and cheats" is that "the baby is thrown out with the bathwater" by voters who tune out what is going on. It is easy to see why people become discouraged when they do not know who is telling the truth. The problem with increased voter cynicism is that people stop showing up to vote, which means they voluntarily give up their right to select the leaders who will determine the future of their social, legal, and economic system.

In British Columbia today, those of us in the middle of the political spectrum are left with no choice for the next election. Much of this is a direct by-product of the systemic attacks on many people who have ventured forward to try to effect populist change, while taking on the entrenched power system. Most of these people have been chewed up and unceremoniously spat out, while armchair critics have filled radio airwaves and letters to the editor columns with vitriolic repetition of the fraudulent allegations against them.

Heck of a way to run a province.

In a democracy we always get the government we deserve.

• • •

My great-great-grandfather, Badruddin Tyabji, was president of the Indian National Congress and fought hard for Indian unity at a time when the country was torn by religious strife, confrontation, and ideological clashes. He recognized that cynicism can be self-defeating, and that in some respects it is our approach to government that will either define us, or define the government we seek to influence. In his presidential address to the congress at Madras in 1887, Badruddin Tyabji stated:

> Be moderate in your demands, be just in your criticism, be accurate in your facts, be logical in your conclusions, and you may rest assured that any propositions you may make to our rulers will be received with that benign consideration which is the characteristic of a strong and enlightened government.

Epilogue

By November 2002, the dust was finally settling on the Clark era in British Columbia. The North Burnaby Inn still did not have a casino licence, but then it never was destined to have one—despite many public assertions to the contrary. The approval in principle that triggered the search warrants on Clark's house was only a preliminary step in the approval process. Had the RCMP started their investigation by checking the process, they would have learned that the input of other agencies would have killed this application long before a licence was issued.

What befell the main characters in the Clark-era story? In the course of writing this book, only three of them did not respond to written requests for interviews: Ujjal Dosanjh, Peter Montague, and Joy MacPhail, but we do know something of their activities. MacPhail was the leader of the NDP opposition and one of two opposition MLAs re-elected in 2001—the other was the NDP's Jenny Kwan.

Ujjal Dosanjh was practising law in a Vancouver firm with two of his three sons who were lawyers. He continued to make the news. A story in the Ottawa *Hill-Times* stated that he was working on Paul Martin's leadership bid for the federal Liberals, helping Martin sign up Indo-Canadians from the Sikh community. There was speculation from "Liberal insiders" that Dosanjh might run for the Liberals if Martin won the leadership.

Staff Sergeant Peter Montague retired from the RCMP after 31 years of service. Before retiring, Montague provided an exclusive interview to Robert Matas of the *Globe and Mail* ("Investigator tells his side of Glen Clark fiasco," October 28, 2002). In the article, Montague said he regretted that the RCMP did not break into Clark's house on March 2, 1999 while no one was home, because if they had, the cameras would not have been present, and there would not have been so much controversy. He also stated that his Liberal party connections were limited to a lunch meeting with Gordon Campbell. This contradicted the testimony of a colleague, Constable Bill Ard, who confirmed that Montague was asked at least twice to run as a candidate. Montague indicated a lack of close contact with the media, particularly reporter John Daly. That seemed inconsistent with the wording on the invitation to his retirement luncheon hosted by Corporal John Taylor. The invitations were sent out to many reporters stating that Montague had spent 31 years in the RCMP and "throughout those years, he has developed numerous friendships with people working in the news media industry. You are invited to join Peter ..." John Daly and Gary Hanney, who covered the raid on Clark's house, accepted the invitation and went one step further, presenting a gift to Montague. Later they refused to comment on the gift's significance.

Montague also indicated in the article that he was reluctant to investigate the case: "We do not want to investigate some of these more high-profile figures. We know we are going to get extreme flak ... no matter what we do. No one likes to go into a situation knowing you're dammed if you do and damned if you don't." These assertions are ironic, in that by all accounts the investigation was going to be shelved for lack of evidence until Montague advocated that the case be resurrected.

In a judgement that appeared to be well-received, Madame Justice Elizabeth Bennett sentenced Dimitrios Pilarinos to daily house arrest from 7 p.m. to 6 a.m. for a period of two years, less a day. She also demanded that Pilarinos surrender his passport and perform 240 hours of community work service. Ian Donaldson read out a letter from Pilarinos to the court that said, in part:

> I deeply regret and feel horrible for what I have done. I realize I have hurt many people due to my actions and for this I apologize sincerely. I have hurt my family and my friends, including the Clarks. I have let them down and again for that I apologize and I hope that one day everyone that has been affected by this ordeal will find it in their hearts to forgive me. I assure you, I have learned from my mistakes. I have disappointed [my family] and have put them through torment. I am not a bad person. I have made terrible mistakes and for this, I will continue to pay forever.

Pilarinos' wife, who is not from Greece, was living in Greece with the children after the children were bullied at school. Dimitrios Pilarinos lost his house and livelihood during the three-year ordeal.

Most of the major players in the NDP government were in private life. Corky Evans continued to live in the Kootenays and worked for Arrow and Slocan Lakes Community Services Society, as a part-time director, and he was pursuing other business interests. Mike Farnworth was working with the Washington, D.C.-based National Democratic Institute for International Affairs, and he was posted in Bulgaria. Paul Ramsey had returned to his life as an instructor and was plugged into the community in Prince George. Moe Sihota hosted a current events television show on CHUM in Victoria, the local Moses Znaimer station. Gordon Wilson was in private business in Powell River, enjoying a quieter lifestyle. Many former cabinet ministers were semi-retired and reconnecting with their families or taking time to travel.

Gordon Campbell was learning about the challenges of leadership. The 2002 Liberal convention held in Penticton generated more protesters than delegates and was notable for its lack of policy debate and for restructuring the party to centralize power. A controversial change to the party constitution meant that MLAs were no longer bound by party policy; conventions would be held only once every two years, and most financial resources would be controlled centrally. Campbell was flanked by three plainclothes RCMP officers throughout the convention, and almost 200 RCMP officers provided a secure perimeter around the conference centre. Campbell referred to the protesters as "special interest groups" and stated that their presence indicated that the Liberals were on the right course. He did not speak about the record debt and deficits of a provincial Liberal government that had increased the provincial debt more in a year and a half than its NDP predecessor had in the previous ten years.

Most British Columbians, desperately juggling the various challenges of their daily lives, were upset that a government that promised them more disposable income, better health care, and a progressive education system, had not delivered. Many despaired at their current situation and asked themselves what went wrong. They thought they had voted for positive change.

The media were demonstrating that they were increasingly open to a re-examination of the players and series of events in the Clark era. The tangled webs of power plays, somewhat exposed through the complex labyrinth of testimony in the Clark trial, were slowly unravelling as some brave journalists delved deeper into the story.

From 1996 until 2000, a series of criminal allegations, investigations, and charges were instigated by the RCMP against prominent NDP members. They have cost the taxpayers millions of dollars and caused damage to the people under investigation. In almost every instance, some time later there was a low-profile dismissal, or in the case of Glen Clark, full aquittal on all allegations and charges. Regardless of the political implications, there has not been an inquiry into the actions of the RCMP, even though an inquiry may assist the RCMP in clearing the air. Unless there is significant public outcry, there is not likely to be an inquiry because the current government would have to call one, and it has little to gain in doing so.

Glen Clark and his family continued to live in the same house featured in the news stories. Clark was working hard for Jimmy Pattison, making up for lost time and ensuring he met the growth targets for the company. Even with the distractions of the trial, he had managed to show improved sales. But in the competitive environment of a Pattison corporation, Clark would have to continue to show growth on growth, or he would be politely shown the door. When I asked him how he felt about this, he looked at me as if I was crazy, laughed and said, "Compared to what I faced in politics, this is a cakewalk. I mean, what's the worst he can do?" Clark shrugged and smiled.

Endnotes

Chapter Two

1. Glen Clark interview, September 12, 2002, Vancouver.
2. Glen Clark interview, December 6, 2001, Vancouver.
3. Ibid.
4. John Laxton telephone interview, September 13, 2002.
5. Glen Clark telephone interview, September 15, 2002.

Chapter Three

1. The "don't split the vote" strategy was used successfully by the Social Credit party as a tactic to attract voters who were perceived to share a common interest in what was referred to as "free enterprise." For decades the voters of British Columbia were told by Social Credit that if the so-called free enterprise vote split, the socialists would be elected. This strategy has been explored in many books on B.C. politics.
2. B.C. Supreme Court Ruling, *Friesen v. Hammell,* 2000-08-03, Vancouver Registry, A962818, paragraph 5.
3. "More Lies!" by Julianna Hayes, *Okanagan Life,* July-August 1997, p. 5.
4. Ibid., p. 6
5. Ibid., p. 1.
6. *BC Free Press,* "B.C. court OK's fraud trial," January 1999.
7. Brian Gardiner interview, November 9, 2001, Burnaby. This quotation and the following Gardiner quotations are from this source.
8. Vancouver, January 18, 2000, Canadian News Wire.
9. B.C. Supreme Court Ruling, *Friesen v. Hammell,* 2000-08-03, Vancouver Registry, A962818, paragraph 4.

10. CP wire service story, April 28, 2000.
11. BC Supreme Court Ruling, Friesen v. Hammell, 2000-08-03, Vancouver Registry, A962818, paragraph 14 and all subsequent paragraphs of the court ruling in this chapter.
12. Brian Gardiner interview, November 9, 2001, Burnaby.
13. Ibid.
14. CP wire service story, August 3, 2000, Vancouver.

Chapter 4

1. www.bcauditor.com/AuditorGeneral.htm
2. 1998/1999: Report 4, A Review of the Estimates Process in British Columbia, March 17, 1999, "General Conclusions," Queen's Printer. This extract and the following quoted extracts are from the report.
3. 1998/1999: Report 4, A Review of the Estimates Process in British Columbia, March 17, 1999, Queen's Printer.
4. Brian Gardiner interview, November 9, 2001, Burnaby.
5. Ibid.

Chapter 5

1. Comments from Elections BC on initiative requirements.
2. Second Reading, Bill 36, third session of the 35th parliament, July 6, 1994, Gordon Wilson in debate.
3. Ibid. Glen Clark in debate.
4. In 1995, Ika Jagic, a Kelowna resident, claimed to be initiating a recall against me, Judi Tyabji, then MLA for Okanagan East. This received frequent and widespread media coverage, although there was little evidence that a recall campaign was underway. No petition was ever filed.
5. Interview with Brian Gardiner, November 9, 2001, Burnaby.
6. Ibid.
7. Quotations from Erda Walsh in this section are from an interview in Vancouver, November 3, 2001.
8. Quotations from Lois Boone in this section are from an interview in Vancouver, November 3, 2001.

9. *WebPosted Newswire* May 7, 1999 6:21 PM PDT.
10. Ibid.

Chapter 6

1. Professor Anthony Hall, University of Lethbridge, presented evidence to address Canada's request to extradite Mr. James Pitawanakwat from the United States for his involvement in the Gustafsen Lake standoff in British Columbia in 1995. The evidence was presented to Mr. Paul Papak, assistant federal public defender in Portland, Oregon, September 2000.
2. Michael Izen interview, March 13, 2002, SFU Harbour Campus, Vancouver—for this and the following two quotations in this section.
3. Quotations from Erda Walsh in this section are from an interview in Vancouver, November 3, 2001.

Chapter 7

1. CBSC Decision 98/99-0440, p. 3. Released Oct. 14, 1999.
2. Ibid., p.3.
3. Geoff Meggs interview, December 21, 2001, Burnaby.
4. John Daly interview, October 17, 2001, Vancouver.
5. Ibid.
6. Richard Fowler interview, April 2, 2002, Vancouver.
7. Ibid.
8. David Gibbons interview, September 26, 2001, Vancouver.

Chapter 8

1. Gordon Wilson by e-mail on September 12, 2002.
2. Fred Steele telephone interview, September 13, 2002.

Chapter 9

1. CBC TV National, Aug 20, 1999.
2. Quotations from Moe Sihota in this section are from a telephone interview on June 8, 2002.
3. Quotations from Rafe Mair in this section are from a telephone interview on May 7, 2002.

4. Quotations from Erda Walsh in this section are from an interview in Vancouver on November 3, 2001.
5. August 21, 1999. CBC online website, www.cbc.ca, "Glen Clark, Mandate Squandered?"
6. Ibid.

Chapter 10

1. Gordon Wilson. *A Civilized Revolution.* Vancouver: Ronsdale Press, 1996.
2. Judi Tyabi. *Political Affairs.* Victoria: Horsdal and Schubart, 1994.
3. Quotations from Moe Sihota in this section are from a telephone interview on June 8, 2002.

Chapter 11

1. Quotations from Corky Evans in this chapter are from a telelphone interview on May 26, 2002.

Chapter 12

1. January 14–15, 2002, *HMTQ v. Pilarinos and Clark,* 2002 BCSC 1267, 20020829.

Chapter 13

1. February 14, 2002, *HMTQ v. Pilarinos and Clark,* 2002 BCSC 1267, 20020829.
2. January 30, 2002, *HMTQ v. Pilarinos and Clark,* 2002 BCSC 1267, 20020829.
3. Cited court documents to the end of the chapter are from February 6, 2002, *HMTQ v. Pilarinos and Clark,* 2002 BCSC 1267, 20020829.

Chapter 14

1. *Globe and Mail,* February 26, 2002.
2. Canadian Press, February 27, 2002.
3. *Globe and Mail,* February 26, 2002.
4. Canadian Press, March 25, 2002.

5. March 20, 2002, *HMTQ v. Pilarinos and Clark,* 2002 BCSC 1267, 20020829.
6. January 16, 2002, *HMTQ v. Pilarinos and Clark,* 2002 BCSC 1267, 20020829.
7. Canadian Press, January 18, 2002.

Chapter 16

1. *Globe and Mail,* June 4, 2002.
2. *Vancouver Sun,* June 6, 2002.
3. *National Post,* June 8, 2002.
4. Canadian Press, June 7, 2002.
5. *Vancouver Sun,* June 13, 2002.
6. *Globe and Mail,* June 13, 2002.
7. *National Post,* June 13, 2002.

Chapter 17

1. June 28, 2002, *HMTQ v. Pilarinos and Clark,* 2002 BCSC 1267, 20020829.

Chapter 18

1. All court citations in this chapter are from August 29, 2002, *HMTQ v. Pilarinos and Clark,* 2002 BCSC 1267, 20020829.
2. David Gibbons telephone interview, September 13, 2002.

Chapter 19

Opening quotation: *King Lear,* Act 1, scene ii, excerpts from lines 109–125.

1. Andy Ivens interview, March 16, 2002, Vancouver.
2. Dave Barrett telephone interview, September 2, 2002.
3. Andy Ivens interview, March 16, 2002, Vancouver.
4. Fred Steele telephone interview, September 13, 2002.
5. Corky Evans telephone interviw, May 26, 2002.
6. Dave Barrett telephone interview, September 2, 2002.
7. Bill Vander Zalm telephone interview, September 2, 2002.

Chapter 20

1. January 16, 2002, *HMTQ v. Pilarinos and Clark,* 2002 BCSC 1267, 20020829.
2. Bill Vander Zalm telephone interview, September 2, 2002.
3. Dave Barrett telephone interview, September 2, 2002.

Chapter 21

The opening quotation is from: Ralph D. Sawyer, *The Seven Military Classics of Anicent China*. Boulder, Colorado: Western Press, 1993, p. 142.

1. Adrian Dix telephone interview, July 10, 2002.
2. Jimmy Pattison telephone interview, August 30, 2002.

Chapter 22

The opening quotation is from ancient Chinese military philosophy.

1. That tax cuts failed to generate growth was a situation predicted prior to the 2001 election by noted B.C. economist Dr. David Bond. In a controversial incident Dr. Bond was released from his position with the HSBC after the publicity from his statements provoked Collins' anger, prior to the 2001 election.
2. Bill Tieleman, "Liberals crow with begging bowl." West Star Communications, September 20, 2002.
3. August 29, 2002, *HMTQ v. Pilarinos and Clark,* 2002 BCSC 1267, 20020829.

For reference material related to this book the author plans to maintain a data base at: http:\\www.daggers.ca.

Photo Credits

Unless otherwise stated all photographs are from the collections of Glen Clark, Leslie Ivens, Judi Tyabji Wilson, and Gordon Wilson.

p. 292(L) B.C. Government, (R) *Richmond Review*.

Index